The Frontiers of Secrecy

Closed Government in Britain

The Frontiers of Secrecy
Closed Government in Britain

David Leigh

JUNCTION BOOKS

First published by Junction Books Limited   1980
   33 Ivor Place London NW1

Copyright © David Leigh 1980

ISBN 0 86245 002 0 (hard cover)
     0 86245 004 7 (paper cover)

Reproduced from copy supplied, printed and bound in Great Britain by Billing and Sons Limited, Guildford, London, Oxford, Worcester

Contents

Acknowledgements

I would like to thank the *Guardian,* from whose staff a good deal of information has been quoted and Bruce Page of the *New Statesman.* For particular pieces of help, I thank Martin Rosen of the Swedish Foreign Office, Patricia Hewitt and Harriet Harman of the NCCL, Laurie Taylor, Jacob Ecclestone, President of the NUJ, Ami Lonnroth, Richard Norton-Taylor, Margaretta Holmstedt, Tony Benn, Christopher Mayhew and Peter Chippindale. Christine King did the typing. The faults in this book are, of course, my own.

I owe a special debt of thanks to Jeannie Mackie.

Foreword

This book is a polemic against secrecy in British life. It is based on the belief that information is power, and that the people with power have a vested interest, not only in hanging on to as much of it as possible, but in obscuring the truth about how much power they have in the first place. It is a book about how we are ruled, written from the point of view of a professional journalist. As a middleman in the information business, a journalist has a fairly good vantage-point from which to observe the trade.

'Secrecy' is a word with an attractively offensive sound. But it would be wrong to give the impression that all human life could or should be lived in a goldfish bowl. As a journalist, I should be as great an exponent of 'freedom of information' as anybody. And yet journalists have secrets. My office does not give out my home telephone number to inquirers because they might make my life a misery. No journalist would allow a passer-by to inspect his desk drawers; they might contain any number of embarrassments.

Sometimes the embarrassments are of the sort that belong to all investigative organizations. Files can reveal the sources of information which journalists would traditionally die rather than disclose. Quite right too: a man who was dismissed or disciplined because it had been found out he 'leaked' information to the press would feel he had been the victim of unethical behaviour. And it makes practical as well as moral sense for the journalist to protect his sources. If they dry up, so does he.

And yet the position is not entirely simple. Sometimes journalists inflate their own sense of importance by mumbo-jumbo about their sources. That is not a good reason for secrecy. Sometimes, as with the police, or debt-collectors, their files are full of scurrilous bits of unproven information. It would certainly be wrong and legally dangerous to let the public see them; should journalists not go further and preserve a proper discretion by refusing to gossip to their friends about what they know, like doctors and lawyers? This is the point at which 'secrecy' (bad word) changes into 'privacy' (good word).

This book makes the case for free access to many internal government documents. Yet I know that totally free access to my own documents could be full of snares. A memorandum explaining legal risks in an article would be gold-dust to the person or organization written about — at least if they had it in advance. A memo from one newspaper executive to another explaining frankly why a politician's speech or a bishop's draft article should be sat on, might lead to completely unnecessary bad feeling if it were made public. I once, for what seemed good reasons at the time, arranged to tape-record a barrister, without his knowledge, as he conferred with his client. It would upset him and me greatly if the circumstances became public. Just like officials of the security services, I and other journalists do not like to discuss our more unsavoury methods of getting information. Harold Wilson, when Prime Minister, once pointed out that in all the fuss about MPs disclosing their own outside interests, no one was making lobby journalists disclose their own outside interests. Some journalists work furtively for other organizations apart from their employer; they would hate to have it known. In Sweden, one can inspect the expense accounts of ministers and civil servants; in Britain, the prospect of seeing his own restaurant bills displayed in the public library would make the average journalist, like any businessman, become desperately thoughtful. Journalists are also often coy about their income (another fact publicly available in Sweden); some are ashamed they earn so little, some that they make so much.

The point is that these exceptions to openness have a variety of justifications, ranging from the principled to the ignoble, from the sociologically vital to the utterly trivial. Some might be blown away in a change of atmosphere, if we ceased to live in a society so besotted with reticence. Some would probably always remain. But no journalist would face up to the implications for his own behaviour unless he was forced to. Nor would any of our masters. That is why this book examines the British system of government in such a critical way. The balances of power need to be changed; but so too does our mental landscape.

May, 1980

1
Information Control in a Nominally Free Society

You shall, in all things to be moved, treated and debated in Council, faithfully and truly declare your mind and opinion according to your heart and conscience; and shall keep secret all matters committed and revealed unto you, or that shall be treated of secretly in Council.

And if any of the said Treaties or Councils shall touch any of the Councillors, you shall not reveal it unto him but shall keep the same until such time as, by the consent of His Majesty or of the Council, publication shall be made thereof . . .

And generally in all things you shall do as a faithful and true servant ought to do to His Majesty. So help you God and the Holy Contents of this Book. [Extract from the Privy Councillors' Oath, still sworn by Cabinet Ministers.]

Common people have been kept under blindness and ignorance, and have remained servants and slaves to the nobility and the gentry. But God hath now opened their eyes and discovered unto them their Christian liberty. [Gerrard Winstanley, extract from a pamphlet by the Levellers, published in April 1649.]

The first state secret is this: who is actually in charge? Britain, nominally a democracy, is in fact a complex oligarchy with a loose system of democratic supervision. This is a different class of political structure from democracy itself — a theoretical model in which we the people, all of us, all the time, would be in charge. All Western countries with parliamentary systems are supervised oligarchies of this kind, although political scientists such as Dr Itzhak Galnoor, in *Government Secrecy in Democracies*[1] tend to be struck by the particularly oligarchic nature of British political culture. Interestingly, when we look for the locations of the real centres of political power in Britain, they appear confusing, or even concealed.

Many British institutions are secretive about their activities to a greater or lesser extent. State industries, government agencies, Whitehall ministries, the Cabinet, 10 Downing St, the Monarch, Parliament and its committees, the courts, the police and the law officers — all these bodies are secretive and, frequently, the more powerful they are then the more secretive.

But the sum of secrecy in Britain is also greater than that of its parts. Because we live in a society whose basic political culture has never been radically up-ended by revolution or war, these secretive components are heaped one on top of the other. They are not like the rings of a tree by which one can simply perceive its age; the whole structure is more like a huge mountain, covered with abandoned monuments, paths that seem to lead to the summit of political power but suddenly twist downhill, and trackless woods.

The monarchy is supposed to be virtually powerless, but it still exists. The people, in the shape of the House of Commons, have a very problematic hold on power, but the Commons still exists as the highest sovereign body in the land. The Prime Minister's office has grown to be almost incomprehensibly powerful without changing its public format. And the bureaucracy has an active role that our constitutional ideas do not really provide for. The great lobbyists for special interest groups are almost invisible. Because of Britain's historical continuity, in which institutions are superimposed or grafted on to existing ones, and because of the habit of secrecy about their own powers and limits within those institutions, the real mechanisms of government are hard to see. Myths and mysteries about government flourish, sometimes deliberately encouraged. If we set out to pick our way through the secrecy of particular institutions, and the myths that surround them, it may be possible to gain a clearer idea of the dimensions of the biggest secret — the real distribution of political power in Britain, and the way it is exercised.

Each autumn for example, Britain holds a solemn ceremony of government — the State Opening of Parliament. The Monarch rides with a military escort through the streets of London, past crowds of onlookers, to the Houses of Parliament. There, in the House of Lords, gorgeous in her crown and splendidly seated on her throne, the Queen is attended by her senior courtiers in various states of fancy dress — the Lord President of the Council, the Lord Privy Seal; the Lord High Chancellor, the Controller of Her

Majesty's Household and The Treasurer of Her Majesty's Household. In front of her stretch the scarlet and ermine robes of the country's most powerful elite — the House of Lords. Beyond the Bar of the chamber skulk a knot of rather suburban looking civilians, middle-aged men in suits and women dressed up in hats, apparently privileged to watch and listen as the Queen announces how she intends to rule the country; what laws she will pass, what alliances she will form, to what political principles she will adhere. Everyone appears extremely respectful and impressed.

We all know, the tourists lining the streets to take photographs, the journalists who sit up in the gallery out of passing curiosity and those of us who idly switch on our televisions, that this is only mummery, a dollar-earner, a demonstration of historical continuity. Some observers, influenced by Walter Bagehot and his laudatory nineteenth-century division of the British Constitution into 'dignified' and 'efficient' parts, even fancy that these pageants function as an obscure political antibiotic, immunizing us against dictatorship by separating the mesmerizing pomp and display of the State from the personalities of those who really are in charge of the government. It is certainly a charming theory, although one with certain drawbacks — such as, for example, that the United States survives although it behaves quite differently; that the theory has been invented in the wake of the pageantry and not vice versa; and that other 'dignified' parts of the system, such as judges and generals, similtaneously wear fancy dress and wield formidable quantities of authentic power.

The particularly characteristic quality of the State Opening of Parliament as a demonstration of governmental style is that the real sinews of state power are supposed, not to be elsewhere, but buried in it, like bones in a fish. Those courtiers in archaic dress do not advise the Queen but some do have important enough jobs in the real government. The Treasurer of Her Majesty's Household for example, although in knee-breeches, is in fact the deputy chief whip of the government of the day — in 1978 one Walter Harrison for Labour, in 1979 John Stradling Thomas, the Conservative MP. His task is to make sure MPs of the ruling party turn up in the right place at the right time, in sufficient quantities to vote through government measures and, by exerting various pressures, to avoid 'backbench revolts' if at all possible. The Lord Privy Seal was one Sir Ian Gilmour in 1979, who deputized in the House of Commons for the Foreign Secretary (a peer, Lord Carrington). In the previous administration the Lord President of the Council was the Cabinet minister in charge of Commons business and deputy party leader, Michael Foot. (He insisted democratically on wearing a lounge suit to these occasions.)

The Queen's speech is, of course, drafted by the Prime Minister of the day, who is one of the rabble of civilians down at the Bar of the House, standing alongside the Leader of the Opposition and those MPs who feel the impulse to share in these events. The rows of peers in ermine are merely a miscellaneous collection which includes, as well as the worthy, descendants of the rich or famous, geriatric politicians and businessmen friends of retired Prime Ministers. Their social status is high; they belong to an agreeable club and get paid expenses for it, and find it easier than most to book tables in restaurants. Their democratic authority is nil, although they are allowed to make speeches, have a minor role in parliamentary business and occasionally find themselves, oddly enough, appointed to such high posts in government as Foreign Secretary or even Prime Minister. The Lords certainly represent an elite of an important kind, but they do not, as such, constitute any longer the governing class.

Buried in the public spectacle then, is what history tells the public is the real system of government, the real home of power. This is the House of Commons — 635 MPs, elected as representatives of the public; professional politicians who have won supervisory control over the monarch, elect her ministers, control their funds, make laws and call the executive arm of government to continuous account, transmitting, not as lucidly as glass perhaps, but as faithfully as possible each democratic impulse of the country.

This attractive idea too is mostly nonsense and flummery, as political scientists will readily observe. But for our purposes, let us try to analyse the situation sidelong, through the spectrum of secrecy. Knowledge about what is going on is an obvious test of real political power as opposed to ceremonial power (there are, of course, other valuable tests, such as the ability to have people taken out and shot). Thus knowledge is valuable, and loses nearly all its value if it is freely shared. Having access to knowledge about affairs of State implies a wish to protect the knowledge from others — secrecy — or to distribute selective bits of it in a self-serving way — propaganda.

The State Opening of Parliament is a good example of propaganda. The regime is ostentatiously presented in a way which suits the governors. It legitimizes and glamourizes them, draping whatever uninspired legislative compromises have been knocked together in the grand robes of history. It is a piece of propaganda in which the citizenry is perfectly happy to share, because it is propaganda by them as well. They too want to identify with a romantic style of government, sanctified by the past and reassuring about the future.

But the bad habit of mystifying the process of government merely begins with the State Opening; as we follow the glimmer of power back into the recesses of Whitehall, this is worth remembering. When the monarch was truly in charge, the propaganda displays were accompanied by real administrative secrecy. This is reflected still in the title of Privy Councillor — someone who was Privy to the secrets of State — and in the Privy Councillor's explicit oath of secrecy, still sworn by Cabinet ministers to this day as a symbol that they are being given a bite of power real enough to be worth hiding. The Queen herself, although largely a figurehead, is allowed to surround her political existence with a residual fetish of personal secrecy.

The Queen's regular meetings with her Prime Ministers and other politicians such as the Leader of the House are never discussed in public. Nor are the political matters which reach the Queen through her private secretary — the routine channel of communication on 'affairs of State'. Not only what flows from the royal lips, but also what reaches the royal ear, is granted the beatitude of secrecy. When Sir Harold Wilson retired as Prime Minister in 1976, he recalled, before going on to quote from his own harmless dinner-table speech,

> On Tuesday 23 March, the Queen and Prince Phillip honoured her retiring Prime Minister by dining at Downing Street, with members of the Cabinet, my own family and friends, including the vice-chancellor of Bradford University. It was a happy and informal occasion ... she in fact stayed until a quarter to twelve. As this was a private occasion, it would not be appropriate to quote the Queen's gracious speech.[2]

A similar fetishism, although with a slightly better reason for embarrassment, was displayed in 1979 when the Palace steadfastly refused to say whether or not the Queen's private secretary, Sir Michael Adeane, had passed on to her the news he had been given that Anthony Blunt, then an honorific member of the Queen's Household, was a Soviet spy. Had Sir Michael not passed on the information, officially communicated to him precisely in order that he should do his job and tell the Queen, he would have been behaving most peculiarly. But, insisted the Palace, 'all communications between the private secretary and the Queen are confidential'.

It can be seen how, in Britain, constitutional theories imperceptibly slide into ideas of good taste. It is a condition of employment of royal servants that they do not retail their memoirs; and it is considered a great solecism to mention the Queen's large untaxed and undisclosed private fortune. Even in its vestigial symbolic form, the secrecy surrounding the Queen looks unhealthy. It also demonstrates, in a simple way, one of the perversions of the press to which secrecy makes newsmen prone. As the Queen's public words, other than in ceremonial speeches, are so rare, her most banal remarks have a disproportionate gossip value. Until quite recently the procedure for journalists even in sophisticated Fleet Street was to accompany the Queen on tours of biscuit factories and so forth, in order to pounce on each operative as the Queen passed by with a gracious word or two. 'What did she say?' we would ask 'What did she say?'

Behind the Queen and her court stands the House of Commons, which is supposedly the true governmental system of Britain. Here the executive is held to account and laws are made. An inspection of the information flow alone would tell us otherwise, however. Except in so far as they belong to the government, MPs are only residually secretive about their own proceedings and have small power to pull back the curtain of government.

To all intents and purposes, the House of Commons' own doings are now part of the open side of the State and thus not very important. Until the mid eighteenth century, the discussions in the House of Commons were indeed kept secret from the public as they were considered part of the private decision-making process of the powerful. It was the intruding zeal of journalists that led to first a grudging acceptance of publicity, and eventually an elaborate institution to record daily, through Hansard, every last tittle of ministerial circumlocution and back-bench clowning. The resolutions of the House forbidding its proceedings to be reported have never been formally rescinded, which is an odd testimony to the British tolerance for keeping fatuous rules and operating them with wide discretion. MPs are touchy about their control over minor information matters, which is perhaps a reflection of their lack of power over major ones. Only recently has it been permitted to broadcast the proceedings of Parliament to a public apparently not greatly impressed. Television cameras are still forbidden to intrude. It is regarded as 'contempt of Parliament' if newspapers get hold of leaks from the reports of parliamentary select committees in advance, even though the reports are to be published. Inoffensive journalists have been solemnly referred to the Committee on Privileges for this as recently as 1978.[3] Similarly and rather childishly government White Papers and such documents are furtively released to the press a few hours before official presentation to the House of Commons. The early release is perfectly logical; it is, for example, so that their contents can be set in type overnight, and so that journalists have a little time to digest what they would otherwise be expected instantaneously to paraphrase. But the furtiveness is not so rational; the papers are issued through the Westminster press 'lobby' stamped 'Confidential Final Revise' with an adjuration not to discuss their contents with any outside party. The idea is to pretend that these documents do not in fact exist, because otherwise MPs would protest that the press was being given government information before they themselves were.

Apart from official government White Papers and announcements and the compost of selective political gossip which permeates through party meetings and cabals to the 'lobby', there are, in constitutional theory, two major ways that MPs can independently acquire information for transmission to the public. These are the parliamentary question, and Commons committees.

Question Time

> Stonehouse was very contemptuous of parliamentary procedure. He said ministers in practice have not got to bother about parliamentary opinion and that in no sense now is the House of Commons a watchdog keeping its eye on the executive. Parliamentary question and answer he described as a farce. [Cecil King][4]

> *The Attorney-General*: If a Minister is questioned, the truth will come out. He must tell the truth to the House. There is no question about that.
> *James Callaghan* (hastily): I apologise for interrupting but the Attorney-General gave an absolute answer that, if a question was put in Parliament, then the name would have to be given. If he did not say that, I hope he will make it clear that this is not what he means. There could be cases in which the national interest would be ill-served by giving the name at that time.

What he is required to do in the House is not to tell a lie to the House. [Hansard][5]

A Cabinet minister has been to visit a government institution in the West Country, accompanied by his principal private secretary. Returning that night in the black government Rover, across the rain and gales of Dartmoor, a bedraggled figure flags them down. 'I'm lost', he cries, 'can you possibly tell me where I am?' 'You're on Dartmoor', replies the civil servant briskly and drives on. After a while, the minister enquires why he had behaved in such a way. 'Well minister', says the civil servant, 'It was the perfect answer as far as I was concerned. It was entirely truthful, and gave away the minimum of information.' [Old Westminster joke.]

The mythology of the parliamentary question in which civil servants scurry nervously on the day 'their' minister is due to be questioned, and the files of Whitehall bulge with vital information preserved in case some MP should take it into his head to make enquiries, is no longer a strong one. The time for verbal questioning of ministers is limited to a few minutes each week and unless the questions are 'planted' ones on which to hang a ministerial statement, the sessions tend to be used for gladiatorial displays of political point-scoring. The much larger sheaf of questions, to which only a written answer is publicly given, can certainly elicit a good deal of factual information — but only if the government feels like giving it.

To choose a day's Hansard at random is to discover many examples of evasion.

Mrs Renee Short asked the Secretary of State for the Home Department whether he is satisfied with the present procedures for dealing with allegations of maltreatment of prisoners by prison staff.

Mr Brittan: These procedures are kept under constant review.

Another MP asked for details of firearms registered in each police area of the country.

Mr Brittan: Such information is not recorded centrally for England and Wales and could not be obtained without disproportionate cost.

The Minister for Education was asked what was the annual cost per pupil for material and tools in the subjects of woodwork, metalwork and pottery.

Dr Boyson: The information is not available as the returns ... do not differentiate between materials and equipment used for different subjects.

Mrs Thatcher was asked how many people were questioned after the 1951 defections of Burgess and Maclean; and how many were asked to leave the Civil Service.

The Prime Minister: ... not all those questioned were themselves under suspicion, and it would not be in the public interest to give numbers. A number of people left the public service or were transferred.

Mr Cook asked the Prime Minister whether ... she will now answer questions on the security and intelligence services.

The Prime Minister: No.[6]

There are types of questions which, as the exchange with Mr Robin Cook suggests, government departments simply refuse to entertain. In 1978, for example, a Labour MP, Jeff Rooker, set out to compile a list of the questions government departments refused to accept. The exercise had been carried out once before in 1972 and, in the interval, some slight openness was discernible on the part of the Treasury. In 1972 the Treasury refused to discuss the sterling balances or its economic forecasts. Another MP had successfully amended the 1975 Industry Act to compel the Treasury to publish its economic forecasts and to make the Treasury economic 'model' accessible to outside forecasters. And the Treasury further declared itself willing to disclose the total size of sterling balances and their broad distribution, although details of individual countries' assets were still withheld.

Otherwise, the list of examples furnished by departments was impressive. The Ministry of Agriculture refused to answer questions on forecasts of changes in food prices, the amount of strategic food reserves, agricultural workers' wages and the day-to-day affairs of such bodies as the White Fish Authority. The Civil Service Department refused to give information used in evaluating tenders for computer projects. They will not disclose figures for outside pay levels supplied by other organizations 'in confidence' to determine civil servants' pay. The Ministry of Defence refused to disclose not only 'operational matters' but also accident rates for aircraft, and the number of foreign soldiers 'training' in the UK. They will not disclose details of arms sales to foreign countries, a politically, not militarily sensitive matter. They will not reveal contract prices, the costs of individual aircraft and other weapons or any details of research and development. The Foreign Office too, refused details of arms sales to foreigners and 'confidential exchanges between governments' (by which they mean all such exchanges).

The terms in which government departments refuse to answer questions from MPs give us a preview of the farrago of reasons presented in support of administrative secrecy. Some, in principle at least, are sound. A common theme is a concern for the privacy of the individual. Thus, for example, Health and Social Security refuse to provide personal information about individual claimants or hospital patients. But Home Office staff refuse information on all 'matters involving privacy'. They define this in practice as, for example, enabling them not to answer questions about individual inmates of prisons unless it suits them to do so.

A remarkably wide area is covered in the Department of the Environment's refusal to disclose all information which they define as 'personal information relating to the employment or appointment of individuals'. And it is entirely reprehensible that the Department of Health conceals to which senior doctors it awards extra pay in the shape of so-called 'distinction awards'. Patronage is a public issue in a way that the personal career files of civil servants are possibly not.

The way judges and other senior legal functionaries are appointed is shrouded in a mystery which gives over a whole area of State activity to an oligarchic group with a narrow social base. The Law Officers refuse to answer questions on 'advice given to and by the Lord Chancellor about judicial and other appointments'. This concealment is further extended to all 'confidential exchanges between the Lord Chancellor and the judiciary', although occasionally a Labour Lord Chancellor will release 'unattributably' a mild rebuke he has delivered to a particularly irresponsible judge. There is a lot of patronage in British government in the shape of individual appointments to paid jobs or peerages; it is all a secret, in the sense that Parliament is never allowed to examine the reasons for preferments, or the histories of the individuals concerned. In the US presidential appointees are subject to examination by what, in theory at least, are democratic committees.

Naturally, the Treasury will not disclose 'the tax affairs of individuals or companies'. Not all countries are as delicate about these money matters — Sweden, for instance, does not disclose the intimate details of tax returns, but it does disclose the gross annual declared income of individuals. They seem to survive. The Department of Industry keeps secret the amount of Exchequer handouts given to individual companies. So too does the government keep secret, on grounds of 'commercial confidence', the leases it purchases on individual office buildings.

The Attorney-General and his colleagues refuse to reveal the legal advice they provide to other government departments. This is an important area of policy and one is bound to wonder what, for example, the 1979 Conservative Government was told about its position under the European Convention on Human Rights when it set about searching for ways to prevent black fiancés entering Britain. Or, to take another case, what advice was given the Home Office when it was under pressure in a civil court to ventilate the murky world of telephone tapping?

'Privacy' and 'commercial confidence' are justifications for secrecy which beg some questions. So does the explicit reluctance of government departments to provide the forecasts which they draw up of likely trends in important matters such as the likely number of future jobless, the number of prison inmates in ten years time, or 'detailed future forecasts of overseas aid'. The Department of the Environment made the most sustained effort in 1978 to provide a generalized basis for refusals to answer questions, as distinct from *ad hoc* examples of matters they had kept secret from MPs at some point in the past:

> Information which is commercially confidential ... some aspects of the managements of the department and the formulation of policy (e.g. personal information relating to the appointment or employment of individuals) and details of the advice given by individual officials; information which is classified for security reasons; matters which are entirely within the responsibilities of individual local authorities and matters relating to the day-to-day management of nationalized industries, government agencies and fringe bodies.[7]

This raises further important points around which the problems of freedom of information legislation will eventually be seen to crystallize — notably 'advice to ministers' and 'classified material'.

Two final points are worth noting before moving on from these bland catalogues. First, 'disproportionate cost', like so many of the concepts used in the secrecy structure, is an entirely subjective idea. In early 1980, the Home Office reaction to questions demanding details of people who had died over the years in police custody was 'disproportionate cost'. When it occurred to the Home Secretary, William Whitelaw, that he was in the firing line for accusations of a cover-up, the cost rapidly ceased to be 'disproportionate' and the information was obtained. When other ploys fail, 'disproportionate cost' is a political fall-back position with no quantifiable meaning.

Second, this list of 'barred questions' merely skims the secrecy system. A list of topics on which ministers, while agreeing to reply, give enigmatic, evasive or downright misleading answers, would be a much longer and startlingly comprehensive affair. Only the Prime Minister's short list of barred topics gives the real flavour of executive secrecy over vast tracts of government. Mrs Thatcher would not answer any questions on: 'security matters; telephone interception; Cabinet committees and detailed arrangements for the conduct of government business'.[8]

Parliamentary Committees

The other channel of enquiry for MPs is the system of select committees. These are not to be confused with the standing committees which study draft Bills. Until recently, the system was incoherent. The Public Accounts Committee, working with the staff of the independent Comptroller and Auditor General is designed to check that money voted by Parliament in the past has been properly spent. Its discoveries often lead to highly critical reports of overspending and waste, and it has the power to investigate administration, to examine witnesses, and call for documents. So too can a second instrument of financial control, the Expenditure Committee, which grew into a series of six subcommittees selecting departmental estimates for invigilation. Other select committees, encouraged to proliferate in the late 1960s, spent their time, in theory, considering broad aspects of policy. One such was the Science and Technology Committee.

These committees suffered from a number of weaknesses. Being inquisitorial rather than politically adversary bodies, they were regarded unenthusiastically by some politicians, as a diversion from the real business of political life — sustaining your own side and abusing the other. Michael Foot, a classic parliamentarian, used to refer to them contemptuously as 'sewing parties'. Unlike the powerful Congressional Committees in the US, they were not given substantial research backing. MPs in Britain are in general badly serviced in this way. The power to extract information by summoning ministers and officials is less impressive than it sounds. In September 1976, the education subcommittee of the Expenditure Committee complained that they were being refused access to major planning papers of the Department of Education, which they characterized as a department unduly secretive in its long-term planning.[9]

Harold Wilson, in February of that year, refused to allow Harold Lever, one of his Cabinet, to appear before a committee looking into the government rescue of the Chrysler company. (The US firm had coolly proposed to cut their losses in Britain by either closing down entirely, or by tossing over the whole collapsing British operation to the government; Lever had been backing Wilson's plan to bail out Chrysler with a £162 million package of subsidies and loan guarantees.)

'The December leaks had featured, indeed greatly exaggerated the role played by Harold Lever, the Chancellor of the Duchy of Lancaster', memorialized Wilson.

What I could not accept was the suggestion that any minister referred to in press stories as having taken a particular line in the Cabinet on the question, having no relevant departmental duties, should automatically be subject to a committee summons. Apart from the fact that such summonses could be based on leaks, there would be a crossing of the lines of departmental responsibility. Such invitations might be based on pure press speculation.

There was a particular problem here in respect of ministers holding no departmental portfolio, such as the Lord President, Lord Privy Seal and the Chancellor of the Duchy of Lancaster, who from time immemorial have chaired Cabinet committees, or have been sent on missions by Prime Ministers. To call them would blur existing ministerial responsibilities, and impair collective Cabinet responsibility.[10]

'Ministerial responsibility' and 'collective responsibility' are in many ways just more of the constitutional myths useful for justifying the practice of secrecy. The bald facts appeared to be that Wilson did not want to see Lever questioned about a trip he made to the Shah of Iran in an unsuccessful attempt to see if the Shah would switch a contract from a folded-up Chrysler to another British-based firm. Wilson was not interested in the gain to public knowledge if splits in his Cabinet were aired, and his own position anatomized. He was in a position to enforce his view.

At the end of 1979, there was an important development in the select committee system which may, possibly, make it a more genuine instrument of accountability. Committees were set up to cover the work of each Whitehall department in a systematic way, and some, such as the Home Affairs Committee, promptly made it clear that it was going to try to sink its teeth into the Home Office. The Committee announced that it would inquire into deaths in police custody, about which some statistics had been obtained from the Home Secretary after persistent questioning. It is too early to evaluate the new system except to predict that the Committee will meet with resistance to full disclosure. The Director of Public Prosecutions was promptly barred from appearing before the Home Affairs Committee by the Attorney-General Sir Michael Havers. This is an interesting veto because one State secret is which prosecutions are ordered or refused by the Attorney, a politician, and which by his nominal junior, a bureaucrat. It was Sir Michael, for example, who insisted on prosecuting the *New Statesman* for interviewing a juror in 1979, not Sir Thomas Hetherington, the DPP. After MPs' protests the ban was eventually dropped. In January 1980, the Manpower Services Commission refused at first to disclose details of its plans and then gave way. The Defence Committee, chaired by a Conservative, set out to investigate ammunition storage in Germany, taking its evidence in secret, at the same time as it was disclosed for the first time to the public that £1,000 million was already earmarked for the Chevaline project to update nuclear missiles in submarines, tests on which had been kept secret during a seven-year programme under three governments. Committees do not have the power to hire and fire their staff, and some at least of the committees' clerks are former Foreign Office men in their late fifties. As one committee member told Colin Brown of the *Guardian:* 'The least you might say about some of them is that they are the absolute opposite of the sort of person you might find as assistant to the Congressional committees in the US.

The latter tend to be young dynamic lawyers with political ambitions, who can actually take a lead in negotiations with departments.'[11]

Plainly MPs are not entirely powerless to discover government policy and its executive activities. But it is the risk of leaks, or the uproar following leaks, which makes ministers and civil servants forthcoming. Sir Robert Cox, head of the buildings section of the Department of the Environment, the Property Services Agency, blandly told the supposedly powerful Public Accounts Committee of Parliament on 14 April 1975, something that was not true. The Committee were troubled that one region of the PSA, the southern, had apparently made vast economies in maintenance changes, but none of the other regions had managed to do the same. Sir Robert reassured them:

The Southern region covers among other things, the Aldershot area and in the years before 1969 there had been substantial redeployment of military resources. There had been a lot of staff moving north. Consequently there were quite a number of opportunities in the Aldershot area and in the Southern region generally for proposing to the Army that there should be economy in the use of buildings, that buildings which were only partly occupied could be closed and that there should be a reduction in heating in buildings that were no longer used or no longer fully used ... other regions did not have the same possibilities because the same redeployments had not taken place.[12]

Equally complacently, the Committee reported to the House:

The Agency told your Committee that ... military resources in the region had been substantially redeployed which had provided opportunities for reducing the number of buildings and areas to be maintained. The same opportunities had not existed in the other regions ... the Agency considered that in general the scope for special maintenance economy reviews in the UK had considerably diminished.[13]

Unfortunately, Leslie Chapman, the man in charge of the southern region, had been a crusading bureaucrat who retired, exasperated with the inertia that had stifled his efforts to spread methods of saving the taxpayers' money. His indignation over-rode the normal gag of the Official Secrets Acts, and he announced, to much embarrassment all round, that not a word of this was true. There had been no troop movements north at all. He eventually wrote a book documenting, among much else, 'the superficiality and ineffectuality of the Public Accounts Committee examinations'.[14]

The affair was highly amusing to connoisseurs of bureaucratic wriggling. A newspaper reporter pointed out to the PSA, in March 1977, that the civil servant concerned would say this answer was false. The Department sat tight, hoping apparently that the matter would go away, and fearing, according to answers Sir Robert later gave, that Mr Chapman might have other surprises up his sleeve concerning misleading answers, which would be revealed in the book he was preparing. A year later, on the point of its publication, the Department realized, from renewed press interest and the preparation of great denunciations of the Civil Service to be shown on television, that they were in trouble. Sir Robert hastily wrote to the chairman of the Committee confessing that he had been 'misadvised' and the Committee misinformed. The Committee, by no means anxious to have it thought they had been made fools of, reconvened, re-examined Sir Robert and said loftily that they were more interested in the future, in any event, than the past.

No heads rolled, Sir Robert explained that he had been wrongly briefed, although naturally he took personal responsibility for uttering these mistaken words. (The 'personal responsibility' did not involve any tangible act, such as resigning.) The author of the incorrect brief had since retired and nothing could be done. No doubt his memory had been faulty.

The Committee recorded, lugubriously:

We think it possible that if Sir Robert had not produced so telling a point regarding the redeployments of military resources as part explanation of the scope for greater economies in Southern Region, the Committee of 1974-75 might well have pressed him further on the respective opportunities open to the various regions. We have carefully re-examined this aspect of the subject in the light of Sir Robert's further evidence and the PSA's memoranda. These memoranda, which we found useful and informative gave up-to-date figures of developments and progress in all the PSA's regions since the late 60s ... the Committee would have been assisted in its enquiry in 1975 if the PSA had expanded their oral evidence at the time with additional information of this kind, as up-to-date as possible ... we believe that had the Committee pursued their questioning ... their report would have included a critical comment on the slowness of other regions to secure similar savings in maintenance expenditure...

We accept unreservedly that Sir Robert Cox believed his evidence to be correct and that he had no intention of misleading the Committee. On the evidence before us, we are unable either to accept or reject the PSA's opinion that the alteration to the earlier draft of Sir Robert's brief was made in good faith, but we consider that as proof one way or the other is unlikely to be forthcoming it would serve no useful purpose to pursue this line of enquiry further.[15]

Cabinet Government

Of course many well-informed people never assume that the House of Commons is the real source of governmental power in the first place. They know that MPs do function as a lobby with which the regime has to contend, and that they do have political influence, if not authority. But, behind the House of Commons there is an organization actually known as 'the Government' — the third tier after the Queen and the House of Commons. Is this the real hub of the British State? Certainly the clouds of secrecy begin to thicken in a way which suggests we are nearing Mount Olympus.

There are about 100 ministers in 'the Government', chosen from the ruling party. The junior ministers, tied to departmental duties, are given one small share of the secrecy mumbo-jumbo. It is not publicly revealed for which segments of the Whitehall machine they are actually responsible — to which minister the Prison Department of the Home Office actually reports, for example, or the immigration section.

This is rather fatuous, because the allocation of responsibilities between say, Home Office ministers, is generally clear enough. A document has to be issued to MPs listing the various sectional responsibilities so that they can direct letters and questions to the right person. But the public may not see the document which is classified, like Whitehall phone directories, 'Restricted'.[16]

Junior ministers are bound to secrecy about the affairs of their departments and at the same time made privy to very little information that is considered undesirable for their ears. Senior ministers take the policy decisions, supposedly in Cabinet, and senior civil servants tend to ensure that the 'departmental view' is not easily upset by some fly-by-night second-rank minister. A succession of junior ministers — Alex Lyon, Eric Heffer, Brian Sedgemore, Michael Meacher — retired from the 1974-9 Labour Government with a dazed and doubtless paranoid conviction that they were excluded and manipulated by their departments. Michael Meacher, former Parliamentary Under-Secretary to the Department of Health and Social Security, confessed to a 1979 conference on hypothermia that his officials had overborne him and insisted he suppress an answer to a parliamentary question on the subject that he had planned to give in 1976.

Meacher, asked about the extent of hypothermia, had planned to quote from an independent research survey showing a ½ per cent of a sample were found to have hypothermia, and thus, a feasible death rate from the condition might be as high as 35,000 a year. His civil servants told him this politically sensitive information 'may be misleading and could certainly be used against the government'. It was almost certain, they said that such a reply 'would be used to bring pressure on the government to improve heating provision for old people'. One presumably should not criticize Mr Meacher, entirely vulnerable to Prime Ministerial patronage and subsequently a champion of freedom of information, for what he did next. He issued an answer to the parliamentary question explaining that only 17 people were recorded on death certificates as dying from the condition in 1974. As to the true death rate, he was unable to give an estimate.[17]

Cabinet ministers, also appointed and dismissed at the command of the reigning Prime Minister are considered, mythologically, to be the real holders of power. In theory, they (and indeed they alone), know everything that is being done in the name of the government, and this knowledge is therefore a State secret. Policy decisions are taken by the Cabinet, a kind of central committee, and announced (or kept secret) as and when the Cabinet pleases. Its agenda, minutes and briefing documents are kept secret before, during and after Cabinet meetings, themselves unannounced. Differences of opinion between its members and the options they consider are never to be revealed, under the doctrine of 'collective responsibility'.

The executive arm of government also rests on secrecy. The public and Parliament may not know what is going on in Whitehall but Cabinet ministers do. Under a second mythical doctrine, that of 'ministerial responsibility', there is no right for the public to know even the names of civil servants administering industrial grants, telephone tapping, or negotiations for oil-company licences. The minister is answerable, and if anything goes wrong, he along will take the blame.

As we clamber higher and higher up Olympus, we find increasing collusion between politicians and civil servants to maintain the fictions of secrecy. It is convenient for both groups to negotiate and administer undisturbed, and great effort goes into presenting the idea that 'collective responsibility' and 'ministerial responsibility' can only be preserved by extensive secrecy.

Ministerial Responsibility

Cabinet ministers are apt to huff and bluster when it is pointed out that they do not know the half of what is going on in their departments, and that if they do find out they always wriggle out of taking the blame. This natural reluctance to lose face is very convenient to the helmsmen in the civil services because they become, as a consequence, responsible to no one but themselves. 'Ministerial responsibility' is stone dead as a justification for bureaucratic secrecy, but it is a pity it will not lie down. The last minister actually to take the blame for administrative malfeasance was the hapless Sir Thomas Dugdale in 1954. He reigned over the Crichel Down affair in which, unknown to him, his civil servants had behaved ineptly, if not improperly, over a compulsory purchase case. Palmerston's Victorian boast is merely a piece of history:

> In England, the Ministers who are at the head of the several departments of State are liable any day and every day to defend themselves in Parliament, and in order to do this, they must be minutely acquainted with all the details of the business of their offices, and the only way of being constantly armed with such information is to conduct and direct those details themselves.

It is startling, therefore to find the government's 1978 White Paper on Official Secrets reform parrotting this hoary claim: 'In the British context ... the policies and decisions of the executive are under constant and vigilant scrutiny by Parliament, and Ministers are directly answerable to Parliament.' Presumably the civil servants who drafted this piece of insolence were hoping no one would recall the authoritative finding of the Fulton Report on the Civil Service a full ten years earlier:

Indeed, we think that administration suffers from the convention, which is still alive in many fields, that only the minister should explain issues in public and what his department is or is not doing about them. This convention has depended in the past on the assumption that the doctrine of ministerial responsibility means that a Minister has full detailed knowledge and control of all the activities of his department. This assumption is no longer tenable. The Minister and his junior ministers cannot know all that is going on in his department nor can they nowadays be present at every forum where legitimate questions are raised about its activities. The consequence is that some of these questions go unanswered.[18]

Even if a minister does know what is going on, there is nothing in the Constitution to oblige him to confide in MPs, the press and the public. Ministers learn some, but not all, of what the government machine is doing in their special area, and they have no way of forcing out of their civil servants what they do not even know to exist. Richard Crossman, when Labour Health Minister in the late 1960s, was startled to discover, when he proposed to publish (against Civil Service advice) a report on scandalous conditions at Ely mental hospital, that his own department had been aware of the situation for some years and had an inspector's report to that effect.[19]

'Ministerial responsibility' was raised as an argument against the appointment of ombudsmen on the Swedish pattern to investigate bureaucratic stupidities in Britain. This ploy, a purely political one, was abandoned in the late 1960s in favour of what turned out to be a more effective device. Ombudsmen were appointed but were so circumscribed in their investigations — they have to operate via MPs, must not name culpable officials, must not name complainants, and publish in obscure and unmanageable bulk — that they have little public impact. The British Civil Service has two standard defence postures: the first is to assert metaphysical doctrines, such as 'ministerial responsibility' and defend them against all comers with a dogged scholasticism. The second is to bury reform in a procedural blancmange, while expressing loyal acceptance of whichever great alteration has been forced upon them.

Ministers are further bamboozled by the 'previous administration rule'. This delightful notion is supposed to protect the political neutrality of the Civil Service by denying incoming ministers the papers of the previous government. The argument is that this prevents a Labour Government, for example, from assuming office and immediately announcing the dastardly plans its opponents had laid in the event of a Tory victory. It enables governments to explore options through a loyal Civil Service machine, which will then offer the same loyalty to its democratic successors. As can be seen, this idea too has a good deal of metaphysics about it. It has the rather strange implication that, apart from the permanent Civil Service, no one at all has the right of access to all government files. As a new Home Secretary acquires his government car, listens to the impressive lectures of MI5 about the need for secrecy at all times, and studies documents such as the list of those whose telephones are currently being tapped, it must be difficult for him to come to terms with the fact that there is a great deal he is simply not being told.

And Cabinet ministers are given to relaxing in their self-important fantasies. There is a remarkably candid passage in the 1964-70 diaries of Barbara Castle, describing the childish delight and jealousy of the Cabinet when Richard Nixon, a considerable while before his resignation as US president in the squalid circumstances of Watergate, paid a state visit:

When I arrived [for dinner at No. 10] I found Michael [Stewart] and Dennis [Healey] there, John Freeman [ambassador to the US], Burke Trend [Cabinet Secretary] and the head of our FO. Downing Street was a blaze of light. We were all very poised and relaxed like people who have arrived into the heart of the establishment. If we're honest, it's moments like this when one is in the inner circle and conscious of not being awed by it, that are the consolations for all the work and strain ... eventually I managed to turn to Burke Trend who, in this informal setting seemed far more boyish and vulnerable than his rather avuncular role in Cabinet ... we had a natter about Cabinet affairs and then he said with impulsive jocularity, 'But it's all great fun, isn't it.'

[The rest of the Cabinet lurked bitterly in the drawing-room, and Nixon had to be brought out to meet them. Each did his best to impress an 'indefatigably smiling Nixon'.] As we said goodnight, I grasped Nixon's hand and said impulsively, 'You are a sport.' There was no other word for it. Dennis tells me he is far nicer than LBJ whom Dennis found repulsive.[20]

Behind all this high life, dreary little bureaucratic secrets are constantly being preserved. Chapman recounts, in the story of his battles to save up to 50 per cent of Whitehall regional maintenance budgets, that he had to deal with three successive junior ministers. In 1968, the Labour Parliamentary Secretary, Lord Winterbottom, ordered the Ministry 'to put forward similar programmes with all speed, and made it clear that he would be watching events closely'. Winterbotham was shortly reshuffled to the RAF. In 1969 Chapman found another sympathetic minister, John Silkin. Persuaded by Chapman, he issued instructions that priority was to be given to Chapman's economy surveys. Civil servants stalled for several months, asserting that the idea had implications and consequences for staffing and allied matters. This is a recognizable Whitehall delaying tactic; at one point it was claimed that staff shortages meant it would take up to 17 years to complete the surveys. As Chapman tells the story, Silkin nagged and insisted, and hopes were high in Chapman's breast that millions of pounds and thousands of staff were about to be saved.

There was a General Election, which the Conservatives won, in 1970. Paul Channon became the relevant junior minister in the newly-organized giant Department of the Environment. He too visited Chapman's pioneering teams:

> He asked several times why it was that these policies were not being applied elsewhere, and I think he must have thought that some of my answers were, if not evasive, then downright inadequate. What I could not tell him was that parliamentary secretaries and ministers alike from the preceding administration had given just such instructions and that they had not been implemented. It is accepted by parliament that civil servants do not tell ministers of one administration about the instructions given by any of their predecessors of a different political colour ... while it may suit ministers in some ways, it certainly makes it easier for civil servants to forget about unwelcome orders.[21]

Channon was reshuffled to Northern Ireland within the year. Chapman, disenchanted and suppressed, asked to retire in early 1973, and eventually set about whistle-blowing from outside (upon which, to the surprise of a few, the fabled Official Secrets Act turned out to be mere bluff, which no one attempted to apply).

Collective Responsibility

British politicians find it embarrassing to have it known that they are sometimes manipulated by outsiders and civil servants, that they frequently disagree among themselves about policies and that they are often kept in the dark by their own colleagues. The notion of the secrecy of the Cabinet Room draws a decent veil over all this loss of face, and Cabinet Secretaries are always ready to be metaphysical on their behalf. As the 'avuncular' Burke Trend explained to the 1971 Franks Committee on the Official Secrets Act:

> The dominant feature ... of Cabinet Government is the doctrine of collective responsibility of ministers ... It is a convention of the British constitution that ministers [are] collectively responsible for the actions of the Government as a whole ... whatever different views or conflicting considerations may have emerged in the discussions leading up to a collective decision, once that decision is taken, it will be announced by the Minister with the main departmental responsibility for the subject and it will have the support of all ministers.
>
> It is essential to the success of the system that ministers and officials participating in the collective discussions of the Cabinet should be able to exchange views freely and frankly among themselves without the risk that their discussions will be made public. Unless business can be conducted in absolute confidence, the integrity with which the Government conduct their business is bound to come into public question. Revelation of the views put forward ... would undermine the essential unity of government, and even after a decision on the question at issue has been taken and announced, it would endanger the Government's collective integrity.[22]

Sir Burke warmed to this task of translating into impressive abstract nouns the traditional British ruling-class habit of maintaining a stiff upper lip. His purpose was to encourage prison sentences for those who disclosed these matters:

> there is a body of opinion which holds that ... the disclosure of the processes involved in policy formation promotes the public interest ... if these processes were disclosed, the doctrine of collective responsibility could not for long be effectively main-

tained ... Reports in the press about differences of view or emphasis between members of the government are far from uncommon and it may appear that they do not cause noticeable harm. We think there are two answers to this argument; first that it is misleading to suppose that casual reports of this kind, based as they are on speculation or inference cause no harm, they do in fact to some degree damage the corporate integrity of the government. Secondly, we think it would be conceded that the harm that might arise ... would be immeasurably greater than the harm done by the casual reports that now appear.[23]

Sir Burke appeared to be glossing over one or two tiny points. Frequently newspaper reports are based on leaks from Cabinet members, often the Prime Minister himself. Cabinet debates, which everyone knows are taking place, are circulated through the 'lobby' as propaganda for one party or another, or as general propaganda on behalf of a compassionate, anguished, far-seeing, or stern collection of ministers. And when Sir Harold Wilson boasted, as he did in his memoirs that a 1976 television reconstruction of a Cabinet debate over Chrysler was completely wrong, how much confidence was he giving the public by telling them they had no idea how they were really governed?[24] Prime Ministers, are perfectly capable, when they feel like it, of suspending 'collective responsibility' and allowing Cabinet ministers to dissent publicly from a particular line. Harold Wilson did so over the EEC in 1975 and Callaghan, his successor, when asked whether he would do the same over EEC direct elections, announced monarchically, 'I certainly think that the doctrine should apply, except in cases where I announce it does not.'[25] The Franks Committee members were unwilling to let Sir Burke get away entirely with these airy statements:

Q: I was not at all sure I understood what you meant by the word 'integrity'. We have heard allegations from members of the public that in fact it is the secrecy with which government is conducted which in their minds sometimes brings the integrity of government into question. They are inclined to think secrecy is being imposed to cover up mistakes or for similar motives. But you are saying the integrity of government demands this extreme secrecy.

A: Well integrity is a difficult word, is it not? It is like 'good government' and 'the public interest' and all these other phrases.

But if you have any body of men who genuinely share collective responsibility for their policies and their actions, surely any premature or unnecessary or unwise disclosure of their discussion among themselves will engender some degree of stress. They will cease to be the united and coherent body that they ought to be, to some extent. Now this is a matter of degree. But if that sort of thing goes beyond a certain point, what one can only call integrity in the literal sense of the word is involved — they cease to be an integer, they become a series of separate and possibly even conflicting entities.[26]

Towards the end of the 1970s, the idea that the threat of prison was a suitable device to protect this 'integrity' was abandoned. Whitehall and Westminster, as they mulled over the idea of official secrets reform, concluded that it was quite enough to threaten leaky individuals with the sack. Otherwise they might have been faced with an embarrassing prospect of mounting court cases against newspapers which were becoming less deferential. Basic attitudes towards Cabinet secrecy were not much altered by this 'liberal' change in the government's 1978 White Paper. The ombudsman is debarred from Cabinet papers, and attempts are still made to censor ministerial memoirs.

James Callaghan, then Home Secretary, and later to become a notably secretive Prime Minister, was much more frank about the vulgar political considerations which lie behind this attachment to 'collective responsibility' and ministerial secrecy in general. Testifying to the same committee he said:

It is inevitable is it not, when you consider that at any one time only half the country is in favour of the government and the other half want to get rid of them tomorrow. So a government is not like an ordinary institution, it is not like a cricket club where on the whole, all the members belonging to the club want it to go on, provided it wins games, and are not so concerned. Whereas frankly, half the people in this country are concerned to find things that will redound to the discredit of the government every day. It is inevitable in this case that a government is going to have some defensive action and say, 'We are not going to tell you anything more than we can about what is going to discredit us' ... and I think this battle will go on, but frankly I do not think altering Section 2 [of the Official Secrets Act] is going to alter it very much. It will depend to a much greater extent upon

the atmosphere and attitude of the Minister, of his advisers, of
the press generally and of the general atmosphere of public opinion. I sometimes think we make it almost impossible for a
government to govern here.[27]

The Cabinet is not, in reality, the power centre it purports to be,
any more than the House of Commons or the Queen's Court. Here
we enter a dense thicket where the very structure of government is
supposed to be a State secret, mappable only by the yelps from
disaffected Cabinet ministers that they are not allowed to see
Cabinet papers, that they are not informed about their colleague's
decisions, and that mysterious events appear to have taken place quite
behind their backs. Such as, to take what some might think a rather
large example, the successive development of a British atom bomb,
an 'independent nuclear deterrent', and its refurbishing over seven
years at a secret cost of £1,000 million. As Tony Benn, a self-
conscious 'democrat' discovered in two Labour governments, the
real political direction of the government is in the hands of three
groups: a monarchic Prime Minister with total power of hire and
fire and general access to documents; a network of interdepartmental Whitehall committees and groups such as the 'Think Tank'
and the Cabinet Office, with their own imperatives and loyalties;
and finally, a secret system of cabinet committees.[28]

Cabinet Committees

Once you embark on this business of striptease of a government,
where do you stop?[29] [Burke Trend, Secretary to the Cabinet.]

Cabinet committees are small groups of Cabinet ministers with
their own administrators. Some are permanent, such as Defence
and Overseas Policy; some experimental, such as Harold Wilson's
'inner Cabinet' (the Management Committee;) and some *ad hoc*,
such as Edward Heath's Civil Contingencies Committee, set up
to find ways of neutralizing strikes and insurrections. They can
take decisions which bind the full Cabinet through 'collective
responsibility', even though other ministers may be sublimely
ignorant even that such a committee exists, or such decision has
been taken. Their personnel are controlled by the Prime Minister,
who can steer a debate in a desired direction simply by excluding
ministers he does not agree with, or packing the committee with

those of his own views. (Benn, for example, despite his well-developed views on official secrecy and the need for less of it, was excluded from the second committee which considered secrets law reform in 1978. It drafted proposals so illiberal that their Tory successors were forced in the end to scrap them.)

Their existence is supposed to be secret, although as with so much in this type of governmental fog, the secrecy is relative. Enough ministers have written indiscreet memoirs for it to be generally known that Cabinet committees exist. What is more jealously preserved is their scope, personnel and activities, on the grounds that how the governmental household is organized is none of the public's business — the public merely pays the bills, votes for or against what it does not understand, and endures the way it is administered.

Burke Trend went out to bat on this unpromising wicket coolly enough in 1971, just as he went out to bat for the idea that Prime Ministers should be allowed to breach all his pieties on secrecy through the 'long and honourable convention' of writing propagandizing memoirs.

Trend: One can only say that all governments, or at least all governments that I have known, have always taken this line, and I think they take it almost by instinct. This is their affair how they choose to organize their business ... at the bottom of it all is this feeling of collective responsibility. They may well delegate X to 3 or 4 members in a committee but whatever that committee decides bind them all and they know that. Why should they have to disclose how they have organized the treatment of that particular subject?

Q: If you keep it so wrapped up, how can you have any pressure on government before decisions are made for good or ill?

Trend: There is nothing to prevent you pressing the government to give attention to that problem — you have an MP, you can agitate, you can do whatever you like.

Q: It is certainly not the point of view taken by foreign governments. I think a strong case could be made out that the public should have this information, that the government ought not to conceal the way in which they organize their business. This is getting rather close to secrecy for secrecy's sake. How would you respond to that?

Trend: I would simply say that I am afraid I could not agree.[30]

What Trend was in fact defending was not a system of privacy, but a system in which, once the real power-centre is identified, it is possible for interested lobbyists to cut out other lobbyists. By cutting out, successively, the public, MPs and other Cabinet ministers, both the Prime Minister and senior civil servants have a much clearer field in which to exert their own influence on decision-making. Trend was speaking, not as a rather crazily obsessional constitutional theorist, but as a Whitehall lobbyist. Behind this specious talk about the need for secrecy, lies, as usual, a claim for power.

Some years later it was James Callaghan again, by now Labour Prime Minister, who put the other half of the collusive attitude to Cabinet committee secrecy. He composed a remarkable document, which is worth quotation in full for two reasons. First, it shows with great clarity how subjective the whole business is, and how manipulative towards their democratic constituencies politicians can be. When I first saw this paper, I tried the experiment of changing the odd word so that it read as a justification for keeping the existence of the whole Cabinet secret from the public, not just its committees. The new version looked just as disconcertingly plausible as the original.

Second, it illustrates the way secrecy is merely a tool of government propaganda. The Labour Government was feeling rather foolish because Judith Hart, Minister for Overseas Development, was being urged to set up a coordinating interdepartmental group to improve aid. Because Cabinet committees are supposed to be a secret, she was unable to tell the Commons Committee concerned that such a body already existed. Callaghan let it be known, in the usual unattributable 'lobby' way, that his ministers had been much exercised about this absurdity, but had jointly decided it was necessary to preserve the system.

In fact, falling in with the Cabinet Office and his own inclinations, Callaghan had sent round a minute giving instructions. Sworn to secrecy, bound by 'collective responsibility', and confronted with this secret document, ministers were to acquiesce in the propaganda charade that they were united in their passionate conviction secrecy was right. Unfortunately for Callaghan's public image, one of them engaged in counter-propaganda, and leaked it:

THE PRIME MINISTER
Personal Minute
MINISTERS IN CHARGE OF DEPARTMENTS

Disclosure of Cabinet Committees

Consistently with the practice of all former Prime Ministers I have always refused to publish details of Cabinet Committees or to answer Questions in the House about them. Hitherto this has led to some allegations in the Press about Whitehall obscurantism but little interest or pressure in Parliament itself. There is however now some evidence that Select Committees would like to interest themselves in the Committee system and may be seeking to erode the present convention. I have therefore been considering the case for taking the initiative and disclosing details of the committee structure.

I accept that the present convention has certain disadvantages for us. In particular non-disclosure makes it difficult to answer charges that the government's policies are not properly co-ordinated. For example the Select Committee on Overseas Development has recommended the establishment of a Cabinet Committee to coordinate political, trade and aid policies towards the developing world largely because the ODM were not able to disclose that such a Committee (RD) already exists. It is also arguable that non-disclosure is inconsistent with a policy of greater openness. In any case some parts of the Committee structure are quite widely known about outside Government; in these cases what is at issue therefore is a refusal to admit publicly what a lot of people know about privately.

It is important therefore to understand the reasons for the current practice of non-disclosure. They are as follows: the Cabinet Committee system grew up as the load on the Cabinet itself became too great. It allows matters of lesser importance to be decided without troubling the whole Cabinet; and major issues to be clarified in order to save the time of the Cabinet. The method adopted by Ministers for discussing policy questions is however essentially a domestic matter; and a decision by a Cabinet Committee, unless referred to the Cabinet, engages the collective responsibility of all Ministers and has exactly the same authority as a decision by the Cabinet itself. Disclosure that a particular Committee had dealt with a matter might lead to argument about the status of the decision or demands that it should be endorsed by the whole Cabinet. Furthermore publishing details of the Committees would be both misleading and counter-productive. The existence of some could not be disclosed on security grounds; others are set up to do a particular job and are then wound up. The absence of a Committee on a particular subject (e.g. agriculture or poverty) does not mean that the Government do not attach importance to it; and the fact that a particular Minister is not on a Committee does not mean that he does not attend when his interests are affected. Publication would almost inevitably lead to pressures for both more and larger Committees, and for disclosure of information about their activities.

I do not believe that we could in any event disclose the existence of the GEN groups. [The *ad hoc* committees set up under each administration. They are numbered with the prefix GEN for 'general'.] This is partly because of their ephemeral nature and partly because disclosure would often reveal either that very sensitive subjects were under consideration or that we had something in train about which we were not ready to make an announcement. Disclosure of the main standing Committees would thus give a partial picture only. Moreover having gone as far as this I do not believe that it would be possible for me to hold the line and refuse to answer any further questions about the composition and activities of the Committees. At the minimum we would be under pressure to reveal the names of the Chairmen. This would make it harder for me to make changes; and it would have implications for the responsibilities of Departmental Ministers since Select Committees would try to summon the Chairmen of Cabinet Committees to give evidence in addition to the responsible Minister. I should also be under continuing pressure to say that a Committee was considering a particular subject (and often it would be a GEN group); and there would be questions about when Committees were meeting, the work they were doing, whether particular Ministers are on them, the details of under-pinning Official Committees, etc.

I have therefore decided that we should not change our stance on this matter. The present convention is long established and provides a basis on which we can stand. Any departure from it would be more likely to whet appetites than to satisfy them. I ask my colleagues therefore to rest on the position that the way in which we coordinate our decision is a matter internal to Government and not to answer questions about the Cabinet Committee system.

February 1978[31]

And so obscurity covers political decision-making both large and small. The chairman of the Association for Disabled Professionals, Peter Large, complained a few months later that there was no way for either the public or professional lobbies to evaluate sensibly the work done by the experimental Minister for the Disabled, Mr Alf Morris. While rumour had it that Morris was effective because he chaired a Cabinet committee covering several departments, with an underlying interdepartmental committee of officials, no one would reveal the truth about this important State secret: 'I and others do not know who all the members of these committees are, or how the committees function. We must be told. We should know who is involved with the Minister in managing our affairs, and we should know how our affairs are being managed.' Some people thought the office depended on the personality of the virtuous Mr Morris, others that the coordinating arrangements were all important: 'It would be easier to assess the arguments if we were allowed to see clearly what the present arrangements are and how they really work'.[32] Poor Mr Large. Little did he realize what a threat his innocent demands represented to the 'integrity of the government' and a Prime Minister's power to manipulate his colleagues.

The Civil Service

Clambering through the swirling mist of these political heights, we emerge at last on to a huge, dim plateau, peopled by nearly a million permanent administrators, great and small, all bound by the Official Secrets Acts never to discuss their work, and all, at least at the senior levels, impeccably 'house-trained' to mesh with their colleagues in a giant bureaucracy.

The Civil Service has grown to be a great power in the State, partly because it is permanent while politicians move on, and partly because there is such a lot of it. In mid-Victorian Britain, when Palmerston could boast of genuine ministerial control, there was no bureaucracy. The census of 1851 showed that only 1,628 clerks and officials manned the central departments of civil government; and the total number of public employees, including the Customs and Excise and the Post Office, was only 75,000. (There were 932,000 in France.) By 1978, after three-quarters of a century of welfare politics, industrial intervention, and the simple increase in the technical complexity of a modern State, there were 737,984 people manning the Civil Service proper, and another 184,000 in various fringe bodies.

The problem, and I think it is true to describe the Civil Service's attitude to administrative secrecy as a problem for the rest of us, began with the Northcote-Trevelyan Report of 1853. It set out, in brisk and untimorous prose to organize a centralized, meritocratic bureaucracy: 'We see no other mode by which (in the case of inferior no less than superior offices) the double object can be attained of selecting the fittest person, and of avoiding the evils of patronage.' Junior Civil Service jobs, the authors observed in a famous passage, were sought by 'the unambitious, and the indolent or incapable'. The top jobs on the other hand, were distributed in a way which patronage still dictates in 1980.

> Numerous instances might be given in which personal or political considerations have led to the appointment of men of very slender ability and perhaps of questionable character, to situations of considerable emolument.

Reform had to come, simply because a competent permanent Civil Service was so important to an elaborate administrative machine nominally under democratic control:

> The great and increasing accumulation of public business and the consequent pressure upon the Government need only be alluded to; and the inconveniences which are inseparable from the frequent changes which take place in the responsible administration are matters of sufficient notoriety. It may safely be asserted that, as matters now stand, the Government of the country could not be carried on without the aid of an efficient body of permanent officers, occupying a position duly subordinate to that of Ministers who are directly responsible to the Crown and to Parliament, yet possessing sufficient independence, character, ability and experience to be able to advise, assist, and to some extent influence those who are from time to time set over them.[33]

What Northcote-Trevelyan perhaps did not see were the dangers of setting up a closed system which could monopolize knowledge and be peopled by middle-class elitists. The Fulton Report gloomily pointed out 105 years later: 'One of the main troubles with the Service has been that, in achieving immunity from political intervention, a system evolved which until recently was virtually immune from outside pressure for change. Since it was not immune from inside resistance to change, inertia was perhaps predictable.'[34] If inertia was the only problem, administrative secrecy might not matter so much. But it is coupled with recruitment from a limited social group — the bland hiring the bland.

And senior civil servants, fortified with grovelling talk from outsiders about 'high-flyers' in the Service, do have a distressing tendency to see themselves as Platonic Guardians. They elaborate constitutional myths in order to preserve a public anonymity, as in this passage by Richard Wilding, a deputy secretary in the Civil Service Department, to a 1979 seminar organized by the Civil Service College:

> It is in theory and in principle, a very democratic system. The authority to determine how civil servants shall behave is totally vested in the elected representatives of the people; there is no basis on which the civil servant, the appointed official, can seek to impose his own values on the course of Government in action … It is a very tight and rather closed system. There is equally no room in it for the character who is known in American literature on the subject as the whistle-blower. In Britain, the aspiring whistle-blower is blocked. And the reason why he is blocked is not fundamentally, and never has been the Official Secrets Act — that doubtful prop of the British Constitution. It is the fact that if he blows the whistle, the player against whom he is registering a foul is his fully responsible Minister. He is therefore committing a politically hostile act, and *ipso facto* doing something inconsistent with his Civil Service status. The whistle-blower in this country must blow his whistle in the privacy of the Minister's room. If that is ineffective, he should resign his post before he blows it publicly.[35]

Wilding's definition of a 'politically hostile act' is an interesting one. His elegant essay makes much play with another concept — 'the generally accepted rules of decent behaviour' — which is even more interesting. It reminds us of Burke Trend's patrician disapproval of ministerial leaks in his evidence to the Franks Committee. Wilding finds some activities perfectly decent; among 'the accepted ways of going about things' he lists these — warning other permanent secretaries what your minister is planning; tipping off fellow civil servants before making proposals (to ministers) impinging on their areas; and remembering that your colleagues in Whitehall will remain, and have backs to be scratched, long after all your nominally commanding ministers have departed. And always, he warns, quoting Talleyrand, 'pas de zèle'. Ministerial policies are here today and gone tomorrow, and all civil servants must therefore be 'Laodicean' (a word my dictionary defines as 'lukewarm').

These precepts are a recipe for information sharing inside Whitehall, and secrecy (or information rationing) outside it. Ministers are told something; departmental lobbyists, such as oil companies, farmers or animal lovers, are told something; Parliament is told a little; and the general public, in such forms as the press, told a little too. But Whitehall knows everything, and has its own preferences. And, as the biggest secret of all is the fact of what is secret, so administrative secrecy makes it very hard to perceive that this is the structure of power in Britain.

It is beginning to be documented, however. Tony Benn, now out of Cabinet office, and no longer needing to collude with secrecy, listed, in a lecture to the Royal Institute of Public Administration in January 1980, some of the ways in which Whitehall rations information upwards to ministers.[36] They brief every incoming minister, he said, in a long departmental document, which purports to show options for fulfilling the winning party's manifesto. But in 1974, the 172-page Energy Department brief, several sections of which were marked 'Secret' or 'Confidential' contained the sentence, 'In principle it is desirable that all new orders for base load power stations should be nuclear'. This is the kind of material classed as 'advice to ministers' which Whitehall is always most obsessional about keeping secret from the public, on the hoary grounds that individual civil servants will not dare advise freely otherwise. In fact, nuclear energy is a controversial issue all over the Western world; if the 'departmental view' in 1974 was that Britain should 'go nuclear', then it was taking a highly political stance.

At one Cabinet he attended, said Benn, the Ministry of Defence presented a draft Defence White Paper showing a huge gap between the military might of West and East. 'This crude misinformation was designed to win public support for a bigger defence budget by suggesting a more serious imbalance than existed.' The MOD had, in calculating the military strength of the West, left out entirely the French armed forces. Questioned by ministers who, claimed Benn, fortunately spotted it in time, the Ministry said NATO did not exercise the same operational control over France as over the rest of the alliance. The White Paper was re-written.

Benn described how his permanent secretary would secretly brief his own junior minister to oppose him at Cabinet committees where they both appeared. He said his permanent secretary would try to 'bounce' him into approving high-technology projects that Benn was unlikely to understand. For example, he presented him with a long paper in July 1966, advocating large spending on two projects — a High Flux Beam Reactor (HFBR) and the High Magnetic Field Laboratory (HMFL) — at the bottom of which the permanent secretary had merely initialled 'I agree'. In 1975, Benn asserted, a similar attempt was made to 'bounce' a Cabinet committee into building a fast breeder nuclear reactor by writing him a paper listing only two options (at the instigation, Benn claimed, of the Cabinet Office). Option one was to spend £2,000 million on building a reactor. Option two was to achieve a position in which a reactor could be built at any given point in the future — at a cost of £1,500 million.

With the power of the Cabinet secretariat and the 'Think Tank', the power of Civil Service patronage to outside appointments, and the power to claim the importance of 'national security', Benn said the Civil Service was a strong political lobby:

Unless this process is stopped in its tracks, Britain could be governed by a commission of permanent secretaries reducing ministers to ciphers only able to accept or reject what is put before them, and the House of Commons will be a consultative assembly which will be able to express its opinions but do little more.

Over all that I have described, an official curtain of secrecy is supposed to be maintained. Why? It is in the interests both of weak ministers and strong public servants, both of whom prefer to keep the public in the dark. Weak ministers because they dare not invite challenges to their policy which they fear they could not answer; strong civil servants because their strength lies in that they cannot be challenged if they can remain anonymous.

I have reached the solemn conclusion that what we have constructed in Britain is the embryo of a corporate state that more resembles feudalism than the democracy of which we often boast.

The Official Secret

Apart from its duty to ministers, exercised in this obscure and unsatisfactory way, Whitehall, the permanent repository of all governmental knowledge and authority, has no obligation whatever to inform anyone of its doings. There is no public right to knowledge about the affairs of government. On the contrary, civil servants are bound by law to silence about their activities, with some scholastic loopholes under which senior civil servants can say pretty much as they like — this is the doctrine of 'implicit self-authorization under the Official Secrets Act', or, in plainer terms, a licence to propagandize on their own behalf. At the same time, the citizen's right of privacy, although often spoken of respectfully, has been barely developed, despite the quantum increase in information-gathering about him in the age of the computer. (The idea of privacy involves, in fact, a specialized right to information by the citizen — information held by others about himself.) A decently functioning democracy would hold these three ideas in balance — secrecy, privacy, publicity. Instead secrecy in Britain has flourished like ivy, with laws, codes and conventions, while the other two doctrines remain stunted. This is why the frontiers of secrecy in Britain, although they are, at the beginning of the 1980s, constantly shifting, are drawn in the wrong places.

The system of executive secrecy as a formal notion can be traced back to 1873. The Treasury, the supervising department of the Civil Service, was angered by leaks about the organization of the Exchequer and Audit Office, and the premature disclosures of a possible pay rise for suburban letter carriers. A circular about these 'breaches of official confidence' was sent round officials, saying they caused 'extensive mischief by sowing suspicion and by discrediting the Service'. Leaks were considered to be: 'offences of the very gravest character'. The permanent secretary wrote: 'The unauthorized use of official information is the worst fault a civil servant can commit. It is on the same footing as cowardice by a soldier. It is unprofessional.' Two years later, after further leaks to the press, another circular threatened civil servants with dismissal for talking to the press. This did not prevent Charles Marvin leaking, in 1878, details of a secret Anglo-Russian treaty from his copyists' stool at the Foreign Office. All the authorities could do (he was only in temporary work) was charge him with stealing the papers on which he had written the details down. The criminal charge simply would not hold up and was dismissed. Leaks continued. In 1884, General Gordon's Proclamation reached the press before it reached MPs. This caused a lot of trouble and provoked a third circular saying secrecy was 'not confined to matters still under discussion, but includes also the unauthorized disclosure of matter finally decided upon'.[37] Three years later some instructions to Naval Intelligence leaked to the press, and immediately afterwards a dockyard draftsman sold confidential warship designs, possibly to a foreign power. The flavour of espionage was enough to trigger legislation which, as can be seen from this short history, was really a reaction to the rise of modern journalism.

The government was fundamentally aristocratic; the press was a vulgar and commercial activity conducted by opportunist tradesmen. It was not seen, despite some self-consciously campaigning attitudes over the years by *The Times,* as inherently valuable. Indeed most of the British press has been seen by the authorities for most of the time as inherently seditious. This is reflected in the extensive legislation about it. And finally, civil servants were perceived as just that — servants — who owed a duty of loyalty and silence to their masters. Indiscretion in a servant was, as the Treasury complained, exactly like cowardice in a soldier. It was unservant-like. The first draft of legislation, in 1888, was even called the 'Breach of Official Trust Bill'. The laws on official secrecy were never primarily about spying but always went hand in hand with exasperation about leaks.

The next 23 years were punctuated by efforts in Whitehall to push forward laws that would efficiently plug leaks to the press. From the 1889 law, rechristened the Official Secrets Act, came the idea that leaks merited not only dismissal but jail. A handicap for Whitehall was left in the shape of a 'public interest' defence. Crown servants or contractors could not be prosecuted unless they leaked matter which they 'ought not, in the interest of the State or otherwise in the public interest'.

Spying continued to be thought of as a problem. So did leaking. In 1900, for example, four years after an unsuccessful attempt to strengthen the spying provisions, news leaked to the press of the Home Secretary's decision to increase police pay. The government made a straightforward attempt to get at the press in 1908, introducing a new Bill which simultaneously strengthened the spying clauses and tried to outlaw publication of information if it was not 'in the interests of the State'. The newspapers, although they stood accused of making profits from disloyal civil servants, protested strongly. The Bill was dropped. But the civil servants kept on trying. Within two years, after information about undelivered pension books reached the press before it reached MPs, and after an apparently infuriating leak of the report of the Welsh Church Commission, the Home Office had a completely new Bill drafted. It also took into account a 1909 report from the Committee of Imperial Defence that the espionage sections of the legislation had to be strengthened, because of the danger of German spies.

'National security' and irritation with newspapers were combined, not for the last time in the Home Office's history, into a neat package that only waited its parliamentary moment to be smuggled by. It came a year after drafting, in 1911. Amid spy fever and a constitutional crisis over the parliament Bill, the press simply failed to notice what the government planned. The government, for its part, pretended the Bill was entirely aimed at spying, and it went through the Commons on an August afternoon, virtually without debate. Although the idea of punishing publication as such had been sidestepped, it was from now on, without any mention of the public interest at all, an offence both to communicate and to receive any official information whatsoever — the number of cups of tea drunk by a Civil Service department, to take a famous example became, in theory at least, an official secret. The idea that government itself was an official secret was born in English law; typically, by a process of mendacity. The 1971 Franks Report allowed itself a gentle sarcasm:

> Government spokesmen explained that the Bill was intended to serve, but more effectively, the same object as the 1889 Act which it would replace. They did not conceal the facts that the new Section 2 was designed to impose a much tighter grip on all unauthorized disclosures of all kinds of official information than its forerunner of 1889, and that it would affect the Press as well as Crown servants. Nor did they think it necessary to draw attention to these facts. Section 2 was not once mentioned in the Parliamentary debates.[38]

The modern apparatus of Civil Service secrecy consists of several parts. The first is the Act itself, described by senior civil servants, in some particularly ripe pages of Franks testimony, as an awesome and inspiring thing. Sir Martin Furnival-Jones, then head of MI5 testified (incognito):

> Some have told me that it is so, that they find a kind of pride in being subjected to the criminal law in this way ... the fact that they ... are picked out as being people who are doing work so dangerous if you like that it brings them within the scope of the criminal law if they talk about it, has a very powerful effect

on their minds … it is not that they are deterred by the fear of prosecution, but in a sense it is a spur to their intent.[39]

This means, presumably, that the Act makes civil servants feel important — or at any event, self-important. The practical purpose of the Act, in fact, is supposed only to cover the marginal employees, those poor enough to be bribed, young enough not to fear dismissal, or old enough to have retired and thus become otherwise invulnerable. The main sanction against leaking, as in all large organizations, is not, of course, fear of the law, but fear of the sack. Civil Service staff discipline rules (the 'ESTACODE') require them not to talk to journalists. Franks was rather disconcerted to find that Whitehall handed out documents for its employees to sign which mixed up the two notions — the law and the employer's rules:

Q: Most of these declarations require the signatory to state that he is aware of various things, one of which usually is that he must not disclose information which he has acquired in the course of his duty without previous consent in writing from the Department. Would you agree with me that while to have consent in writing may be a prudent precaution, it actually is imposing a requirement which is not imposed by the Act?

Sir Phillip Allen, Permanent Under-Secretary of State, Home Office: Entirely.

Q: And similarly most of these declarations require that the person concerned shall submit two copies of the proposed publication, which again it appears to me goes further than the Act?

Sir Phillip: Yes.

Q: Do you agree that it is a fair comment to make that these declarations are imposing, or putting further obstacles in the way of publication, which go beyond the Act?

Sir Phillip: Yes I do.

Q: And in fact that most of these declarations, given that they ask the signatory to say he is aware of various obligations, mis-state the effect of the Act and exaggerate its importance?

Sir Phillip: Yes.[40]

Classification of Documents

There is, within the general secrecy of government paper, a somewhat more realistic system of 'classification': the grading of

documents in four ways. The purpose of this is to try to limit the
burden of secrecy which logically would demand the maximum
effort to stop material falling into outside hands — files would
have to be booked in and out; locked in safes at lunchtime; never
taken home; limited in distribution; hidden from the window-
cleaners on their regular rounds; and kept off desk tops. No one
would ever get any work done for the rigmarole of locking,
unlocking, signing and checking. So, apart from 'unclassified'
material, papers are graded (a) hardly secret at all; (b) mildly secret;
(c) rather secret; (d) secret. Or, as Whitehall officially puts it: '(a)
Restricted; (b) Confidential; (c) Secret; (d) Top Secret'.[41] These
words have no objective meaning; one could tune the semantics
another way and grade documents (a) secret; (b) very secret; (c)
very, very secret and (d) earth-shatteringly secret.

This subjectivity does not prevent Whitehall from attempting
definitions, themselves equally meaningless. Thus: 'restricted'
means material whose leaking would be 'undesirable in the interests
of the nation'; 'confidential' means 'prejudicial to the interests of
the nation'; 'secret' means 'serious injury to the interests of the
nation'; and 'top secret' means 'exceptionally grave damage to the
nation'. There is obviously a certain common sense idea of more
and less behind this verbiage; any innocent can see that the internal
phone directory of the Department of Health and Social Security
('Restricted') is less of a secret than the list of exact circumstances
in which Britain would start a nuclear war (although, on reflection,
perhaps it would be safer for all concerned if our enemies had this
information somewhere to hand). There is after all, no such thing
as the absolute secret which, if revealed, would destroy the nation,
unless suppose our rulers took a decision that they would fire all
our Polaris missiles at the Russians in 24-hours time, come what
may — the consequence of leaking that could reasonably be
expected to be catastrophic. If the Russians believed it of course. In
the 1939-45 War, our possession of the Ultra secret, the continuous
ability to crack German codes, was a vital secret *at the time.* No
secret is forever.

The classifications are based on the idea that political
embarrassment can be as bad for 'the nation' as a disclosure which
helps the Russians or enables drinkers to stock up with whisky the
day before the spirits' tax is doubled in the Budget. Despite the
urgings of the Civil Service Department that classifications should
be kept low and regularly downgraded, they tend to be routine. In
1979, I remember a senior Treasury civil servant describing to me

with some amusement how he had stamped 'Secret' on a proposal that Britain should guarantee £200 million of White assets in Rhodesia, to facilitate a constitutional settlement. The next morning he was intrigued to read of the proposal in the *Financial Times*. It had obviously been leaked by a minister. The Foreign Office, probably the most secretive ministry, stamp a security classification on a full 95 per cent of their papers.[42]

The 'Top Secret' stamp can only be authorized at assistant secretary level. When it was decided to impose direct rule on Northern Ireland in 1972, the plan was stamped 'Top Secret'. So too are plans for 'the military use of space'; negotiating positions which 'would prevent our achieving highly important national ends' (such as, presumably, the 1979 scheme for achieving a pro-Western cease-fire among the combatants in Rhodesia); and a number of types of defence documents.

The second-rank 'Secret' stamp goes on 'highly embarrassing disagreements with a friendly government'; the Cabinet's legislative priorities; forecasts of future economic developments such as inflation or unemployment 'which might damage confidence'; planned tax changes or details of pay negotiations which might provoke strikes in important industries; emergency plans to deal with strikes in essential industries; the full list of wartime government bunkers; cryptographic keying material; plans for new weapons of all kinds; vital military information such as photographs of important military sites; and (rather oddly) 'adverse reports on general morale affecting major operations'.

The two minor classifications, 'Confidential' and 'Restricted' are interesting because the 1971 Franks Committee, trying to bring some sense back into the discredited idea of Official Secrets Acts, implied they could safely be scrapped. Thus, all draft Bills, Cabinet committee memoranda; routine office circulars and instruction manuals; routine files on military stores; and telephone directories, are automatically stamped 'Restricted'. All assumptions about prices, wages or unemployment figures which 'might prejudice the government's ability to develop suitable policies'; all exchanges with foreign governments and Foreign Office minutes about other countries; all matters of wage-bargaining policy and unemployment policy; all discussions of future policy on fuel; industrial subsidies; the balance of payments and long-term investment; all local government, regional planning and land development documents; all information about weapons design and development; and all 'routine political reports' — everything on these subjects for example is automatically stamped 'Confidential'.

Whitehall staff have a second system of 'Privacy' markings to cover information they extract from commercial firms; information about their own bureaucratic ups and downs; and recommendations for that characteristically furtive British institution — the Honours List. The markings are 'Commercial — in confidence; Staff — in confidence; Honours — in confidence'.

As can be seen from all these lists, Whitehall is immensely thorough about censorship. A civil servant will be prevented from seeing many documents. Even if he sees a totally unimportant document, he faces the sack for leaking it. Even if he is prepared to be sacked, he faces prosecution at a minister's discretion, under the Official Secrets Act.

Censorship of the Past — Memoirs and Research

But this is not quite the end of the story. We have seen how senior politicians collude with the secrecy system while they are in office. Out of power, they tend to become amateur historians or the authors of boastful memoirs, and it is rather hard to stop them. Since the 1916 beginnings of the Cabinet Secretariat, its head, the Cabinet Secretary, has also been Chief Censor (as the Lord Chamberlain used to be over other theatrical performances). He vets ministerial memoirs and crosses out the parts which offend him. Ministers are given a special dispensation to consult the records to 'refresh their memory' before writing, but since the first of the notorious Crossman *Diaries* in 1975, they have had solemnly to promise to behave themselves and not 'publish information destructive of the confidential relationships on which our system of government is based'.[43] This means that they should not disclose differences of opinion with their fellow ministers, and they should not reveal what advice individual civil servants gave them until at least 15 years have passed. (They have to be censored for 'national security' as well.) 'The conventions are to be regarded as concessions made to the author, rather than restrictions imposed on him.'[44]

As with much of the secrecy apparatus, the system of vetting ministerial memoirs was, at the end of the 1970s, looking rather shell-torn, if not exploded. Asserting that people had a right to know what had been going on in their own government, Crossman had, before his death, given what the Cabinet Secretary described woundedly as 'blow-by-blow' accounts of Cabinet meetings and altercations with his own civil servants. The particular battle is discussed later in this book in the section about the press. Its conclusion was a court case to try to ban the memoirs, which the Attorney-General lost.

As usual in the secrecy structure, the legal position had been extremely vague prior to the case, resting as it turned out, largely on bluff and the willingness of the Cabinet Secretariat to make up the rules as it went along, according to its own notions of the constitution, and of gentlemanly behaviour. After the case, unsuccessfully brought under the Civil Law on confidence (originally designed for trade secrets) matters were not much clearer legally. But ministers were from then on made to sign pieces of paper accepting an 'obligation of honour'.[45] The theory of the Radcliffe Committee, set up to propose this, appears to be that if you can't take a chap to court, you can at least make him feel a cad.

As far as professional historians are concerned, the records stay sealed for at least 30 years. This is bad enough from the point of view of public knowledge, but particularly interesting (the Whitehall phrase is 'sensitive') files can stay closed for much longer, even up to 100 years. The documents concerning the abdication of Edward VIII in 1936 stay closed, for example, as do all post-war documents mentioning the activities of MI5 and MI6. Worst of all, some particularly embarrassing documents may be fed into the shredder and be lost forever; there is widespread cynicism among the participants that the full truth about Eden's dishonest and disastrous 1956 Suez venture will ever emerge into the Public Records Office. Metropolitan police records showing how they had spied on the hunger marchers of the 1930s were put in the Public Records Office after 30 years, and later withdrawn when it was discovered that some of the men they had once characterized as dangerous were still alive.

Crown Privilege

The final loophole stopped up by Whitehall is in the courts. Like Parliament, the courts in Britain are, in constitutional mythology, an independent power centre. They too claim the right of secrecy to a surprising extent over their own doings, citing their own mythologies, such as *'sub judice'*, 'the secrecy of the jury room', and the introverted traditions of the Bar.

They too collide with Whitehall, like MPs, about the amount of information to which they are entitled to lay claim. Until 1968, a ministerial certificate was enough to prevent government documents being disclosed in a court case, the courts accepting that such a certificate marked the frontier line beyond which disclosure 'would be injurious to the public interest'. Naturally enough, Whitehall invariably took the view that whole classes of documents, such as Cabinet minutes, diplomatic exchanges and 'policy papers' were immune from the courts, and so was anything which upset the smooth process of government. An army doctor was not allowed to testify on a report about a soldier's condition; 'national security' was accepted as a reason for keeping secret messages to a military commander-in-chief; wartime details of submarine construction; and a letter from the Admiralty to an oil company in the First World War. The Home Office has stopped the production of reports about a prisoner's mental condition, and the release of a letter written by a deputy police chief to the Gaming Board, making unpleasant remarks about a gaming licence application.[46]

The Lords, as Supreme Court, started to be sceptical about ministerial assertions in the case of Conway v. Rimmer in 1968. This was an action for malicious prosecution in which policemen's reports led to the dismissal of a police cadet for suspected theft, and in which the Home Office refused on principle to release the reports. The Law Lords demanded to see the reports, read them and ordered their disclosure. Since then, as in most matters to do with common law, the precise position has been rather enigmatic. But as recently as 1980, the Home Office could be observed doggedly refusing to produce a whole series of documents about the way they had set up so-called 'control units' in prisons, claiming privilege for 'policy formation' and 'advice to ministers'. The judge overruled them in a civil case brought by a prisoner. He read the material and said it could back the prisoner's claim that the units were unlawful.[47]

The Mystery of Government

This then is the formal outline of mystery-making in British government. At every turn, for reasons of self-importance, political convenience and bureaucratic camouflage, it is made elaborately difficult for the ordinary member of the public to work out precisely how he is being governed. It is a closed system, in which a great deal of trouble is taken to prepare authorized versions of events and direct them through controlled channels. Secrecy and propaganda are two sides of the same coin.

The way institutions develop in a country is rarely the result of a conspiracy, or even a single impelling historical force. It is generally through the interplay of forces, some strong, some weak, some permanent, some fleeting — some with the ability to correct their own imbalances and some, like the secrecy fetish, exasperatingly self-sustaining. It is very hard for a society to educate itself unless it can see what is happening to it. This is why the biggest secret of all is the precise extent of secrecy in government; are civil servants too powerful? It is not easy to tell unless we can see when they advise, how they come to conclusions, how much influence they actually have. The same problems exist in judging senior politicians.

Secrecy has some strong forces behind it. There is a tradition of aristocratic government in Britain which is older and more powerful than universal suffrage. It runs on a notion of mystique, not of democratic legitimacy. There is a century-old tradition of an elite permanent bureaucracy into the hands of which has unintentionally fallen a gigantic interventionist machine which ministers lack the expertise and the longevity to control. And there is a long tradition of fear. Since 1939, Britain has been in a state of war, openly with Fascism, and then in a silent way with Russian Communism and the former Imperial possessions of the Third World. This has given an unhappy plausibility to the phrase 'national security', with its corollary that politicians and officials must be allowed to act parentally, knowing the public's interest better than it does itself.

Over the last decade, other forces have begun to assert themselves and there is now a fairly general recognition among 'opinion-formers' that Britain is out of step with many of the Western democracies. We apparently live in a country where huge projects can be conceived in a huddle between officials, pressure-groups, international companies, ministers and foreign governments, without proper consultation. Although they persuaded the then bomb 18 months before it was announced in Parliament in 1948,[48] and decided to spend £1,000 million on updating Polaris submarines without any public announcement during the preparatory period between 1973 and 1980.[49] More than £800 million was spent on building an Anglo-French prestige supersonic airliner, Concorde; the mounting costs were concealed on grounds of commercial confidence until the project passed the point of no return.[50] Civil servants in secret interdepartmental committees decided in 1967 to build a third London airport at Stansted, without proper consultation. Although they persuaded the then Conservative minister to agree, it was subsequently accepted that they had chosen the wrong place.[51]

We apparently live in a country where unpopular and probably undesirable major policy changes can be proposed by 'neutral' officials who do not wish the public to know what they are recommending. The Department of Transport, for example, felt entitled in 1972 to urge ministers to lop 40 per cent off the railway network,[52] and in 1979 to allow the size of heavy lorries to be increased, complaining self-righteously in both cases that those who exposed their attitudes were criminals.[53]

We apparently live in a country where Cabinet ministers feel they stand a good chance of deceiving the public. It was pretended in 1956, that a military attack on Egypt was for 'peace-keeping' purposes when it was a secret plot between Britain, France and Israel; and it was pretended in 1976, that child-benefit welfare payments to mothers were being cut because of the attitude of trade unions. Cabinet minutes later made clear that the government was simply looking for an excuse to save money.[54] Again, the people who exposed these particular dishonesties were accused not only of criminality, but of threatening the constitution.

We apparently live in a country where safety reports are frequently suppressed on grounds of commercial confidence or political nuisance value. Road tests on old-fashioned invalid tricycles; factory inspections and pollution reports; car safety defects figures; reports on meat-packing plant hygiene; reports on food-poisoning outbreaks — all these have been hidden in the past.[55] Many of them have been brought to light because other countries, notably the US, are much more free with the release of information — and it is often the very information which is being kept secret in Britain at the same time.

We apparently live in a country where a subcommittee of MPs is required to say in 1976 that the range of the Tow anti-tank missile is 'xxx' and the Dragon missile 'only xx'. (The US military announced to Congress at about the same time that the range of Tow was about 3,000 metres and the Dragon was medium-range, 60-1,000 metres.)[56]

We apparently live in a country in which a labour-exchange clerk who reports discriminatory firms to another government body, the Commission for Racial Equality, can be threatened with the

Official Secrets Act and then sacked[57] — in which one government body, the Manpower Services Commission, can be refused unemployment forecasts from the Treasury and have to commission its own from a university[58] — in which an official government committee studying data protection and privacy can be refused details of the Metropolitan police computer[59] — and in which a Cabinet minister can complain that his mistrustful officials, pushing for nuclear power stations, omitted to brief him that the Russians had a catastrophic nuclear accident in the Urals in the 1950s; that 200 tons of uranium had disappeared probably to Israel in 1968 by way of unplanned nuclear proliferation; that British uranium was being ordered from South-Africa occupied Namibia in 1970; and that a leak of nuclear waste was occuring in 1976 at the Windscale nuclear reprocessing plant, at the point when it was being planned to step up its activities.[60]

This does not sound like a very satisfactory country in which to live. Later in this book we will look at the detailed interplay between democratic rhetoric and silent misconduct in three especially secretive areas — the Home Office Prison Department; the justice system; and the large empire of the secret services.

But first we must deal with another shining star of British mythology. The government may be furtive, but we have a countervailing institution, surely? We have the Fourth Estate — fearless, shameless, exposure-minded. We have a Free Press. Why isn't that enough?

2
Manipulating the Press

Nor is it to the common people less than a reproach; for if we be so jealous over them that we dare not trust them with an English pamphlet, what do we but censure them for a giddy, vicious and ungrounded people, in such a sick and weak estate of faith and discretion as to be able to take nothing down but through the pipe of a licenser? That this is care or love of them we cannot pretend when as in those Popish places where the laity are most hated and despised, the same strictness is used over them.

...truth is...a streaming fountain; if her waters flow not in a perpetual progression, they sicken into a muddy pool of conformity and tradition...give me the liberty to know, to utter, and to argue freely according to conscience, above all liberties. [Milton, *Areopagitica.*]

Where blasphemous, immoral, treasonable, schismatical, seditious or scandalous libels are punished...the liberty of the press, properly understood, is by no means infringed or violated. The liberty of the press is indeed essential to the nature of a free state; but this consists in laying no previous restraints upon publications...to subject the press to the restrictive power of a licenser as was formerly done...is to subject all freedom of sentiment to the prejudice of one man...but to punish (as the law does at present) any dangerous or offensive writings...is necessary for the preservation of peace and good order, of government and religion, the only solid foundations of civil liberty. [Blackstone, *Commentaries,* Book 4.]

The British media are not strong willed. This is partly for historical reasons. Despite the lip-service paid to the idea, genuine freedom of the press has never been seen in Britain as part of the constitution. Newspapers have been seen as seditious; as house magazines for the ruling class; as vulgarly commercial. But never since the penny and halfpenny papers multiplied a century ago on the joys of steam technology, have they really been seen as the Fourth Estate. Journalists have been surprisingly ready to take themselves at the valuation of their betters and to submit to a web of legislation and restrictions which borders on the ludicrous. They have as a consequence become extremely dependent for information on some of the more secretive power-holders of the Western world, and because of this are often channels for official or political propaganda. At the banquet of power, journalists tend to be polite guests, fed maggoty bread — the alternative is to starve.

Two fundamentally democratic ideas about information have never really been accepted in Britain even among many professional journalists — first, that liberty is indivisible, and crass, irresponsible or simply loathsome publications are inescapably part of it; and second, that knowledge about public affairs should be a right and not a privilege. We have to look at Sweden with its venerable Freedom of the Press Act providing for access to State files, and to the US where press freedom is written into the Constitution, to see this belief in action.

At the same time, newspapers, radio and television companies do have a great deal of ephemeral political impact in Britain, where there is little advance censorship of an open kind. All the frontier posts of official secrecy, which have moved about a great deal in the last ten years, have been planted after particular confrontations with journalists. It is only when we look at the frontier lines in other countries that we see how far forward the British State is still allowed to string its barbed wire.

The Official Secrets Act

As described in Chapter 1, the Official Secrets Acts were supposed in 1911 to be simply about spying, and no one said anything to the 1911 Parliament to disabuse the public of this deliberately misleading idea. The Acts are indeed about spying; they were also a government device to stop leaks to the press. Civil servants were wary enough of angry journalists to drop their 1908 proposals that printing information should of itself be a crime. They did get through measures which were drafted in a very wide and vague way, and were extended in 1920 to be even wider and vaguer, with a clause forcing journalists if need be to disclose their sources.[1] The 'Section 1' spying clauses of the Acts are a testimonial to the sheer slipperiness of information. Before they would feel safely covered, government lawyers had to invent some extraordinary concepts. Letters to an address 'reasonably suspected' to be that of a foreign agent constituted 'communication with a foreign agent'. Someone 'reasonably suspected' to be a foreign agent constituted, *ipso facto,* a foreign agent. Trying to send letters to a 'suspected' address of a 'suspected' foreign agent proved that someone was trying to get information which might indirectly be useful to a potential enemy, for a 'purpose prejudicial to the safety or interest of the state'. Collecting or publishing any information relating to a 'prohibited place' was enough to convict unless the alleged spy could prove his innocence, a reversal of the normal burden of proof.

Journalists treated these 'spying provisions' complacently enough until they were dug up like some rusty bomb and exploded under two young journalists in 1978, in the ABC affair analysed in Chapter 5. All laws against information and 'enemies of the state' are capable of being turned against the press. Although the ABC 'spying' prosecutions under Section 1 of the Act were eventually dropped in the course of two hard-fought Old Bailey trials, Section 1 in all its oppressiveness is still on the statute book. Another government may try to use it again and freedom of information campaigners have so far been squeamish about trying to reform it. Whitehall lobbyists busied themselves at the time whispering that the victims of the prosecution were virtual agents of the KGB and not to be troubled about; I can remember the message being dutifully passed on by 'establishment' journalists to pressure groups drafting liberal model information Bills in 1978. These hints were, not to put too fine a point on it, all lies.

Section 2 has, however, been the notorious anti-press clause, asserting as it does that the uttering and receipt of any information learned by a civil servant, no matter how lowly, in the course of his job, is a crime. As with all government secrets, the real nub of the Act is buried in misleading verbiage. It reads:

If any person having in his possession or control any secret official code word or pass word or any sketch plan, model, article, note, document or information which relates to, or is used in, a prohibited place, or anything in such a place or which has been made, or obtained in contravention of this Act, or which has been entrusted in confidence to him by any person holding office under Her Majesty, or which he has obtained or to which he has had access owing to his position as a person who holds or has held a contract on behalf of Her Majesty, or as a person who is or has been employed under a person who holds or has held such an office or contract:

(a) communicates the code word, pass word, sketch plan, model, note, document or information to any person other than a person to whom he is authorized to communicate it, or a person whom it is in the interest of the State his duty to communicate it; or

(b) uses the information in his possession for the benefit of any foreign power or in any other manner prejudicial to the safety or interests of the State;

(c) retains the sketch plan, model, article, note or document in his possession or control when he has no right to retain it or fails to comply with all directions issued by lawful authority with regard to the return or disposal thereof; or

(d) fails to take reasonable care of, or so conducts himself as to endanger the safety of the sketch plan, model, article, note, document, secret official code or pass word or information;
that person shall be guilty of a misdemeanour.

(1A) If any person having in his possession or control any sketch plan, model, article, note, document or information, which relates to any munitions of war, communicates it directly or indirectly to any foreign power, or in any other manner prejudicial to the safety or interests of the State, that person shall be guilty of a misdemeanour.

(2) If any person receives any secret official code word or pass word or sketch plan, model, article, note, document or information, knowing or having reasonable grounds to believe at the time he receives it that the code word, pass word, sketch plan, model, article, document or information is communicated to him in contravention of this Act, he shall be guilty of a misdemeanour, unless he proves that the communication to him of the code word, pass word, sketch plan, model, article, note, document or information was contrary to his desire.[2]

The one civil liberties achievement between 1920 and the 1939 war was to knock out the clause in the 1920 Act depriving suspects of the right to silence. A Stockport journalist, E.D.G. Lewis, was fined in 1937 for refusing to tell police his source for a 'wanted' description printed by his newspaper. Then a much more important person, the MP Duncan Sandys, was questioned about his source for facts he had discovered about anti-aircraft defences.

The House of Commons mounted its high horse about 'parliamentary privilege', and this collision with Parliament led to the Act being modified, in 1939.[3]

Beneath its dishonest flatulence, Section 2 has a fine simplicity. Everything except official statements, it says, is secret, and if the Attorney-General feels like it he can prosecute any of those who speak about the way the government is run. Civil servants do not know what is really secret and what is not, except by asking formal permission in writing. Therefore, apart from very senior officials, no civil servant dares to speak to a journalist who rings him up, without such permission. Hired public relations officials flourish, sent to these exposed positions like ambassadors.

Newspapers do worry about the Official Secrets Act, although 'receipt' is tricky to prove and the legislation has been heavily discredited by ludicrous occasional prosecutions, political abuse and promises of reform offered but never fulfilled between 1970 and 1980. Inside a newspaper or broadcasting company, the anxious huddles with the office lawyer often involve a kind of political guesswork: 'What we are about to print is technically illegal, but is an Attorney-General likely to act?'

Direct threats to newspapers are rare, although book publishers, with large amounts of capital tied up in a single project, are more vulnerable to hints. The Act works primarily by frightening official sources of information and inducing a 'clearance mentality' in them; it is best to say nothing dangerous unless it is cleared with one's superiors. Within newspapers and broadcasting companies, I have never in my own recent experience seen an article directly vetoed for fear of the Official Secrets Acts. What does happen is that sources of information are heavily disguised, one tries to avoid quoting directly from official documents and sources, and a generally muffled air surrounds the provenance of a piece. I once had publicly to apologize for printing an item of information I knew to be true (details would run into the law of libel) because the government official who had given it to me would have faced prosecution if he was called on to testify. But this is just as much the fault of Civil Service disciplinary codes as of the Official Secrets Acts: the man concerned not only feared prosecution, he feared the sack.

The retired defence journalist Chapman Pincher gives in his memoirs two direct post-war examples of the use of the Act to intimidate in advance. In 1950, he says, the permanent secretary at the Ministry of Supply, Sir Archibald Rowlandson, rang the *Daily Express* and asserted it would be prosecuted under the Acts if it printed Pincher's discovery that embarrassing and expensive repairs were needed to a nuclear reactor being built at Windscale to make bombs. Poor workmanship was to blame. A year later Rowlandson admitted to the *Express* that his successful threat had been mere bluff. In the same decade, Duncan Sandys, Conservative Aviation Minister, used the Acts to stop the *Daily Sketch* printing pictures of the 'flying bedstead', an ungainly prototype of the jump jet. He wanted to announce the development personally two weeks later at the Farnborough Air Show.[4]

In 1967, Sir Anthony Nutting, former Minister of State at the Foreign Office, wrote a book about Suez after keeping secret for ten years the reasons why he had resigned from the Conservative Government. He said secrecy 'allowed a government to deceive Parliament and people and sheltering behind that deception to lead the nation into war'. The Cabinet Secretary, Sir Burke Trend, was displeased: 'He told me in effect that the book could not be published. Sir Burke went through the book with me page by page objecting to almost all ... He referred to the oath taken by a Privy Councillor and also to the provisions of the Official Secrets Acts as being the bases of his objection to publication.' Sir Burke also sent a letter to *The Times,* which planned to serialize extracts, telling the editor, William Rees-Mogg: 'Objection was taken to these memoirs on the grounds that they infringed official secrecy'.[5] Neither Nutting nor Rees-Mogg were frightened off by these threats.

But unpublicized bullying beforehand is always a much more efficient censorship tactic than efforts at revenge after the event. Those inevitably have to be conducted more or less in the open, in a courtroom, and be unsympathetically reported by the professional colleagues of the people in the dock. Before the last war, such figures as Compton Mackenzie and the son of the Labour Minister George Lansbury, fell foul of the Act for describing long gone intelligence activities and Cabinet meetings. In the post-war period there was the occasional minor prosecution or threat of prosecution against young left-wingers for printing military material. (In 1958 there was a case suppressing an article on radio eavesdropping. See Chapter 5.) But most actual prosecutions were properly aimed at leaks to foreign intelligence agencies, or dishonest dealings by policemen, prison warders and postmen. Between 1946 and 1971, there were 20 'Section 1' cases, almost all about Russian intelligence-gathering. There were 22 'Section 2' cases under the blanket clauses making all government information a theoretical secret — only three were aimed at publications.[6]

In 1970, however, the Labour Government lost its head and let Sir Norman Skelhorn, the DPP, prosecute the *Sunday Telegraph* and a young man called Jonathan Aitken (later to become a Conservative MP) for printing an official report on the civil war in Nigeria which annoyed the Nigerian Government. Government troops were winning at the time, and had the backing of the British, despite an emotional campaign on behalf of the breakaway insurgents in Biafra, which Aitken supported. It became a *cause célèbre* — there had been growing public unhappiness about the Official Secrets Acts and other instruments of press censorship since the Vassall Tribunal of 1963, which jailed two journalists for refusing to name their sources in an uproar about Whitehall's competence at winkling out blackmail-prone homosexuals.

Technically the case turned on the culpability, under the law as drafted, of members of a 'chain' passing the key document from hand to hand. Written by the Defence Adviser posted to the British High Commission in Lagos, the report went through several hands. Only two links in the 'chain' were put in the dock along with the newspaper and its editor, the others acting as witnesses. All the defendants were acquitted and the judge, Mr Justice Caulfield, remarked caustically that Section 2 was a legal mess which should be 'pensioned off'. This affair was nectar to secrecy's opponents; Aitken wrote a sarcastic book about the Official Secrets Acts[7] and the Franks Committee, set up to study them as part of a secretive Whitehall's slow retreat under fire during the 1960s, began to work in an atmosphere of controversial excitement.

The last decade has left journalists relatively carefree about prosecution under the Acts. Franks discredited them, and proposed they should be confined to properly classified areas of security and privacy, but after ten years of Whitehall foot-dragging and unacceptable proposals, nothing has yet been done.

The only attempt to mount another trial of journalists came at the end of the decade in the ABC affair, and that too was a legal and political fiasco. By the spring of 1980 journalists and newspapers were acting as though the Acts were a total dead letter. Duncan Campbell, one of the ABC defendants, printed, for example, a long, accurate account of the Government's secret and extensive telephone-tapping system in the *New Statesman* magazine, based on leaks by a GPO engineer.[8] He was clearly in breach of the 'receipt' clauses of the Acts and did not try to disguise this. The Conservative Government made no move to prosecute, although the D-notice Committee (see below) sent a plaintive 'private and confidential' letter, asking him to stop.

Unfortunately, contemporary displays of journalistic machismo have a flimsy basis. A journalist is only as good as his unofficial sources, and these sources still have much to be scared about. Whenever sensitive information reaches newspapers, the government aims as a rule for the vulnerable source, not the self-righteous and vociferous journalist. It sets up what Mrs Thatcher insouciantly termed in 1980 'the customary leak enquiry'.

The *Railway Gazette* affair of 1972 is a case in point. The magazine was shown a railway policy review document classified 'Confidential', from the Department of the Environment, which had found its way to one of the best campaigning newspapers in Britain, the *Sunday Times.* The *Sunday Times* published a story[9] pointing out, to some public debate, that civil servants were urging the Transport Minister to close down 4,600 miles of the 11,600 mile rail network. Scotland Yard were summoned by the Department under a Conservative Government. The *Railway Gazette* was raided and its editor complained that staff telephones were being tapped and one young employee threatened with embarrassing personal disclosures unless he named sources. Under the Franks Report proposals, published only the previous month, no one would have been committing any illegality by viewing departmental documents about railways.

Harold Evans, the editor of the *Sunday Times* was interrogated and cautioned under the Official Secrets Act. The offices of the *Railway Gazette* were searched, under it was claimed, the provisions of the Theft Act. The document might, it was explained, have been stolen. No prosecutions ensued. They had never been likely.

Nor were prosecutions the real point of the 1976 Frank Field affair, in which all the Labour Government's young political advisers were solemnly finger-printed in an effort to discover who had leaked a set of Cabinet minutes to the magazine *New Society.*[10] The minutes detailed the Labour Cabinet's rather shabby efforts to postpone the costly introduction of child-benefit payments and palm off the blame on to trade-union leaders (typically, by unattributable 'lobby' briefings of journalists). A Whitehall source passed the minutes, which had been quite widely circulated, to Frank Field in a London restaurant. Field was then heading a welfare lobby, the Child Poverty Action Group. His informant told Field to print them in *New Society,* which was done anonymously after Field burnt his documents. Field's authorship rapidly became known. No proceedings were taken against either him or the magazine, although all Cabinet documents had been recommended by Franks for continued protection by the criminal law. The indignant Whitehall source was never traced by police. Field subsequently became not only an ardent campaigner against official secrecy, but also a Labour MP. Some time afterwards, the Government dropped the Franks scheme to make all Cabinet document disclosures a criminal offence, marking a small political retreat. Field asserted proudly: 'It was only the leak which persuaded the Government, shamefacedly, to introduce the child benefits scheme.'[11]

In the same spring, Sir Phillip Allen, retired permanent secretary at the Home Office, was called in to conduct a 'customary leak enquiry' into the disclosure that some names on the resignation honours list of Sir Harold Wilson had been queried. The leaks named as honours candidates, accurately enough, a right-wing financier, James Goldsmith and a businessman friend of the Prime Minister's who later left Britain after a Customs investigation — Sir Joseph Kagan. These leaks caused some pain to Sir Harold and even more distress to naïve Labour supporters up and down the country. Mr Callaghan set the mark on his prime ministerial style by ordering this inquiry. Sir Phillip interrogated more than 15 witnesses, but no prosecutions followed.[12]

In 1976 I had my first personal experience of the direction these leak investigations take. One of the things the Official Secrets Acts are supposed, properly, to protect, is the confidentiality of police records about individuals. In fact, this being an issue of privacy and not of bureaucratic convenience, secrecy is not scrupulously observed. Police used to assert in public that there was little danger of details of criminal records falling into unauthorized hands because they were never handed out by telephone, but only transmitted to police stations.

A young man from Swindon, who in the interests of his welfare I had better call George, gave me a personal demonstration that this piece of public relations was simply untrue. He had various petty convictions himself and, claiming to be motivated by outrage at the way his background always leaked and prevented him gaining honest employment, he found out how Criminal Record Office records were released. Simply by getting hold of the ex-directory phone numbers of central and regional CROs (which he did originally by accident), he rang up, announced he was a PC from various police stations, and obtained CRO details for any sample name one gave him.

The Times, for whom I was working at the time, printed this disclosure of police malpractice. Scotland Yard with gratifying speed appointed a chief superintendent to investigate. But he did not investigate the police abuses; he started investigating me and my source. Policemen arrived in the *Times* office armed with a long questionnaire aimed at discovering the source. Belonging as I did to the staff of a relatively powerful establishment newspaper, I merely sat comfortably through the interview, flanked by a Times Newspapers Ltd solicitor, not answering dangerous questions, and declining on the lawyer's instructions to make a statement.

George, on the other hand, who had foolishly been checking on his own CRO file by phone, which enabled him to be traced, rang up a few days later. He was distraught and tearful: 'I confessed', he said. 'This superintendent comes round to my house with four big officers, runs me upstairs and pushes me face down on the bed. He got out this electric soldering iron, sticks it up me and threatens to switch it on. So I confessed!' I naturally dismissed these unprovable and no doubt entirely baseless and malicious allegations against a senior police officer who my contacts assured me would not hurt a fly — but there was no doubt George had been rumbled. Later the chief superintendent informed me with some satisfaction that George had met his just deserts, being arrested in Swindon for 'obtaining a curry by deception' at an Indian restaurant. In Sweden it is considered unconstitutional under the Freedom of the Press statutes to try to trace the source of leaks to the press about government. This is a genuine restriction: in Stockholm visiting journalists will be proudly told that a finance minister who sought to trace a recent budget leak was prevented from doing so. The 'customary leak enquiry' is merely part of the authoritarian British governmental tradition, not an integral feature of democratic systems.

D-Notices

There is a second front-line of advance censorship for the press on so-called national security matters — the D-notice system. Unwholesome in principle because it involves secret collusion between the press and government officials to keep news from the public, the system has been occasionally abused in practice and is sliding into a graceful decline in the 1980s. It still encourages an attitude of pleased furtiveness, especially among provincial newspapers, but it is unlikely to survive the 1980 retirement of the then secretary to the D-notice Committee, Rear-Admiral Kenneth Farnhill. The public rightly see something potentially sinister in a censorship system which is itself made a mystery of, and the Official Secrets Acts which underpin its operations are now treated with increasing contempt. The D-notice system can only work in an atmosphere of trust that government officials mean the same thing by the phrase 'national security' as do professional journalists. That trust (or deference) is simply no longer there, and being a purely voluntary arrangement, the D-notice system is consequently dying. In some ways this is a pity because it does mediate between the secrecy obsessions of Whitehall officials and the more rational attitudes of the outside world.

The system, like so much else in Britain, has developed a formal and informal side. The formal side is enshrined in a green ring-bind folder stamped 'Private and Confidential' issued to newspaper editors and generally kept locked up. In the 1950s and 1960s individual D-notices used to be sent out in double envelopes marked to show they were for the Editor's eyes only. Once read and memorized, they were solemnly destroyed. Other journalists were of course unable to censor themselves in the Editor's absence, which rather defeated the system's object. (The Editor of the *Spectator* described this rather embarrassedly as 'I suppose ... an excess of zeal for security'.)[13]

The folder contains a set of a dozen D-notices consolidated in 1971 and reissued with only minor alterations and additions ever since. They come from the 'Defence, Press and Broadcasting Committee' which is based in the Ministry of Defence and consists of 17 people. The chairman is the permanent secretary who heads the Ministry of Defence, and the Secretary a retired naval man, Rear-Admiral William Ash. Until 1980, his predecessor was Kenneth Farnhill, who conducted a review of defence intelligence for Sir Dick White (former head of MI5, MI6 and the security arm of the cabinet secretariat) before taking over the DPBC in 1972. The secretary's stand-in is a Ministry of Defence public relations man. There are three other senior officials on the government side of the full committee which rarely meets: the head of the Home Office, the head of the Army section of the MOD and a senior representative from the Foreign Office. Between them they cover the full range of spying, 'internal security' and ordinary military activities. The other side of the committee consists of eleven pressmen (mainly from the proprietors' associations whose role is to agree with requests for suppression: two provincial newspaper executives, two pressmen from Fleet Street, one from Scottish newspapers, one each from commercial broadcasting and the BBC, two from magazines, and one each from the main domestic and commonwealth teleprinter news agencies.

The D-notices are supposed themselves to be kept secret on the grounds that they help the Russians to know what we are most furtive about in this country. In fact, any marginal advantage given to our enemies is outweighed by the public suspicion generated by this secrecy. Which helps the Russians more — the knowledge that we fear they will eavesdrop on our defence radio signals, or the mistrust of the British general public for its government? Nigel Lawson, editor of the *Spectator,* tried to explain to a Tribunal of three elderly Privy Councillors in 1967 that it was bad enough keeping the existence of the whole system a secret for so long:

> On the whole, newspapers do not like their readers to know they are accepting any kind of censorship; they like to give the impression of being bold, fearless and free, so they may well want to keep this fact quiet, that there is this system of censorship, and certainly it was kept very quiet for a very long period of time, presumably with press collusion.[14]

However, the Privy Councillors were most upset that the *Spectator* had published part of a D-notice, in order to explain to the public what a current political row was about. And the press side of the committee itself was mortified. One Mr L.J. Dicker, representative of the Newspaper Proprietors' Association, spoke of his closeness to the mighty. He had been trained in radar and such like during the war in the Royal Artillery.

> I have had a certain amount of security responsibility... I was transferred to Press communications ... and attended many top secret briefings and worked in close liaison with the field press censors and field security services. My appointment to this committee was on the recommendation of the late Lord Burnham who was a big figure in the NPA and managing director of the *Daily Telegraph,* and who had been during the war director of public relations at the War Office.

The press side would have no objection to being 'positively vetted' by MI5 he assured the Tribunal, adding: 'I should imagine on the quiet we have been vetted already — I should be surprised if we were not.'

He wanted the *Spectator* dealt with, going on to call melodramatically for the dispatch of D-notices in double envelopes by fast motorcycle, 'officer to officer', and the issuing to himself and other members of the committee of scrambler telephones: 'The security of D-notices is a thing which is very close to our hearts and we do not want them made available to all and sundry ... They are made as watertight as possible, but you cannot avoid giving some clue as to what is going on.'[15]

The Radcliffe Committee fell in with these attitudes, announcing without any effort to weigh the public interest:

> We think that this is one of these issues on which the security consideration ought to prevail. After all, the system has been operating for more than 20 years with the assent of a great many editors of a wide variety of journals, and it does not appear that in that time any editor has felt that his public duty has required him to violate that confidentiality or to protest against it.[16]

The simplest way to demonstrate that the D-notices do not need to be kept secret is to print their contents. Since 1971, they have not been rushed out on an emergency basis which would suggest to the Russians that some specific and exciting secret was suddenly coming into being. Apart from aircraft specifications and so on, where it is explained what figures are still on the secret list, the D-notices are entirely generalized. There are 12. They give an interesting insight into the way Whitehall would define real military secrets if it had to justify classifications instead of merely stamping them on most pieces of passing paper. But the D-notices are still very vague, like most of these censorship operations. They are saved from absurdity in the usual way by an informal system of *authorized* concessions.

D-notice No. 1, headed 'Defence Plans, Operational Capability and State of Readiness' is a conspectus of the security field. It points out that censorship is lifted if material is officially released or published abroad. The information listed, it says 'is always of great interest to a potential enemy'. There should be no disclosure of information about detailed subject matter covered by the following paragraphs without seeking official advice; such a lot has already been published that without asking for advice 'an inadvertent breach of this notice can easily happen'. This list reads:

Information relating to:

(a) defence policy or plans which would enable a potential enemy to deduce details of our strategy or intentions.

(b) the operational capability and state of readiness of individual units or formation; actual service manpower strengths by specialities, categories or trades; the degree of implementation of defence equipment policy; or our logistic resources.

(c) the organization, functioning, techniques, equipment personnel or cost of the Intelligence and Security Services and of the Special Forces [this is a reference to, respectively, MI6, MI5 and the Special Air Services, the SAS].

(d) future movements or intended destinations of HM ships or RAF, or moves of Service units or formations (as distinct from normal peace-time reliefs) except immediately prior to the movement taking place.

(e) current or projected tactics, trials or operational techniques (including electronic counter measures).

(f) the present and future organization of our military control and reporting system, including the location, techniques, covering zones and special functions of radar stations and communications centres within the system.

D-notice No. 2 urges consultation with Whitehall before giving details of weaponry trials, design details and stocks, including 'material relating to defence against biological and chemical warfare' (the 1950s pilot production plant for nerve gas at Nancekuke, Cornwall, has now been pulled down, rather gingerly, and turned into a radar station.Britain does not officially make nerve gas, although the US does; it merely defends itself against it): 'The mutually satisfactory application of this notice rests on a precise knowledge of whether or not the subject is classified.'

D-notice No. 3 lists in a similar way the types of naval items which, if classified, 'must be safeguarded in the interests of national security'. They are straightforward enough, including silencing devices and diving depths for submarines; mine disposal techniques; weaponry; port defences and communication or electronic warfare equipment.

D-notice No. 4 divides aircraft and engines into three groups.

The 'Initial Publication List' allows journals to say who manufactures the plane, what it is supposed to do, how many crew it carries and the name (but not the codings and mark number) of the engine. In 1977, no planes or engines were listed in this section. At 'roll-out' planes move onto the 'Part Publication List' when photographs and measurements are normally released. The weight and some details of performance and engine components are also permitted. The 1977 part-publication list, for example, lists four planes — the Harrier and Sea Harrier jump-jets, the Nimrod and the Tornado fighter bomber. Eight engines are listed with the details that are acceptable; the Tornado engine, for example, must be described as having a pressure ratio 'over 20', and a thrust/weight ratio of 'over 8'. No details are permitted of the Rolls-Royce/Allison XJ99-RA-1 engine except to say it is in the '9,000 lb thrust class'. Planes that go into squadron service are automatically downgraded to the 'Open List', although not all cancelled projects do. The British Aircraft Corporation's TSR-2 is the only such listed.

D-notice No. 5 lists 14 types of information about nuclear weapons it would normally be 'contrary to the national interest to publish ... without first obtaining official advice'. The notice points out that printing information about transport of nuclear material is highly likely to give away information about stockpiles, storage sites and secret plans for their use; information about such movements is always classified as 'Secret'. In practice the D-notice system is more flexible than this would suggest — it has been frequently explained that Polaris missiles are moved from Faslane in Scotland to be re-armed at Burghfield in Reading. And once when one of the Navy's nuclear items was involved in a lorry crash, it was unable to persuade the D-notice secretary to do anything about it. Indeed, under the system, there was nothing specific he could do. The D-notice also argues that secrecy is in the interests of non-proliferation: 'with the increase in knowledge of the application of nuclear techniques to military weapons'.

D-notice No. 6 covers photographs 'you are requested not to publish without seeking advice'. Once again, the categories are unsurprising. General views of districts with government bases are allowed and aerial pictures of warships, but old pictures of sensitive bases are not because, 'hostile intelligence may find it useful for the purpose of comparison'. Royal Ordnance factories, submarine bases, naval dockyards, airfields, radio/radar sites, military storage depots, firing ranges and the nuclear research units at Aldermaston and Foulness are not to be freely photographed.

D-notice No. 7 is rather peculiar. It is headed 'Prisoners of War and Evaders' and deals in fact with torture and brainwashing. 'In the interests of national security' editors are asked not to write about army and security men receiving what is termed 'anti-interrogation training'. Nor are they expected to disclose what the training consists of or where it is done; it is classed as 'information that a potential enemy is likely to seek'. There have been reports of soldiers being seriously injured by sensory deprivation and beatings; the D-notice deals obliquely with this issue:

> There would normally be no objection to stating that regulations are in force with the object of ensuring that men are not subjected to undue or damaging stress, that the training is carried out under constant medical supervision, that the medical authorities have absolute authority to withdraw any individual who does not appear to be fit to continue the training, and that any man can find himself withdrawn at any stage.

This D-notice is disquieting for obvious reasons. One cannot teach resistance to torture without studying the techniques of torture. The European Court of Human Rights found evidence of systematic 'maltreatment' of IRA suspects and it has been conceded that more than 1,000 officers and 267 civilian security and intelligence agents received 'psychological warfare' training between 1974 and 1977 at the Joint Warfare Establishment, Old Sarum, Wiltshire.

D-notice No. 8 is headed 'National Defence — War Precautions and Civil Defence'. It is detailed in Chapter 5 on the secret government underground in Britain, and stifles discussion of civil defence. It lost much of its force in the famous 1963 disclosures when supporters of the Campaign for Nuclear Disarmament named as one of the 'Regional Seats of Government' a bunker at Warren Row, Berkshire. There was a demonstration outside it and the *Guardian,* alone among newspapers, decided to over-ride the pleadings of the D-notice committee and report the facts.

D-notices Nos. 9 and 11 cover the same ground from different directions. They are headed 'Radio and Radar Transmissions' and 'Cyphers and Communications' respectively. What they are concerned with is radio eavesdropping. 'HMG' intercepts communications 'as a means of obtaining secret information concerning foreign powers ... publication of any information about our interception arrangements tends to stimulate other countries into taking measures which could make the work of our security and intelligence services more difficult'. Likewise: 'Communist countries intercept our radio, communications and other electro-magnetic transmissions for the purpose of obtaining information.' There is a veiled reference to Britain's junior partnership with the US 'National Security Agency': 'In these matters, many of the security interests of our allies are identical with our own.'

There is an unexceptionable request for silence about Britain's own codes and ciphers and an admission that there is no point in trying to conceal the whereabouts of such tracking stations as the gigantic missile warning dome on the Yorkshire moors at Fylingdales. There is also a general request for censorship of details about our own signal-transmitting installations. But the most controversial request is the blanket effort to censor 'the nature and extent of interception by HMG of any form of communications ... for the purposes of national security'. One cannot examine the true purposes of our rulers without discussing their activities, and over the period 1975-80, 'Signals Intelligence' disclosures became a battleground (discussed in Chapter 5) which largely shredded these D-notices.

Secrecy won an early battle, none the less, in disturbing circumstances. By 1973, a book by Geoffrey McDermott, *The New Diplomacy and its Apparatus,* had already named Cheltenham and the 'Government Communications HQ' as the seat of British code-breaking, and pointed out that this was known to the Russians. The Granada Television company were none the less ordered by the Independent Broadcasting Authority to delete their references to Cheltenham, including an address taken from Whittaker's Almanac, in a programme on the Official Secrets Acts. This followed a claim by the D-notice secretary that Granada were in technical breach of D-notice No. 11. The D-notice system is supposed to be voluntary; what occurred in fact was direct censorship of speech by a statutory and unaccountable body, the IBA.[17]

As the ABC secrets affair gathered momentum, and radical sheets printed increasing details about SIGINT and its personnel, the D-notice committee badly lost its way. To avoid the absurdity of information being printed in foreign papers but censored from Britons, the D-notices allow republication, unadorned, of foreign material. Was republication of material in the newly lively radical press also to be allowed? Rear-Admiral Farnhill staunchly said 'No' in public to journalists. In private, he asked the committee for advice in 1978. They temporized, hoping the trial in progress at the

Old Bailey would force back the lid. When the trial failed to do so, Whitehall attempted to legislate. Its Official Information Bill proposed to declare downright illegal the republication of any information about signals interception, as well as about spying, the political police and classified defence and foreign material. These over-ambitious plans had to be dropped. In 1980 the position is that critical journalism, on a spectrum occasionally including the *Guardian* and then moving leftward through the *New Statesman,* regularly ignores D-notices, making its own moral decisions. The nationalistic media continue self-censorship with occasional exceptions.

D-notice No. 10, headed 'British Intelligence Services' is the most famous and, by 1980, the most ragged, attempting as it does to drape both MI5 and MI6 in a voluptuous aura of secrecy they are unlikely to deserve. (Britain's secret intelligence apparatus is discussed in detail in Chapter 5.) The notice asserts:

3. Attempts are made by foreign powers to plant stories in the British Press. [Similar attempts are made by British intelligence, which are not mentioned here.] A variation of this technique, which must be taken into account where activities of foreign intelligence services are concerned, is the planting in an overseas newspaper or other publication of a piece of information about British intelligence matters with an eye to stimulating the British press not only to republish the story, but to expand on it.

4. You are requested not to publish anything about:

(a) secret activities of the British intelligence or counter-intelligence services undertaken inside or outside the UK for purposes of national security;

(b) identities, whereabouts and tasks of persons of whatever status or rank who are or who have been employed by either Service;

(c) addresses and telephone numbers used by either service;

(d) organizational structures, communications networks, numerical strengths, secret methods and training techniques of either Service;

(e) details of assistance given by the police forces in Security Service operations [this is a reference to the Special Branch];

(f) details of the manner in which well-known intelligence methods (e.g. telephone tapping) are actually applied or their targets and purposes where they concern national security. [On the face of it, this would allow discussion of abuses which do not concern national security.] Reference in general terms to well-known intelligence methods is not precluded by this sub-paragraph;

(g) technical advances by the British Services in relation to their intelligence and counter-intelligence methods whether the basic methods are well-known or not.

The 1963 Profumo sex scandal demonstrated sidelong what the attitudes of unscrupulous politicians are to this tempting apparatus of censorship. Sir Roger Hollis, then head of MI5, described (anonymously) to an inquiry about the Conservative War Minister, how he 'formed the impression that Mr Profumo's object in asking to see him was to get a D-notice or something to stop publication, which was a vain hope'.[18] The existence of the D-notice system had been discussed the previous year in the Radcliffe study of Civil Service security procedures, but it was only four years after Profumo that D-notices became the subject of a full-scale official enquiry.

The 1967 'cable vetting' row was, in essence, simple enough. Members of the government were highly displeased because, despite efforts to stop it, the *Daily Express* printed a story describing how MI5 examined all foreign cables — part of the general sweeping up of communications in which British intelligence engages. By coincidence, it appeared that a specific operation involving cable-checking was under way at the time, and there was great outrage up to the level of the Labour Foreign Secretary, George Brown.

Chapman Pincher, who wrote the *Express* story, maintains that the subsequent row, with a Privy Councillor's inquiry,[19] a Government White Paper rejecting it and the eventual departure of the extrovert D-notice committee secretary, Col. Sammy Lohan, was merely a political intrigue by Harold Wilson to punish Lohan for his hostility to Labour. From our perspective, the interesting points are these. The D-notices, with their references to 'well-known intelligence methods' were ambiguous — but MI5 and the Foreign Office preferred to try a mixture of deceit and bullying to stop publication, rather than to confide in either the D-notice secretary or Pincher himself, a right-winger of self-consciously patriotic views. Second, it became clear that a cosy system of self-censorship can rapidly turn to rancorous misunderstanding. And third, a wealth of usually mystified information about the machinery of D-notices was made public for the first time — an unqualified political good, although the Privy Councillor's report was, of course, heavily censored. It offers some fine examples of sanitized prose for that reason:

> Following the telephone call from Mr Taylor [the Ministry of Defence chief press officer, on the receiving end of Pincher's questions] Mr —— got in touch with Mr —— Security Service and passed the story on to them. Mr—— was subsequently told by Mr—— Security Service that the matter had been referred to Mr—— who would shortly be getting in touch with him. The advice subsequently given to Mr—— by Mr—— was that the story was undoubtedly untrue and that our Press Office should be instructed to say so to the newspapers.[20]

This is nearly all mumbo-jumbo, concealing as it does the spying roles of MI6 and GCHQ Cheltenham. Newspapers were solemnly prohibited from mentioning telephone tapping until the Birkett Report on the subject was published. Then newspapers were equally solemnly instructed that they were now allowed to mention telephone tapping. In 1968, D-notices were issued in an attempt to stop the *Sunday Times* writing about the Philby affair by banning all mention of ex-MI6 men. Once again, and rightly, they were ignored.

D-notice No.12 is headed 'Whereabouts of Mr & Mrs Vladimir Petrov' and is a continuing request not to say where in Australia the well-known 1954 defector may be living. Petrov disclosed that the 1951 flight of Burgess and Maclean was a well-organized Soviet plan. There have been other sporadic efforts to keep the lid on defectors; in 1963 another row had occurred when a request not to name the important defector Dolnytsin was urgently rushed out over the Press Association teleprinter, giving all newspapers the information that the *Daily Telegraph* had had to itself before consulting the D-notice secretary. The *Telegraph* was so furious it immediately printed the name; Dolnytsin (not even his real name, it later transpired) seemed to survive.

Behind the formal D-notice system is an informal one, partly consisting of 'P & Cs' — 'Private and Confidential Letters' — and partly of personal chats between Rear-Admiral Farnhill, his successor and 'responsible' journalists. In 1974,[21] a P & C was sent out to all editors about North Sea oil rigs. It warned, unexcitingly: 'Security problems could possibly arise if the method of operating allocated forces or the duties of and capabilities of weapons and equipment intended to be used in the defence of the installations are discussed.' In 1976,[22] the full committee decided to do their bit against 'the IRA and its various maverick offshoots' pointing out that the practice of republishing names printed abroad of the heads of MI5 and MI6 could lead to terrorist interest: 'Physical 24-hour protection as given to the more prominent public figure would not be practicable and would in any case, frustrate the normal intelligence work of the principal people involved, especially their ability to move about freely and unobtrusively' (presumably wearing the traditional cloak and pulled-down hat).

Other Information Laws

The D-notice system, for all its elaborations, is only one variant of the many official appeals to journalists not to print news. Police occasionally persuade newspapers to postpone giving details of kidnapping, and in 1978 the Scotland Yard head of information, Deputy Assistant Commissioner Peter Neivens, sent a successful appeal to editors not to disclose in advance that the Police National Computer was about to be shut down while new equipment was added: 'There is a slight risk that some subversive elements or criminals might attempt to take advantage of the reduction of this facility, should this become publicly known', he wrote.[23] Efforts to pressurize journalists in the interests of government propaganda in Northern Ireland are well-known; the BBC has been publicly and privately reproved for interviews with 'terrorists' and I know personally of one distinguished journalist whose editor was told privately that he was having an affair with a Catholic girl, in a back stairs effort to get him withdrawn from the province. When the state-owned British Leyland car company was pilloried for safety defects, ironically in a BBC TV programme contrasting US open government with British secrecy, Leyland simply exerted pressure on the BBC not to repeat the programme, while accepting its factual accuracy. All this wheedling and leaning merely constitutes politics as usual, but there are a surprising number of further laws in Britain against information.

The 1934 Incitement to Disaffection Act, for example, is used to try to maintain information control over servicemen by the Ministry of Defence. While young men are enticed into long terms of service by government propaganda, they are shielded from contact with journalists thereafter. No moves have been made against newspapers since a 1945 prosecution of an anarchist paper for urging 'hold on to your arms' but in 1975, 14 pacifists were lined up in the dock of the Old Bailey for distributing leaflets telling soldiers how they could desert to Sweden instead of going to Northern Ireland. The prohibition on material likely to 'seduce soldiers from their duty' was attacked by civil libertarians at the time of its introduction. Like so many of these rusty laws it has never been repealed. The jury acquitted all 14 pacifists,[24] after a trial punctuated by accusations of contempt of court against those handing out political leaflets, and against the BBC for screening a programme critical of the Incitement Act during the course of the trial. The BBC on that occasion rejected the judge's attempt to censor their programmes, but it was not the last time such an attempt was to be made. Pat Arrowsmith, a pacifist earlier convicted under the same law, was in the process of testing this law under the European Convention of Human Rights in 1980, five years later. It is a long process conducted rather dismayingly considering the European Commission's generally robust attitude, entirely in confidence until findings are announced.

The law of confidence is also used occasionally to gag newspapers in advance, although it is a concept of civil litigation properly belonging to trade secrets. The censorship of ministerial memoirs, carried out by the Cabinet secretariat, has relied in the past on whatever weapon came nearest to hand — the Official Secrets Act in the pre-war Lansbury memoirs and the Nutting Suez memoirs, or the weight of Attlee's prime ministerial authority in the case of Churchill's 1948 war memoirs. Attlee was 'most apprehensive' that Churchill might quote documents written by Chiefs of Staff because that could lead to a general call for such publication as a result: 'Publication of some of these papers, e.g. those relating to the fall of Singapore would be most embarrassing', minuted the Cabinet Secretary, Sir Norman Brook.[25]

In 1974 the *Sunday Times* forced the issue by serializing the unbowdlerized diaries of the late Richard Crossman, a Labour Cabinet Minister. The newspaper had steeled itself for a prosecution under the Official Secrets Act; to their surprise the Attorney-General, Sam Silkin, decided the Official Secrets Act could not stretch to fit because Crossman was dead. Instead he sought an advance injunction under the law of confidence to stop full publication of the diaries as a book: 'I hope to be able to satisfy your lordship that it is ... an expanding doctrine.'[26] He quoted for good measure the words of Lord Reid in Conway *v.* Rimmer in

1968 (claiming the court's right to decide whether certain State papers should be disclosed but also putting the case for secrecy over such general classes of document as Cabinet papers):

> To my mind the most important reason is that such disclosures would create or fan ill-informed or captious public or political criticism. The business of government is difficult enough as it is, and no government could contemplate with equanimity the inner workings of the government machine being exposed to the gaze of those ready to criticise without adequate knowledge of the background and perhaps with some axe to grind.

Silkin called in aid the Argyll divorce case of 1967,[27] in which the Duchess of Argyll stopped a Sunday newspaper printing her husband's tale of her interesting life on the grounds it constituted marital confidences, analogous to trade secrets.

The *Sunday Times* and Crossman's publishers had to risk perhaps £60,000 in costs to fight this rising tide of mystery-making. They won, pointing out that other ministers such as Harold Wilson had been given much latitude, and that the argument that ministers would never dare to speak out again in Cabinet were nonsense. But Lord Widgery's judgement left the law of confidence still in play. He said in effect that eleven years after the event was a long time to be thinking of banning disclosures and having read the first volume of the diaries, he did not see the harm in it, being unimpressed by claims that it would inhibit future Cabinets, and further, that civil servants had a right not to be exposed or criticized by their political bosses. Nevertheless:

> The expression of individual opinions by Cabinet ministers in the course of Cabinet discussion are matters of confidence, the publication of which can be restrained by the court when this is clearly in the public interest ... [but] the court should intervene only in the clearest of cases, where the continuing confidentiality of the material can be demonstrated. In less clear cases — and this in my view is certainly one — reliance must be placed on the good sense and good taste of the Minister or ex-Minister concerned.[28]

Reflecting on the limits of their victory, Hugo Young, political editor of the *Sunday Times,* said perceptively:

One phenomenon the diaries exposed was how many people in this country do not want to know what is going on. From Cambridge professors to political journalists themselves, many educated men expressed varying degrees of horror and regret that the diaries had been written and then published ... some editorials supported the attempted suppression. More strikingly still, fewer than half a dozen MPs showed any interest ... This is a measure of the depth to which the cult of secrecy has embedded itself in British life. Even those most badly incapacitated by secrecy seem most anxious to defend it.

...The publishers and the newspapers held to the simple conviction that what they did was in the public interest. They did not deceive themselves that the majority of the public, or even that portion of the public most directly concerned, would necessarily see publication in the same light. In challenging the cult of secrecy in Britain today, hard is the way and strait the gate.[29]

Contempt of Court

The common-law crime of contempt of court — in so far as anyone knows what it is — is a huge, cloudy barrier to investigation of an important part of government: the justice system. Like all information laws, it is wide, vague and unpredictable; despite many calls for reform, notably after the Phillimore Report of 1974 and the adverse 1978 finding of the European Court of Human Rights in the *Sunday Times* thalidomide case, nothing had been done about it by 1980. Contempt, and its accompanying notion of *sub judice* are supposed to protect the British courts from interference, thus affording all citizens a fair trial. In practice it stops journalists from describing truthfully what is going on in the course of prosecutions and litigation, not so much through direct confrontations, as through the unwillingness of newspapers to risk potential and expensive trouble. Geoffrey Robertson, a barrister with wide experience of free-speech issues, accurately described in 1978 the noxious impact of the newspaper lawyer in a world where all laws are vague: 'The lawyer's advice creates a broad penumbra of restraint, confining the investigative journalist not merely to the letter of the law but to an outer rim bounded by the mere possibility of legal action.'[30]

In the thalidomide *cause célèbre* the government had tried, in 1972, to assert the principle that any issue taken before the civil courts is immediately taboo for public discussion. Once again the *Sunday Times* fought a long, expensive and lonely battle which they eventually won in Strasbourg. The articles they wished to print describing how the Distillers Company made and sold the horribly deforming drug thalidomide a full eleven years earlier, were injuncted in advance and banned, while the thalidomide parents and the drug company continued to haggle unequally in actions that — due to the inability of English common law to get to grips with the legal liability problems — were never likely to come anywhere near a courtroom. The doctrine of contempt was operating in its usual way, erecting 'keep off' signs over anything which strayed into the mystified and self-regarding maze of the British courts.

On the criminal side, all explanation of events must cease once charges are laid and probably even when charges are 'imminent'. Phillimore's efforts to tidy this up had not been enacted six years later. In Scotland, where judges are always fiercer, newspapers and TV companies have suffered a series of swingeing fines in the last two years for overstepping a vague borderline. Distasteful as it is to see newspapers baying sensationally and perhaps unfairly about unadjudicated crimes and criminals, the whole idea of 'prejudice' to future juries on which these prohibitions are based is probably nonsense. There is no evidence that juries are prejudiced by advance publicity, although it is the kind of thing defence lawyers like to earn their fees by suggesting.

It is probably 'contempt' to delve into the reasons why bail is granted or refused after an arrest. It is probably 'contempt' to investigate why some charges have been laid and not others, although this is an area where the most subtle and sometimes dishonest 'deals' occur between prosecutors and felons. It is certainly considered dangerously near contempt to disclose offers of 'plea-bargains' made to defendants; in 1979 the *Guardian,* for example, rightly felt it was an unacceptable legal risk to expose in advance the fact that although the Attorney-General claimed two journalists in the ABC secrets case were serious criminals, he was perfectly prepared in secret counsel-to-counsel haggles to drop the serious 'spying' charges in return for Guilty pleas on minor Section 2 charges. Some judges claim it is contempt to report any courtroom exchanges that take place in the absence of a jury, or even in open court — journalists find themselves reduced to asking permission about what they can report or not report, the judge setting himself up as *ad hoc* censor.

In preliminary hearings, known as committal proceedings, there is a quite fatuous restriction under the Criminal Justice Act 1967 against reporting the proceedings without special permission, on the ostensible grounds that it is unfair to defendants to have the case against them publicized without their defence being heard. It is said to prejudice juries: in two sensational recent cases which were reported fully at committal, the Bodkin Adams murder case which led to the original legislation and the Jeremy Thorpe conspiracy to murder case, both juries in fact acquitted. So much for 'prejudice'. Juries are not stupid: if they were they could not be expected to adjudicate between two sets of barristers paid to give thoroughly partial accounts of events. Sir David Napley, Mr Thorpe's solicitor and former president of the Law Society, announced afterwards that he had never known a jury be prejudiced by this publicity. He said: 'I have been practising for 47 years and I have been in some unusual cases. But I can say without any doubt that I have never seen a case in which I believe that the reporting of committal proceedings adversely affected the trial.'[31] The Thorpe jurors themselves explained that the news coverage had not swayed them in the least.

This did not prevent some remarkable efforts to widen legal secrecy during and after the Thorpe trial. The Thorpe committal was reported because one of the defendants, George Deakin, asked for publicity — his right under the Act. Peter Chippindale of the *Guardian* and I decided to try to push back the frontiers of secrecy a tiny way by writing an 'instant book' of the committal hearings, trying to put the daily newspaper accounts into a shape that ordinary citizens could understand before the trial of the former leader of the Liberal Party came on at the Old Bailey. After all, the hearings had occurred in public in the first place. Never were two innocent authors so harassed by supporters of the cult of censorship.

The first publishers we approached consulted their lawyer; such a scheme would be contempt of court, he assured them. The second publishers we tried, Hutchinson, were more relaxed. I do not think it even occurred to them that such a simple project would run into so many taboos. They accepted the book. We wrote it in what we hoped was a balanced and neutral way. In case there was any legal difficulty, we carried out the project quite independently of the *Guardian.* Hutchinson's lawyers now began to confer anxiously and pored over the statutes.

Was it libel? After all, court reports are only protected by privilege if they are strictly contemporaneous. No, they eventually decided, that did not matter. Even non-contemporaneous reports have what is called qualified privilege against libel, provided they are fair, conscientious and in good faith. The lawyers went through the book line by line removing any work that might carry a whiff of approbation or disapproval about anybody concerned in the whole bizarre affair. But was it contempt of court? The jurors could read the book up to the moment the trial came on, and although common sense said their heads were already full of lurid newspaper accounts of the case, who was to say what a judge might call contempt? We studied the wording of the Criminal Justice Act and it seemed to say clearly enough that, provided one of the defendants wanted publicity, reports were lawful. It did not say they had to be newspaper reports. After hesitating, Charles Clark, managing director of Hutchinson, decided to go ahead and publish.[32]

Then the printers lost their nerve. They did not relish any pioneering legal ventures in which all concerned could find themselves standing in the dock. A second printer who only had limited capacity was hurriedly found. The print order had to be cut by half. We eventually published; the key distributors, W.H. Smith, decided they would not stock it. Their lawyers, it seemed, had told them this harmless repetition of well-known facts was 'material calculated to prejudice a jury'. Mr Thorpe's lawyer, Sir David Napley, and the solicitor of his co-defendant David Holmes, joined in the fun. Sir David, while carefully expressing no exact opinion as to the book's legal status, duly sent a copy to the Attorney-General. Eminent QCs such as Louis Blom-Cooper opined that the book was a disgrace and ought not to be allowed. Other book shops took fright, expecting no doubt to be hauled up before the Old Bailey themselves. It was all the purest nonsense which reached its apogee at the opening of the trial when Mr Thorpe's counsel complained about our book and another by two investigative journalists, Barry Penrose and Roger Courtiour who had weathered even greater legal harassment on their own account. The jury were only allowed to be sworn when it was established (rather to our disappointment) that none of them had read either of the two books.[33]

In a way the story was a funny one; in another way, it told a great deal about Britain's attitudes to information. In what other country could publishers, printers, distributors and bookshops be so tyrannized by unreal bogeys as to attempt acts of censorship at every turn? After the acquittal, a Liberal peer, Lord Wigoder, tried to restrict the law even further to close the publicity loophole which could be opened by a single defendant in a case involving several people. This was all quite cock-eyed, and seemed to rest on some obscure notion of good taste. In Sweden, where privacy principles are not so primitive as in Britain, newspapers do not normally report the names of defendants at all, but only the circumstances of their cases. This avoids 'double punishment' but the self-denying ordinance is lifted for prominent public figures. It was hard to avoid the impression in Britain that, confronted with a prominent public figure such as Mr Thorpe, newspapers were expected by some to adopt the opposite principle and maintain a respectful if embarrassed reticence.

The contempt bogey continues after the verdict is reached. In the Operation Julie 1978 LSD trial, the editor of the *Daily Express,* Derek Jamieson, had to rush to Bristol with his lawyer ready to explain himself, because his newspaper had printed a background piece about the defendants, after the jury had convicted, but before the judge had sentenced them. Mr Justice Park had warned against press comment before gaoling the LSD distributors, saying that it would not influence his sentences, but people might think it had; yet another novel idea in the arsenal of vague novelties that constitute contempt.

Later in this book, we will examine the way the contempt fetish has collided with disclosures about jury-vetting, about the fog of unreal secrecy in the ABC secrets case and about the deliberations of juries. Each of these three cases was fought by journalists plucking up courage to sail into what Anthony Whittaker of the *Sunday Times,* one of Britain's most expert and hardened information lawyers, calls 'a storm-zone of the law'. The *Guardian* was investigated by Scotland Yard for the first of these; *The Leveller, Peace News* and the *National Union of Journalists'* magazine had to fight up to the House of Lords to be acquitted over the second; and the third was the subject of an unsuccessful prosecution of the *New Statesman* by the Attorney-General. The bloated doctrine of contempt is a bigger nightmare to journalists than any other law except one — the law of libel.

In ten years of debate, the formal legal position has improved little, although self-assertion by newspapers has won a few beach-heads. The Phillimore Committee, appointed in 1971, made some mildly sensible proposals for freeing information. The general definition of contempt should be, it said: 'whether the publication complained of creates a risk that the course of justice will be seriously impeded or prejudiced'.[34] There should only be restrictions on comment, the report said, in the limited *sub judice* period between the laying of charges (or the actual moment of setting-down for trial in more drawn-out civil cases) and the moment sentence is passed. It ought to be a defence to contempt charges, it said, that general discussion was going on in the public interest which only accidentally impinged on particular legal proceedings — that, for example, one could debate fire precautions in hotels, even though a particular hotel was charged with neglecting fire precautions at that time. Phillimore said, rationally: 'The law ... falls short of the certainty it ought to have ... the law as it stands contains uncertainties which impede and restrict reasonable freedom of speech'.

Phillimore may have been rational, but as has perhaps already become clear, rationality does not determine the way these questions work out in the body politic. The courts, like Whitehall, prefer propaganda about their activities to independently-formed analysis of them. The argument about contempt has hinged, since Phillimore, on the idea of 'balance' between the claims of the lawyers and the claims of knowledge; and the claims of knowledge have often been presented as though they were merely the claims of a commercially self-interested press.

In the *Sunday Times* case, the High Court wanted to ban the piece; three judges so decided. The Appeal Court wanted to lift the ban: three judges so decided, saying the litigation supposedly being interfered with was obviously dormant. The Attorney-General appealed to the Lords who reimposed the ban; five Law Lords unanimously so decided, giving a variety of reasons. The newspaper took the case to the European Commission of Human Rights. Five of the thirteen commissioners thought the ban was right, the other eight thought it wrong. The matter was referred to the full European Court of Human Rights. The court voted eleven to nine that the article should have been freely published. In these conflicting votes, there was an unusually clear demonstration of the fact that judges are merely men. As Lord Diplock rather transparently put it:

Trial by newspaper is wrong ... As in so many other matters strong feelings are based on one's general experience rather than on specific reasons, and it often requires an effort to marshall one's reasons. But public policy is generally the result of strong feelings, commonly held, rather than of cold argument ... if people are led to think that it is easy to find the truth, disrespect for the process of the law could follow.[35]

The processes of law sometimes have very little to do with finding the truth, a fact judges could have a vested interest in not advertising. Anthony Lester, the *Sunday Times* barrister, told the Strasbourg court the state of the contempt laws induced: 'timidity and inertia in the public expression of even the most vital information and ideas'.[36]

The court ruled that the ban was not a restriction prescribed by law for the protection of the judiciary which was 'necessary in a democratic society'. It therefore violated Article 10 of the Convention on Human Rights: 'Everyone has the right to freedom of expression. This right shall include freedom to hold opinions and to receive and impart information and ideas without interference by public authority.'

Judge M. Zekia, concurring, asserted that the uncertain idea of contempt of court as it stood was not even 'prescribed by law', as one could see from the contradictory notions of the various English judges about it: 'The exercise of the right [to free expression] cannot reasonably be attained or achieved if [citizens] are handicapped and restricted by legal rules or principles which are not predictable or ascertainable — even by qualified lawyer.'[37]

Even as they sank to defeat in Strasbourg, the Attorney-General's staff composed and issued, not a reformed law, but a stalling 'discussion document'. This attempted to undermine Phillimore at every turn, seven years after that restrained official body began its work.

Phillimore, it discovered 'raised difficult and important questions of public policy'. We have seen above, of course, what secretive lawyers mean by 'public policy' — their own beliefs writ large ('Strong feelings commonly held'). The discussion paper said, of the proposal not to invoke contempt until charges had actually been laid: 'There is ground for the view that the Phillimore recommendation goes too far ... the authorities concerned with the prosecution of offenders have serious doubts.'[38] The recommendation that, in civil cases the starting-point should be the date of setting-down for trial (itself often several months in advance), 'poses ... technical difficulties'. The recommendation that there should be a defence that a journalist was discussing matters of legitimate public interest in a general way, 'may tilt the balance too far'. Phillimore had not allowed enough room to punish people like the journalist Paul Foot, who named witnesses in a blackmail case because he thought they were being protected for political reasons. Contempt should be widened beyond particular trials to protect the lawyers' idea of justice 'as a continuing process'. In recommending that lawful attempts to influence a litigant (such as the Distillers Company) should not be banned: 'it may be contended that the Phillimore recommendation would tip the balance too far'. The government lawyers' paper quoted a helpful Lord Diplock: 'the practical result would be to substitute government by the media for government by Parliament.'[39]

· There is indeed a demarcation dispute, but Lord Diplock's definition of it was misleading. The media do not govern any more than they conduct trials and award punishment. They inform the public and are not permitted to tell lies. The real danger in this field is not government by the media but government by an introverted trade union of self-selected bourgeois lawyers with all the prejudices of their trade and background. By the spring of 1980, the Thatcher Government had finally drafted new legislation on contempt and the press. The omens were that like their draft Bill on official secrets, it would again read as a charter for secrecy and prejudice.

Libel

The libel laws in Britain are, like all the other information laws, vague and unreformed. They encourage the habit of secrecy because they make the risks of criticizing or exposing the powerful unmanageably high, and journalists face great uncertainties.

Their effect, as with contempt laws, is, in practice, to stand proper principles of decency and privacy on their heads. In several countries, such as the United States, public figures are less well protected from defamation than private ones. This is reversed in Britain: obscure and improverished people can be libelled almost with impunity while the rich and powerful can employ lawyers to drag a newspaper through tedious, drawn-out and esoteric libel proceedings with the fairly confident expectation that, if a jury does not award a monstrous (if random) sum against the newspaper, then the legal costs alone will have caused it great pain. A short libel action by the millionaire Jack Hayward against the *Sunday Telegraph* in 1979 established that the newspaper had barked up the wrong tree in implying Mr Hayward had been involved to his discredit in the Thorpe affair. It later became clear to the public that his role was innocent in the course of two sensational court hearings. The *Telegraph,* which had churlishly refused to apologize, was in the wrong, but it was hard to say they had destroyed Hayward's standing, or indeed done more than temporarily put a question-mark over it. The proper course in a civilized country would have been rapidly to take the *Telegraph* before an authoritative press disciplinary body, such as operates in Sweden. It could have ordered a retraction and apology and perhaps fined the paper an appropriate amount, say, a thousand pounds or so. Such a body, much more sophisticated than Britain's toothless and far from authoritative Press Council, would protect the small as much as the great. Instead the *Telegraph* was saddled with damages of £50,000 and legal costs of more than £60,000.[40]

There is no defence in Britain that defamatory remarks are published in good faith, after diligent inquiry, on a matter of public interest and subject to instant retraction and apology if necessary. Such a defence, coupled with a proper disciplinary body for journalists, ought to be the basis of a civilized country's press law. But libel in Britain belongs to the lawyers and woe betide a journalist who makes his employers liable for these maverick costs and damages. Better by far for him to sanitize every word, to dance on the graves of the disgraced and dead and never give the public an inkling of the misdeeds of those still influential and alive.

Thus Reginald Maudling, a genial Tory Cabinet minister and friend of 'lobby' journalists, was a man who nearly became leader of the Conservative Party and Prime Minister of Britain. He died in 1979 to fulsome obituaries, having managed, thanks to the libel laws in general, and the judicious issue of a few slow-moving writs, to avoid systematic exposure of his financial morals. To dance on the graves of the dead for a moment: Maudling was on the take, at various points in his political career, from three prominent dishonest businessmen — Jerome Hoffman, later to be convicted in New York for business fraud; John Poulson, who bribed a wide spectrum of State officials and politicians to help get building contracts, and was jailed; and Sir Eric Miller, who shot himself during a police inquiry into his thefts from a property company he chaired. It has been rightly said many times that the US Watergate exposures, difficult enough as they were in Washington, could never have happened in Britain where there is little formal right to knowledge and an arsenal of potential legal restraints.

Lawyers often say, sanctimoniously, that the libel laws merely require the press not to print lies — an obvious public good. In a newspaper office, long after the authenticity, or likely authenticity of a statement has been accepted, the argument rages over whether such-and-such a person is rich, litigious and likely to sue. It is a casino. A newspaper must prove the truth to legal standards of what it prints: it is not for the plaintiff, who may have deliberately refused to give information in the first place, to demonstrate the lie. An action can be begun up to six years after the alleged libel, and it could be a decade before it comes to trial. Witnesses may change their circumstances or their minds or quite conceivably die during such a grotesque stretch of time. Many informants cannot testify in any event, or will refuse to. Any journalist investigating a malpractice knows he is going to be greeted with a shower of threatened writs; it is the first line of defence, and often a very good one. The pressure is always there to settle out of court if a writ comes in, and most libel actions are conceded in this way.

The situation, as with official secrets and contempt, was sufficiently appalling to generate a full-scale inquiry — the Faulks Committee — at the beginning of the 1970s. Nothing has been done to reform libel for the full decade, so little do governments care for the liberty of the press.

Faulks was establishment-minded enough. It rejected as incomprehensible and alarming the US position arrived at by the Supreme Court in 1964 and based on the constitutional enshrinement of a free press — that to get damages for a remark of public or general concern, an aggrieved public official must prove not only that the statement was false and defamatory, but also that the author had at least serious doubt as to its truth at the time.[41] Faulks even rejected milder versions of this defence. The committee found itself proposing actually to extend libel to the recently dead. All they eventually offered was to reduce the time-limit for actions from six years to three; to make it a little easier to dismiss dormant or time-wasting actions; and to take assessment of damages, the most obvious unfairness, away from juries. (Juries artlessly expose the subjectivity of all claims that information causes quantifiable harm: they award guesswork damages. What else can they do?) It was proposed to make it harder for the casual issue of a writ to ruin a publisher's launch by making it difficult to force the withdrawal of all books without becoming liable to pay compensation later.[42]

Faulks was untroubled by the existence of criminal libel. This rusty offence is quite distinct from the civil wrong of libel: it is a crime, to be punished by fine and imprisonment, which can be brought as a private prosecution. The burden on the journalist is even greater than in the civil court — he must prove that each part of his assertion is true. He must then prove further that its publication is in the public interest. This is the origin of the hoary tag, dismissed until recently as of purely historical interest, 'the greater the truth, the greater the libel'. Truth alone is not a sufficient defence to a charge of criminal libel.

Faulks committee, put simply, could not be bothered to propose the necessary reforms. It said they were too complicated and criminal law of some sort was needed to stop poison-pen letters and rude remarks about policemen made by those with no money. Also it could be used to stop libels on the Royal Family. Faulks did not notice that all these 'public interest' cases could quite well be brought by the Director of Public Prosecutions just as Official Secrets cases are.

All laws against information, no matter how obsolete, can be used as sticks with which to beat the press. Towards the end of the 1970s, Sir James Goldsmith, a wealthy industrialist and would-be newspaper proprietor, was angered by suggestions in the magazine *Private Eye* that he connived at the flight of Lord Lucan, a gambling peer wanted for the murder of his family nanny. He set out as a private prosecutor to exact drastic compensation. His cases would have ruined the magazine entirely, with actions against its distributors and retail outlets, as well as against the sheet itself. The magazine was in grave difficulty when Sir James was persuaded to drop his actions on the grounds that they would stand in the way of his project to buy a Fleet Street newspaper.[43] But already the idea had been sown in the fertile mind of one Roger Gleaves. While serving a prison sentence for sexual offences against boys, Gleaves refined a remarkably successful scheme to drag two Yorkshire TV journalists who had exposed his activities and written a book about them, up and down through the courts. He brought a private prosecution for criminal libel (representing himself) saw his rights to do so vindicated by the House of Lords and forced the two journalists to undergo a full-scale trial at the Old Bailey. Exhausted and inevitably out of pocket, the two were finally aquitted by the jury.[44]

Privacy

When journalists complain of these variegated legal harassments, a common reply is to abuse them for invasions of privacy. This is unfortunate, because the types of newspaper which try to conduct

serious investigations are usually not those who filch photographs
from the drawing-rooms of bereaved widows, or expose the sexual
oddities of vicars. The viciousness of one type of newspaper is
often used as an excuse to suppress the serious inquiries of another.
This makes particularly hypocritical the claims by some politicians
that there is a trade-off available: that if only the press would
accept its duty to privacy, it could be freed of other shackles. In
fact, the government is no more interested in privacy than it is in
real press freedom — it wishes to interfere with the privacy of
citizens on its own account — to tap their phones, store dossiers
about their politics, catch illegal immigrants if they go to see a
doctor, put police tittle-tattle on computers, and vet jurymen
behind their backs. A comprehensive Freedom of Information law
in Britain would be bound to include, as it does in the USA, a
Privacy Act as a corollary. This would allow individuals access to
their own files held by government departments, employers and
other officials, with a right to correct them, and it would firmly
limit the misuse of material stored in and shared between
computers.

Harold Wilson put the trade-off theory very clearly in a 1976
speech which he described as 'an important offer to the press,
because of their understandable concern about restrictions on their
freedom under the Official Secrets Act'. In return for enacting the
various proposals on contempt and defamation, 'which would, in
the interests of the press and the public, increase the right of the
press and the broadcasting authorities to comment on issues of
public concern' he demanded a voluntary self-denying code of
privacy. Far from giving citizens a specialized right to information
held by others about themselves, for checking, control and
correction, what Wilson seemed to have in mind by 'privacy' was
some sort of embargo on gossip columnists and the investigations
then going on, quite rightly, into the career of the Liberal leader
Jeremy Thorpe. He characterized this episode as 'the private lives,
real or imagined, of public figures ... highlighted by the headlines
and comments which followed a recent outburst in a Devonshire
court of summary jurisdiction'. Three years later, Wilson lamented
that nothing had been done to institutionalize a privacy law:

Nor have press problems in relation to defamation and contempt
been eased. From my own experience since leaving No. 10, I
would suspect that certain organs of the press have shown that
they cherish the right to invade privacy more than they would

welcome any easements of the law in relation to defamation and contempt.[45]

It is true that both the 1972 Younger Report on Privacy, and the more recent 1978 Lindop Report on Data Protection, urging some increase in our control of computers to bring it nearer European levels, have mouldered on the shelf and look likely to continue to do so. There have only been one or two primitive developments of privacy law — the Consumer Credit Act, for example, allowing inspection of credit agencies' records of debtors, the Rehabilitation of Offenders Act allowing long-gone minor offences to sink into oblivion, and the legislation allowing anonymity for the victims in rape trials. But privacy law is not the enemy of the serious press to be bartered off against other relaxations in free speech. Privacy is a public good; so is freedom of information — it is a mistake to try to negotiate their introduction with the types of newspaper already so corrupted as to care for neither.

The Lobby

Having had their hands tied, journalists in Britain are then made to dance. Deprived, in theory at least, of independent right of access to information about public affairs, the journalist depends on what he is told as a favour. The frequent reason for claiming secrecy on power-holders' operations is to allow them to present their own, unchallenged version of reality: the obverse of the secrecy coin is always propaganda. From the point of view of a bureaucrat or a politician, the ideal journalist is one who will accept misleading statements and disguise their source.

When mistrust of the legitimacy of much British journalism is voiced, it tends to focus on the parliamentary lobby system. In one way, this is slightly misconceived, because the lobby system of journalism is almost universally widespread and the Westminster part only a small fraction of it. But it does serve as a useful emblem for a whole structure of unattributable briefing. Every Thursday, about a hundred accredited political correspondents — demure guests, bound by ideas of etiquette and carefully traversing only those corridors in which they are by special favour allowed — slip up a flight of stairs in an obscure corner of the Palace of Westminster. There they are allowed to question the Prime Minister of the day's Press Secretary, and later the Leader of the House who is in charge of the following week's parliamentary business. They enjoy the same ritual with the Leader of the Opposition, with individual Cabinet ministers, and the parties' representatives in the House of Lords. Round this skeleton of formal briefings there is an entire nervous system of lunch parties (lobby men are great ones for luncheon clubs to which they invite guests); chats on the riverside terraces; discreet words with the chief press officers of Whitehall in the gallery rooms behind the debating chamber; and drinks in Annie's Bar, and the Strangers Bar. These drinking dens, of which there are several scattered through the Palace, are governed by conventions which exude the characteristic atmosphere of Westminster — something between an old-fashioned gentleman's club and a hierarchically organized boarding school. Thus the Stranger's Bar tends to be occupied by a *hoi polloi* of MPs. Journalists can only enter as the guests of MPs. Annie's Bar is reserved for lobby journalists — those holding one of a limited number of newspaper 'lobby tickets' — and politicians. Other journalists, even those who report debates in the gallery, and outsiders, are not allowed entry. Contrariwise, the Press Gallery Bar is open to all journalists holding the less exclusive 'gallery tickets', and to MPs invited as their guests. The word 'lobby' is a reference to the anteroom outside the chamber where MPs and whips gather during votes, and to the short stretch of carpeted corridor between there and the MPs' tea-room. Lobby journalists are allowed to hang about these spots talking to politicians.

The essence of the system is its anonymity. Everything that is said is 'unattributable'. The public will be treated to a series of pronouncements in their newspapers, often virtually identical, saying 'Westminster circles felt last night the Prime Minister was about to move decisively against trade unions', or 'Senior ministers are saying the Home Secretary is deeply concerned about dishonest policemen', or 'It is felt in Whitehall that important security reasons lie behind these deportations'. The system becomes elaborated as all such systems do; it is agreed by lobby men that everything they hear in the Palace of Westminster can be printed, shorn of its identifying source. But the journalists' status as guests, it is accepted, prevents them reporting everything they *see*. A minister who falls down drunk is invisible, as is a minister making a pass at his secretary.

It is a very good system for flying governmental kites, spreading disinformation, and getting good publicity for oneself at the expense of one's ministerial colleagues or at the expense of the truth. Under this system, a good lobby journalist is a man who can persuade ministers he is reliable: and reliable means discreet. Harold Wilson describes in his memoirs how he 'planted' a story that he planned to kick out a left-wing Cabinet minister, Tony Benn, who was upsetting various financiers, without taking the responsibility for making it known on his own shoulders:

> During the Jamaican conference ... the High Commissioner gave a reception for the British press corps in the garden of his residence. At an appropriate point I asked Harry Boyne, political correspondent of the *Daily Telegraph,* a paragon of discretion [the *Telegraph* was implacably opposed to all that Wilson purportedly stood for] to disengage himself for a little while and go to a room the High Commissioner had reserved. I was waiting there and I stressed that while he could use the story — that Tony Benn was going to be moved sideways to another department — it should not be datelined 'Jamaica' ... the *Telegraph* accordingly ran a story 'from our parliamentary staff' that Tony was to be moved to pastures new.[46]

Peter Jenkins of the *Guardian* testified to the Crossman *Diaries* hearings how great quantities of so-called secret information about the internal workings of the government were in fact leaked in order to manipulate public opinion:

> For example — and there are many others — on Thursday April 3 1969, the Prime Minister's Press Secretary was instructed to reveal to the press, through the usual non-attributable channels of the lobby, that Mr James Callaghan had been reprimanded in Cabinet that day by the Prime Minister. Ministers attending that Cabinet subsequently disclosed to the press that no such reprimand, or at least none matching the press accounts of it, had been delivered in their hearing.[47]

As James Callaghan himself reminded the Franks Committee, when he was being pressed on the apparent willingness of ministers to dish out unattributable information which would be illegal for the journalist to obtain on his own account: 'You know the difference between leaking and briefing: leaking is what you do, and briefing is what I do.'[48]

The briefing system spreads right through government: permanent secretaries do it in Whitehall — economic, defence, education and labour-relations journalists all have their own exclusive-membership groups which set about constructing 'special relationships' with power-holders on non-attributable terms. The Westminster lobby is not necessarily the most important of these lobby groups, although it suits its members' self-esteem and the impulse to mystify of senior civil servants to have it believed so. The beauty of the lobby system is that power-holders can choose with whom they will share knowledge, colluding with a favoured few. The journalists drawn in develop a sense of professional mystique and will even argue against freedom of information as a result. Their stock-in-trade is privileged access to a store of selective gossip and they become expert at deducing from hints and guesses some half-grasped picture of what is going on. This is saleable in the form of 'exclusives', ' scoops' and 'revelations', with the further unhealthy result that all the major prizes in journalism go to those who are most favourably situated simply to find out information. In an open society, most knowledge would be freely available and the prizes would go to those who analysed and discussed it most intelligently. The idea of the State secret corrupts those who hold knowledge and those who obtain it from them: both sides engage in self-aggrandizement at the expense of the public.

It is not possible in Britain to ring up an official who knows the facts and ask him about them without him getting special clearance. Public relations officers — who cost the taxpayer a great deal more money than a Freedom of Information Act ever would — are engaged to issue departmental or ministerial versions of events. Some, such as the career diplomats in the Foreign Office, are explicitly employed, not to make facts available to the public, but to manipulate the flow of information in what is taken to be 'the interests of Her Majesty's Government' — unattributably of course. This was not, of course, quite the way the FO put it when they made extravagant submissions to the Franks Committee about the importance of keeping everything they did under the umbrella of the law: 'The FCO [Foreign and Commonwealth Office], in the interests of stimulating informed public discussion of foreign affairs and Britain's part in them, constantly promotes through its News Department, Information Departments and in many other ways, the highest possible degree of *authorized* disclosure.'[49]

Some of the Foreign Office's propaganda enterprises are discussed in Chapter 6. Their approach is so manipulative that I doubt whether they even understand the concept of freedom of information. In 1979, I went to Sweden where the immigration department showed me the texts of correspondence they had had with the British Ministry of Defence in an effort to get a sensible explanation of Britain's attitude towards soldiers who did not want to go to Northern Ireland for conscientious reasons. (The Swedes were faced with the occasional problem of whether to grant asylum to these soldiers.) I printed a story in the *Guardian* about the stalling attitude of the British to Swedish pressure; some weeks afterwards I was shown a Foreign Office telegram that had been sent to Stockholm, much troubled about this mild disclosure: 'Leigh maintains in his article that he discovered this under Sweden's freedom of information laws. I suspect this is in fact a cover for some covert source he has ...'

Most unattributable briefings are not, of course, outrageous attempts to tell lies. They are merely misleading pieces of special pleading, solemnly written up by those privileged to be present as if they were Mosaic tablets from the Sinai of government. In May 1978, to take a small example, a tanker called the *Eleni V* capsized off Britain's east coast, spilling a good deal of oil and resisting for days various attempts to tow her away or, eventually, blow her up. The Tory Opposition were complaining that there might be a whitewash, as there were charges of incompetence. Sir Leo Pliatski, then permanent secretary of the Trade Department, called together a few journalists he considered suitable for an off-the-record briefing — including *The Times, Telegraph* and *Economist,* but mysteriously omitting both the 'gutter press' and the *Guardian.* I gatecrashed, having heard about the briefing by accident — there is no easy way Whitehall can say 'go away' once caught out in these manoeuvres. Sir Leo did his best to exonerate himself, hinting that the Department had been previously warning that dispersants were inadequate to deal with big tanker crashes, and managing to convey without ever spelling it out that if there was any fault it lay not with the leadership of the Department (himself), but with the introverted and badly-staffed Marine Division. It was a rather boring occasion, enlivened only when Peter Hennessy of *The Times* pointed out that the Government had been making noises about the virtues of open government. Would Sir Leo in those circumstances, release the daily log of the incident so we could all see exactly how the Department had conducted itself? Sir Leo appeared disconcerted: 'It would be consistent with the PM's statement', he said grudgingly, 'I think it might be right to release it. But the Prime Minister should have the report first.' It was not released.

There is nothing wrong with a system of unattributable briefing in conjunction with a relatively open system of government embodying strong rights for the press. The USA is notorious for the transparent fictions by which 'A senior official travelling on Dr Kissinger's plane' gives self-justifying press conferences as he flies through the air. There is nothing wrong with the sound of anonymous axe-grinding, provided (a) a large number of information-holders are allowed to do it, not just the top men and (b) the press has some independent rights of access to information.

In Britain we have too much secrecy and too much news-management. In some ways such a corrupt system is more trying than an openly totalitarian apparatus of censorship because the evil is harder to see. While journalists childishly boast of their special relationships, and lawyers spout nonsense about 'government by the media', the creaking Coach of State rattles along with its blinds drawn. Who is sitting inside the carriage? Where do they think they are going? Let us look, in detail, at a few cases of secrecy in action.

3
A Closed System: the Home Office Prison Department

Sometimes a window opens into British prison attitudes. Take, for example, the ruminations of a traditionalist prison warder, tape-recorded for Tony Parker in a book about Grendon Underwood, a psychiatric prison into which the Home Office allowed Parker more or less as he pleased.[1] (This commendable openness is an occasional flame which flickers in the breasts of civil servants. It rarely lasts long though before defensiveness sets in again.)

The warder is describing the practice of 'ghosting' which is widely used in prisons to keep control. Inmates are spirited away in the night or early morning to another part of the system, perhaps hundreds of miles away. It is used as a punishment, by its disruption of visits, education classes and social relationships; and as a means of breaking up protest movements, or hampering outside inquiry into riots or allegations of beatings.

As he begins to wake up, you say, 'OK son, come on, you're on your way. Get your things packed.' More often than not he's half dazed and you can get him out without any trouble at all. He can see there's two of you and he knows bloody well there's four more waiting outside, so he hasn't got much chance. He's not dressed, he hasn't got his shoes, there's no point in him trying to kick you; he hasn't even got his trousers on . . . there's always the tenth one though, the one whose mind's working before he's opened his eyes; he's going to wake everyone in the prison up even if he is going to lose the fight. But you're already prepared, everyone with you has always got a job to do if necessary; he knows what it is and he'll do exactly that and no more. My job, for example, is to take the right leg, concentrate on that, nothing else, pay no attention to what's happening elsewhere — simply immobilize that right leg. Another one's responsible for the left leg, another takes the right arm, another the left. The fifth one has a towel; he'll have it round the felon's mouth if he can, and if he can't, he'll have it round his neck and give it a few twists to let him know he's in for a throttling. The sixth one on the team, well, his job's to put in a punch here and there if it becomes absolutely necessary ... There was one fellow once, I remember, even with all of us hanging on to him like decorations on a Christmas tree, somehow or other he was still managing to heave us all about ... I said to him, 'And the next movement I make will be to break your fucking arm. Have you got it? All right now its up to you how we go on from here.' Of course that was it, he packed it in then. You'll often find that a threat is far more effective than actually hurting someone. That's what I mean by using a bit of psychology, sir.

British prisons are not concentration camps, but the drift of the last ten years makes it important to stress that we are discussing a social institution based on force. As with the police and the army, there is a special public importance in very closely supervising such organizations. There have been a number of well-documented riots and confrontations in prisons in which inmates may have been beaten up gratuitously, and the facts only emerged with great difficulty — at Hull, Birmingham and Wormwood Scrubs, for example. Misuse of drugs in prisons, the denial of what are considered to be basic human rights, and the takeover by the embittered NCOs of the system — the prison officers — are now common areas for debate.

Methods of punishment are introduced without public disclosure, such as the 'control units' used at Wakefield in 1974 which with their recurring 90-day cycles of solitary confinement appear to break the published prison rules, and probably contravene the European Convention on Human Rights as well. The units were only abandoned after press disclosures and protests. In 1978 a similar secret tactic was conceived; prison warders were trained to break up demonstrations, even peaceful ones, by controlling prisoners while kitted out with three-foot clubs, visored helmets and riot shields. These were christened MUFTI squads — the letters standing with Orwellian cynicism easily worthy of the Ministry of Truth, for 'Minimum Use of Force Tactical Intervention'. The Home Office scheme for institutionalizing violence as a method of bureaucratic control was repeatedly used, but successfully kept secret for almost a year from the public and the House of Commons.

It is particularly shameful that secrecy should have become the universal method of administrative problem-solving in the prison system, precisely because it is a system which runs on physical coercion. The inmates of prisons do not wish to be there and if they refuse to cooperate final discipline is enforced quite simply by assaulting them.

This stress on violence might seem exaggerated, but I will give one example of which I had personal experience, of how secrecy works in practice. People can die violently inside the system. In 1979, as one of the 'liberal' journalists who write about prison conditions, I heard in a roundabout way that one of the prisoners' rights organizations had information on the death of a prisoner. In the usual cautious fashion, I contacted them, and eventually found myself one breakfast-time in the quarters of a senior provincial prison officer. I had checked his background in unofficial circles, and he had the reputation of an honest and thoughtful man.

Some of his fellow warders worked in the prison hospital, he said. They had come to him for advice because an incident had got out of hand and they feared there was going to be trouble. A long-term 'violent' prisoner had been put in the hospital wing. One night, he had been making a considerable row, shouting and banging the door of his cell. It had been decided to quieten him down. 'About ten officers tore into his cell and set about him.' The prisoner was a big man, the cell was tiny. The prisoner died. The medical staff on the hospital wing were well aware of the circumstances, the prison administrators were in a suppressed uproar of anxiety, and no inquest had been held. My senior prison officer thought this kind of episode did not show traditional prison discipline in a morally tolerable light, and he wanted the facts to be known.

He failed, and I failed. We could prove that the man had died two months previously; a paragraph had appeared in the local paper quoting a brief and misleading Whitehall statement that a man had been found dead in the hospital wing (with the implication that he had died of some disease). Having discovered the prisoner's name, it was possible to inspect the death certificate which the authorities had been obliged to deposit with the local registrar. It showed the cause of death had been 'asphyxiation'. But the coroner, when asked about the death, said the inquest had merely been delayed through the consequences of an industrial dispute. The authorities had explained that the prisoner had indeed died in a struggle — he had been himself attacking prison officers. It was during 'efforts to calm him' that the unfortunate accident had occurred. While the official statements could not of course be made public, it was hinted that one or more of the prison officers had accidentally fallen on the man in the mêlée. The only evidence that could contradict the prison officers' official version came from my source who was unable to testify. Not only did the Official Secrets Act debar him from disclosures; the Prison Officers' staff discipline code makes it an express offence to communicate with the press. It was dangerous enough to arrange a meeting with me; impossible for him to put his name to a statement. Both the Prison Officers' Association and the prison doctors were behaving in an increasingly litigious way as the number of allegations about prison life increased.

The dead man had no close relatives to make a fuss on his behalf. If a newspaper printed an unsubstantiated accusation, it would run the risk of heavy libel damages from warders or doctors who claimed to recognize themselves in the description. There was to be no police investigation. Many would take the view that such a man was no great loss to society in any event, short of absolutely irrefutable evidence of murder or manslaughter. And so, the man died violently, in 1979, in a British prison, and the circumstances of his death were successfully covered up.

Secrecy in the prison system is a particularly full-blown habit, because of the nature of the organization. As Pat Arrowsmith, insistent political protestor, wrote from jail in 1975:

> You are ignorant of our customs and our language
> don't realize we too have a social system
> marriages, leaders, tribes, work teams, committees
> that your villages and cities don't concern us
> we have our own which you have scarcely heard of
> Askham, Risley, Holloway and Styal.[2]

Every prison system is an archipelago, and although smaller and far less infernal than Solzhenitsyn's, often almost as remote. The chain of prisons spread through Britain constitute another country from the one inhabited by ordinary citizens passing within feet of those deliberately massive Victorian doors. It is a totalitarian country; every aspect of its occupants' lives is regulated, not by common law, with its notions of habeas corpus and natural justice, but by officials. Curiously, the regime professes a kind of constitutional monarchy; the Home Secretary is king, but he is a monarch who abdicates every few years to be replaced by someone else, and who has many other duties to perform in the world.

The Home Office has administered these internal colonies for just over 100 years, in the course of which they have acquired some striking features. The prison system is violent, overcrowded, mismanaged, and above all secretive. It represents the most mature form of bureaucratic administration in Britain today in the sense that a professional civil service is in a position to control the details of 44,000 lives, 24 hours a day, spend £270 million a year and employ 25,000 staff on behalf of a public which is not terribly interested in what it does, and on behalf of politicians who will never catch many votes for its work.

The habit of secrecy began in 1878 when the professional central Civil Service took over the patchwork of locally administered prisons. As the Webbs pointed out in their 1922 study of English prisons:[3]

Since 1878, the prison has become a silent world, shrouded, so far as the public is concerned, in almost complete darkness. This is due in the first place, to the policy to which every well-ordered administration is prone, of 'No admittance except on business'.

The Webbs were discussing Home Office reluctance to allow independent inspection of prisons and publication of the results — a reluctance still visible in 1979, when the Home Office tried hard to block the same proposal from the May Committee. Local government could be inspected by outsiders, the Webbs noted: 'It is seemingly only when the administration is its own that a government department finds that inspection and public criticism by disinterested outsiders are incompatible with discipline and the best administration.' They went on:

When the prisons were administered by local authorities, the Home Office saw no reason why its inspectors' reports should be treated as confidential documents and withheld from publication. However scathingly the inspectors criticised the prison governor or the prison administration generally, the Home Office of 1835-77 did not find that it was destructive of discipline or inimical to good administration to issue these reports to the world. We are inevitably led to the conclusion that it is not the character of the service or any peculiarity of the Home Office, but the very nature of direct administration by a central government department that leads to this systematic denial of publicity.

Before analysing in any detail the Home Office's system of border control over the flow of information, it is important to interpret the dogma of 'security', frequently introduced into these debates. Since the Mountbatten Report of 1966, which followed a number of prison escapes, the emphasis and activity in the prison system has concentrated on security, with the growth of high-security 'dispersal prisons' for those considered dangerous, and the (fairly arbitrary) grading of prisoners into four categories of dangerousness. A Category A prisoner, for example, cannot move anywhere unescorted and has his activities limited and his visitors specially screened. This kind of subjective division into four categories seems to be part of a common bureaucratic conceptual structure — classified documents are similarly divided into four categories of dangerousness, and as with them, it is safe to accept that the bottom two categories are not very dangerous at all. Prisoners in Category C, 'who cannot be trusted in open conditions, but do not have the ability or resources to make a determined escape attempt', and in Category D, 'Those who can reasonably be trusted to serve their sentences in open conditions', make up a full 69 per cent of the total prison population.[4] The Category A men, 'whose escapes would be highly dangerous to the public or the police or to the security of the state', still number only some 400 prisoners, although the numbers thus defined keep growing. The great majority of British prison inmates are serving short sentences and are not 'dangerous men', as the 1979 May Report makes clear. The Report also grasped another nettle, if only to release it rapidly; the inmates of the British prison system do not represent the total 'criminal element' in British society — they represent a number picked at random by the prejudices and inherited tendencies of the criminal justice system. Pointing out that Britain jails more people than other West European countries, and dramatically more than Holland and Scandinavia, the Report says: 'the fact that other advanced societies have achieved an imprisoning balance qualitatively different from ours cannot be set aside'. Between 1974 and 1978 apart from three men who were immediately recaptured there were no escapes at all from high-security prisons.

Thus, the prison secrecy system can scarcely be said to rest on an overriding need to protect the public from a horde of terrifying malefactors — any more than obsessive secrecy about the security services rests on a need to protect us all from imminent Russian invasion. What we are studying primarily is the feeding and fighting habits of bureaucratic systems, as they grow, flourish and defend themselves.

The imperative of the Home Office is to maintain a closed organization, at every level, not in order to keep the facts of the prison system totally unknown — that would be absurdly over-ambitious — but in order to preserve power to manipulate the flow of information. Wherever the problems emerge — among prisoners themselves, the warders, MPs, journalists, or their own ministers — it is the Home Office which claims the right to extract whatever advantage it can from turning the information tap one way or the other. On the inside of the prison gates, there are at least six different categories of inmate: the prisoners themselves; the prison officers; the local administrators (governors and assistant governors); professional workers such as doctors and psychologists; the chaplains; and the senior administrators at regional headquarters and in various parts of the Home Office itself. There are also groups of people who, for professional or personal reasons, are allowed across the border and thus gain access to information: Boards of Visitors, official visitors; teachers; relatives; lawyers; journalists; academic researchers; politicians; and such official inspectors as the authors of the 1979 May Report. The Home Office tries to exercise a panoply of information control over all these groups of people.

The Prisoners

Here the principle is a common one, that the inmate should have little information about his circumstances and the authorities should have an all-seeing eye. Two sociologists, Stan Cohen and Laurie Taylor, analysed the Kafkaesque maze through which a prisoner must proceed in a withering book called *Prison Secrets*.[5] Their interest began when the Home Office tried to control publication of research they had carried out on long-term prisoners. In theory a prisoner's daily life is regulated by the Prison Rules, statutory documents presented to Parliament and composed by the Home Secretary. As one legal academic puts it: 'They prescribe certain minimum standards, confer a few rights, impose duties, allocate responsibilities, but their striking feature is the discretion conferred (notionally) on the Home Secretary as to nearly all matters excepting a prisoner's right to food, clothes, shelter, and medical treatment.'[6] The rules begin with the well-known piety, promoted to Number 1 position in 1964, 'The purpose of the training and treatment of convicted prisoners shall be to encourage them and assist them to lead a good and useful life.' Prisoners do not even have a right to see the rules themselves; they are given a Home Office summary of those parts thought to be applicable to them. This does not include, for example, the information that their letters will be censored. Prisoners are in fact controlled by administrative discretion; there are literally hundreds of standing orders, circulars and instructions to governors which control the minutiae of their lives. Not only are these documents kept from the prisoner himself; they are not available to the public. And even should there be a breach of the public statutory rules, as Zellick points out: 'the courts have held that, however worded, neither the Prison Act not the Prison Rules themselves confer rights on a prisoner in the vital sense that if they are denied he can bring a legal action either to claim the rights or compensation'.

A prisoner is in the hands of the State. He is liable to be transferred to any prison in the country — the 'ghost train' being used as a method of enforcing discipline. The kind of regime he undergoes is decided by an arbitrary security classification over which he has no control, and which is determined for reasons he may not understand. May said mildly:

> The Home Office acknowledged that the criticism that there was a tendency . . . to match inmates less against the training criteria than against the available training prison vacancies had some validity . . . they admitted too, that there were aware that the process of recategorisation leaves something to be desired.[7]

Mr Justice Cantley, however, dismissed in May 1977 an attempt to sue the Home Office, because a man had served nine years classed as Category A and thought it unfair that he did not know why. The judge observed:

> To allow prisoners to make representations against their classification would seriously hamper and in some circumstances completely frustrate the efficiency and proper government of prisons . . . to give prisoners access to information which might have been supplied by prison staff could do widespread damage to relations inside.[8]

A prisoner is not allowed to consult a doctor of his own choice, but must rely for all medical treatment on the overworked prison doctors — drawn from outside the National Health Service, from the thinning ranks of ex-military and colonial medical officers and the subject of occasional allegations that they prescribe major tranquillizers for disciplinary reasons. A prisoner does not have the right to a second opinion or an independent examination, although important matters of parole, transfer or drug treatment can easily be at stake. Cohen and Taylor quote one particularly bland letter from the Home Office explaining its refusal to allow a life prisoner an independent psychiatric examination:

> The medical officer responsible for Mr W does not consider a further psychiatric examination to be clinically indicated, and there is the danger that examination by another medical practitioner chosen by Mr W or his legal advisors would upset the existing doctor-patient relationship to Mr W's detriment. If the other doctor were to reach a different conclusion to that reached by the prison medical officer and the psychiatrist who have examined Mr W, it would not follow that the Parole Board would accept his views in preference to theirs and on that basis, recommend Mr W's release, or that the Home Secretary would accept such a recommendation. In that event Mr W would remain in prison in the care of a medical officer in whom his confidence would inevitably be lessened if he knew — as he almost certainly would — that another doctor had expressed different views.[9]

One narrow legal gateway was opened when a prisoner complained to the Ombudsman that he was not allowed to sue for medical negligence, and the subsequent Home Office concession was used by another prisoner, George Ince. After a campaign alleging he had been maltreated by continuous doses of heavy tranquillizers, Ince succeeded in obtaining the entry of an independent psychiatrist to the prison by issuing a writ alleging negligence.

But the achievement in this single, prolonged case was more theoretical than real. The administrative obstacles placed in the way of access to lawyers are very great. A prisoner does not have the right of access to a lawyer in any practical sense. Rule 34 (8) says: 'A prisoner shall not have the right to communicate with any person in connection with any legal ... business except with the leave of the Secretary of State.' The Home Office uses this rule to prevent any proceedings or ventilation of prison conditions, and showed a subterranean determination to defend its position even against an adverse ruling of the European Court on Human Rights, in the 1975 Golder case. Sidney Golder, thinking he was unfairly hampered from getting parole because a false accusation had been made against him, was refused permission to see a lawyer with a view to proceeding for libel.

The European Court was unimpressed by the Home Office arguments for imposing 'a reasonable restraint on recourse to the courts . . . in the interests of prison order and discipline'. It ruled: 'It was for an independent and impartial court to rule on any claim that might be brought.' The Home Office, preoccupied with information control, merely informed governors that prisoners could only exercise their new right after exhausting the internal prison grievance procedure — that is to say, after submitting a petition to the Home Office, which could await a reply for up to a year; after disclosing the details of their complaint to the very people complained against; and after laying themselves open consequently to Rule 47: 'A prisoner shall be guilty of an offence against discipline if he makes any false and malicious allegation against an officer.'

The public step was to issue an amended prison rule: 'Subject to any directions of the Secretary of State a prisoner may correspond with a solicitor for the purpose of obtaining legal advice . . . or for the purposes of instructing a solicitor.' The secret step was to send confidential circular 45/75 to prison staff, explaining their method of negating the practical impact of the ruling of the European Court. Pleased with themselves, the Home Office said in that circular: 'By virtue of the arrangements explained . . . above, it does not appear that staff should in practice feel at substantially any greater risk of involvement in litigation than now.'

The whole air of clumsy obsessiveness the Home Office brings to these contests may be explained by its fear of the prison officer staff associations, which have much to be rightly resentful of in their employers. But the Golder affair was devoid of both morality and logic. Even if prisoners were allowed to consult lawyers whenever they liked, they would find it extremely hard to bring successful civil court cases. A solicitor would have to think their case well-founded enough to take on; and a local legal aid committee would not allow legal aid without being convinced of a reasonable case. There is no legal aid in libel cases, in any event.

Problems with lawyers and doctors are part of a larger deprivation of civil rights. Prisoners do not have the right to legal representation at internal discipline hearings, nor necessarily to call witnesses on their own behalf, although they may lose long periods of remission at these secret hearings, conducted by the prison's Board of Visitors. After a confrontation with prison officers at Albany on 16 September 1976, one man was awarded the equivalent of a three-year ordinary prison sentence and more than four months solitary confinement. The public limits under the prison rules are that only 56 days 'solitary' can be awarded, but the Home Office blandly pointed out that it had been decided to award consecutive sentences on several charges in this case. Only very recently has a court shown itself willing to review such hearings to see if they are conducted at all fairly.[10]

The most crass insistence on secrecy is in the general censorship of prisoners' correspondence. It helps to put it in perspective if we bear in mind that in a Swedish prison, the inmate can write letters as he pleases (although there is a right to censor on security grounds). Every prison has a coin-box from which the prisoner can ring up whoever he likes. (This is a piece of information which can be relied on to astonish British prison officials, should you happen to find yourself standing next to one at a cocktail party.)

It is not for reasons of security that censorship is imposed; one would not propose that inmates could be allowed to spend their time composing elaborate escape plots by mail, but if they wish to do so, it is relatively easy to smuggle letters and messages out of prison. Confronted with a 'smuggled letter' unless it has something particularly interesting to say, the average journalist feels no great excitement. It is as easy to get letters out as to smuggle tobacco in. The censorship rules merely operate as a confusing, dispiriting pattern of secrecy which muffles complaints and submerges a prisoner's personality.

The Prison Rules say simply 'the governor may, at his discretion, stop any letter or communication on the grounds that its contents are objectionable, or of inordinate length'. The restriction on length, like the restriction on numbers of letters to two or three a week seems to rest largely on the administrative needs of the censors. Too many letters mean too much reading. The standing orders, never disclosed to the prisoner, explain what is considered objectionable. A prisoner is not allowed to complain about any aspect of his treatment in prison, make allegations against the officers, 'attempt to stimulate public agitation' or send material out for publication. Thus, when in 1979, a squad of officers wielding three-foot staves controlled more than 50 prisoners holding a peaceful demonstration (as actually happened) the Home Office standing orders prevented any attempt to describe events. Just as the prisoner has no idea what has been found 'objectionable' in a returned letter, so the recipient has the fact of censorship concealed. The censor does not cross out material, but makes the prisoner rewrite it. Erasures, say the standing orders, 'are liable to cause misapprehension and suspicion in the minds of the recipients'.

Using the bureaucratic multiplication of rules in standing orders, one can amuse oneself by composing perfectly reasonable specimen letters which break as many as possible of the Home Office rules against free speech. For example:

Dear Uncle George,
I didn't think my aunt Rose would get married at last, especially to someone I'd never heard of in my life. But as she says you're a writer, I wish you'd put in your next book an account of the experiences people like me have to put up with in prison. A life of crime seems exciting when you're young, and my cell-mate Harry who's in here for robbing a post office still spends his time planning to do his next job more efficiently (instead of stealing a getaway car that broke down in the street outside!).

But as far as I'm concerned the game's not worth it. If you don't give the police an 'earner' to let you have bail, they keep you banged up for months; your trial's a farce; and when you arrive here you discover that all the clap-trap spouted by the Home Secretary about 'training' is just to impress the voters.

I'd like to learn to read properly while I'm in here, so that my period of 'bird' isn't totally futile, even if it's horrible. But the Home Office are so incompetent that I'm kept locked up 23 hours a day because the screws are having some protest about overtime. Greedy bastards. Six of them smashed up my mate's cell the other day, and broke his radio, pretending to search it. I'd like to do the same to them. I think Margaret Thatcher and her crew have got a lot in common with these thickheads; and the nancy-boy chaplain is no help at all. Do you think you could get anything done about my literacy classes, such as write a letter to the papers? If my experiences of prison life are of any use to you, maybe you could send me in a few quid?

Every word in this letter offends against some confidential standing order and constitutes grounds for stopping the letter should the governor be so inclined. The European Convention on Human Rights allows restrictions on correspondence 'necessary in a democratic society . . . for the prevention of disorder or crime . . . or the protection of the rights and freedom of others'. The Home Office, on the other hand, has developed a tradition of information control which might be designed to encourage any prisoner in a personal war with authority. There are 18 offences in the specimen letter:

1. Attempting to write to other than a close relative.
2. Attempting to write to someone not known before entering prison, without special permission.
3. Intending material for publication.
4. Discussing crime in general.
5. Discussing criminal methods.
6. Discussing offence of others.
7. Complaining about the police in 'a deliberate and calculated attempt to hold them up to contempt'.
8. Complaining about the courts in similar fashion.
9. Complaining about the Home Secretary in like fashion 'in his responsibility for prison administration'.
10. Complaining about the prison authorities in the same way.
11. Complaining about prison treatment.
12. Making allegations against officers.
13. Threatening violence.
14. Making objectionable references to persons in public life.
15. Using 'grossly improper language'.
16. Making scandalous statements about private individuals.
17. Attempting to stimulate public agitation.
18. Making 'begging requests for money'.

Even letters to one's MP, the traditional right of every other citizen, are censored. This frontier rolled back somewhat after the 1975 Golder case, with the Home Secretary's announcement: 'I am anxious that communications between prisoners and members should be as free as possible.' Merlyn Rees added pointedly: 'I also recognize the legitimate interest that prison staff, whose association I have consulted, have in this matter.' The new standing order made it impossible for an inmate to ventilate any issue about his own prison conditions, without displaying his hand to the authorities, incurring possible punishment and certain delays: 'A letter to a member may not include a complaint or a request concerning prison treatment', said the new standing order. A prisoner was only allowed to write such a letter after the issue 'had been raised and considered through the normal internal procedures'.

The prisoner then, is classified, moved, regulated and isolated from outsiders, even outside authorities, in a secretive way. Apart from the injustice and incompetence such a system breeds, its sheer frivolity is interesting. Cohen and Taylor quoted extracts from governors' handbooks they have obtained, about the way to handle petitions to the Home Secretary. Petitions can be amusing to read, says one: 'And who knows, an accompanying report to the Secretary of State, if entertainingly written, may well serve to cheer him or one of his servants merrily upon his way, even if it is not successful in assisting the petitioner to gain his request.' Another extract reads:

> By and large petitioners tend to omit various pieces of vital information and the writer of the report should be at pains to supply these ... as certain prisoners conduct running battles with authority ... it is vital that a copy of any report should be carefully filed so that in years to come successive writers may be able to establish with ease the history of the battle to date ... those dealing with petitions, particularly in large recidivist prisons, will need a fount of patience but because of the infinite variety of prisoners' requests, and their quaint way of expressing them, the work is not without its rewards.[11]

For an outsider, it is quaint to see the Home Office's paternal way of expressing itself when not speaking in front of the children. It is perhaps fortunate for the rest of us that we are not reduced to dealing with our domestic complaints via, for example, petitions to the Gas Board. If we were, the servants of the Secretary of State for Energy might well find us to be 'quaint' or 'objectionable' or even 'scandalous'.

There is one further important aspect of prison secrecy: the control of information given to the prisoners themselves. Prisoners are refused explanations as to why they have been turned down for parole. This is psychologically painful, as all the uncertainties generated by the Home Office must be. It may well also be straightforwardly dishonest. It must be an extremely useful control mechanism for the prison administration to be able to dangle the prospect of parole before an inmate, in order to give him the impression he has something to lose. If it were admitted to a long-term prisoner that he will not get parole for a long time, or ever perhaps, because of the nature of his crime, or the impossibility of his getting employment, then his incentive for good behaviour has gone.

The Parole Board asserted in 1969:

> the essential difficulty in the situation is, of course, that the reasons for parole decisions are not exclusively focused on the prisoner himself. The range of factors taken into account is extensive and reasons emerge from collective assessments. In some instances a prisoner would not be helped by the disclosure of reasons and to discriminate in any way by giving the reasons to some and not to others, would be unfair.

Cohen and Taylor offer one interpretation of this singularly opaque piece of prose — that it is a reference to a parole dossier (SCF 2) which they obtained; a confidential document quite possibly out of date by now, and full of amateur psychologizing of a rather meaningless kind. The governor's handbook, also confidential, gives hints on the kind of indirect questioning designed to elicit some of the material, and adds: 'The more the inmate is able to feel you are genuinely interested in him as a person, the more of himself he is likely to show and the more reliable your estimate will be.' (This disingenuousness, if exposed, would presumably teach the prisoner that honesty is only considered a virtue in him, not in others.)

Ten years later, in 1979, the Parole Board was increasingly defensive, but still holding firm. 'There is substance in some of the criticism made, notably the uncertainty suffered by prisoners and their families', noted the annual report. But Lord Harris, former junior Home Office Minister just appointed to head the Parole Board, announced that he had been converted to the Parole Board view that secrecy was essential. Otherwise, he said: 'you would be driven to change the whole system of parole in this country'. He had visited New South Wales where he found that the decision to give broad explanations had led to a campaign to be given details. If this were conceded it would be 'an immense burden ... I think a whole series of court cases would arise because of it'. Lord Harris

Parole Dossier SCF 2

Name
National Number
C.R.O. Number

PART TWO: ASSESSMENT AND RE-ASSESSMENTS
Factors which may change

G   Reactions to sentence

Re-assessments

	Not yet clear		i.e. dazed, shocked, confused	1
	Seems to reject	(i)	by serious appeal/petition	2
	Seems to reject	(ii)	with aggressive defiance	3
91.	Seems to accept	(i)	with defeated submission, grudgingly	4
	Seems to accept	(ii)	calmly, as occupational risk	5
	Seems to accept	(iii)	with readiness to plan constructively	6
	Seems to welcome	(i)	as return 'home' to familiar environment	7
	Seems to welcome	(ii)	as escape from immediate difficulties	8
	Seems to welcome	(iii)	as deserved punishment	9
92.	Blames his predicament on:		Bad planning	1
			Authority (e.g. police, judge, pre-cons)	2
			Other persons	3
			Bad luck, drink, drugs, gambling	4
			No blaming	9
93.	Desire for revenge		Seriously expressed	1
			Half-hearted or none	9

enter code/rating

1st 2nd 3rd 4th 5th 6th

H   Expected behaviour in prison

(Actual behaviour)

Seems likely to: Seems likely to:

94.	Seek approval of staff	1	2	3	4	Not care about staff opinion
95.	Be self-reliant	1	2	3	4	Make constant demands on everyone
96.	Be independent of inmates	1	2	3	4	Be eager for acceptance by inmates
97.	Be amenable to authority	1	2	3	4	Be resistant to authority
98.	Be controlled	1	2	3	4	Be aggressive
99.	Be acceptable	1	2	3	4	Arouse hostility
100.	Remain in touch	1	2	3	4	Withdraw into himself
101.	Be stable, calm, placid	1	2	3	4	Be unstable, anxious, disturbed

I   Training needs

102.	Visits/letters not important	1	2	3	4	Visits/letters important
103.	No resettlement problems	1	2	3	4	Serious aftercare problems
104.	Educational level adequate	1	2	3	4	Needs educational help
105.	Work-patterns satisfactory	1	2	3	4	Work-patterns need developing
106.	Working skills sufficient	1	2	3	4	Skills could be improved
107.	Insight adequate	1	2	3	4	Needs help to understand self

maintained that, as one factor in parole decisions was a prisoner's home situation, a prisoner given this reason might become worried. He might fear, correctly, that his wife was having an affair, or that one of his children was seriously ill.[12]

These remarks can only rest on the belief that anything is justified to manipulate the behaviour of prison inmates. What then, is one to make, given this immense range of manipulations at the disposal of the Home Office, of the disturbances at Parkhurst (1969); Winson Green (1975); Gartree (1976); Albany (1976); Hull (1976); and the large number of rooftop protests and demonstrations (many of them kept secret) on a smaller scale? Is the system so ineptly managed that only cynical and dishonest forms of 'man management' keep the constantly bubbling pot from exploding? Or are the secretive and authoritarian habits of prison staff themselves a trifle counter-productive? What is to be said for a parole system which led 646 prisoners to refuse to be considered for parole in 1978, some at least (it is admitted) because they could not face the anxiety of the decision-making system?

Prison Staff

The other inmates of the prison system are free men: the warders, doctors, chaplains, assistant governors and temporarily seconded career civil servants in Whitehall. With them, bureaucratic secrecy operates in the usual way. According to their status, secrecy is imposed upon them, and they have varying amounts of power to claim secrecy about their own doings.

The Official Secrets Act applies in all its catholicity to all the staff and professional officers. This makes it an offence to communicate any information gained about prison without authorization. The Home Office quite arbitrarily extends this to a requirement that anyone connected with prisons should submit anything they wish to say about prisons to the Home Office for advance censorship. The Act has been applied to prison staff just often enough to demonstrate its reality. In 1926 a retired governor of Pentonville wrote for a London evening newspaper a series of articles containing his reminiscences, in the course of which he disclosed a confession made to him by a convicted murderer on the morning of his execution. He was fined at the Old Bailey for breaking Section 2 of the Official Secrets Act, despite an attempt to claim that the Act must be limited to the disclosures of information 'contrary to the public interest'.

It is an express condition of employment that nobody working in the prison service should talk to the press. This is a much more important sanction than the Official Secrets Act except to those who have retired. Put bluntly, if you talk out of turn, you get sacked, and the same would apply if all the Official Secrets Acts were abolished tomorrow.

Inside prisons, the warders themselves know little of the system within which they work and complain bitterly of the bureaucratic maze. Representations by the Prison Officers Association about some local matter, have to traverse up and down the chain between Whitehall, regional headquarters and the local governor before the simplest issue can be ventilated.

The muddled attitude of ministers towards disclosures by prison officers was well seen in the remarks of former Conservative Home Secretary Henry Brooke (by then ennobled) giving evidence to the 1971 Franks Committee:

Q: Clearly it would be desirable to preserve maximum secrecy in prison security; but it has been put to us that Section 2 has been used to try to prevent the press getting information about prison conditions. Would you think that was a reasonable view?

Brooke: ... The specific difficulty, the difficult area in connection with prisons, is that the best way of getting information about a prison is to go to any of the pubs which are near a prison, and give drinks to some of the prison officers who are there. Prison officers are warned obviously, that they must not disclose anything they know; but prison officers are human and certainly an amount of information as to recent events in the prison does get out that way. One just has to ride that one. But I do not think the prison side should cause you any great anxiety, because if any information reached the press which would aid prisoners to escape, I should be very doubtful whether the press would use that.[13]

In this way, Brooke encapsulated the problem as seen by Whitehall — 'disclosure' (or ordinary discussion) by prison officers is unlikely to be dangerous to security but could well lead to irritating publicity for 'recent events in the prison'. What struck the authors of the May Report, on the other hand, was the excessively isolated life they found among prison staff — a testament no doubt to the obscurantist style of the Home Office: 'It has been constantly borne in upon us that they are one of the most isolated [groups of workers in the public sector]'. As well as observing that they were ill-educated and badly-trained, the May Report set out to justify its theory that prison officers complained unnecessarily about their pay and conditions, inadvertently demonstrating lack of contact with the outside world for which their employers must be partly at least to blame:

> All prisons, even open ones, are closed institutions in the way in which the term is ordinarily understood. Traditionally, the staff have lived very close to the institutions themselves, and this reinforced by the nature of their work, has perhaps led them to mix only among themselves ... whatever the cause, we have found members of the service (including governors) a somewhat inward-looking group ... in particular, they are prone to concentrate on their own terms and conditions of service without a well-informed knowledge of what obtains elsewhere. Further, their beliefs of what applies outside the prison services tend to be unrealistic as well as restricted.[14]

Ill-informed by remote employers and resentful of their poor working conditions (amply documented by May) the prison officers have a natural tendency to seek their own solutions, treating the Home Office and the inmates in their power alike as 'the enemy'. This leads them to resent outside investigations of their own behaviour. The May Report accepted that the Home Office was behaving badly as usual: 'The Home Office fully accepts the need to consider revisions of the Code [of discipline] which has been in its present form since 1963, and that only the pressure of other business has so far prevented this from being undertaken.' But it also appears to have been alarmed by POA attitudes:

> Sections of the public have become increasingly concerned about what is done in prisons, and are naturally suspicious of anything that hints at secretiveness or a desire to prevent the proper investigation of complaints. In their own interests, the POA must beware of any policy in regard to police investigations which suggests that they are anxious to create for themselves a privileged position or to prevent the proper discovery of the truth.[15]

The governors themselves are specially recruited, not normally allowed to explain themselves to the press or public, given extremely limited local administrative authority, and generally treated by Whitehall as something of a lower form of life. The London Branch of the Society of Civil and Public Servants slightly took the May Committee's breath away on this topic:

> While accepting the high degree of professionalism of a governor in one breath, the London branch of the Society went on to comment in the next that the task was essentially a 'fairly parochial one with no requirement to acquire a vision for the wide scene'. Such a sentiment, with which we do not agree, no doubt nevertheless explains some of the relationships and attitudes we have discovered in the present organization.[16]

The Committee discovered that not only did the Home Office regard itself as the company headquarters from which all explanations and decisions must come; it also deprived governors of the simplest pieces of knowledge, such as how much it cost to feed their inmates. This was, of course, part of a wider nonchalance: 'We were surprised to learn that the Home Office was unable to tell us how much each prison costs to run each year.' Governors were without knowledge and authority. They were also, in the areas they did control, protected from the consequences of their behaviour: 'Managers in control of quite substantial resources . . . are fully protected in what they do and yet answerable to no one . . . we cannot believe that the present situation is a healthy one.'

From the point of view of everyday journalism, which controls the public's perceptions, this swaddling of the key functionary in the system does not do good. If there is a comparison, perhaps it is with large state institutions like hospitals. When there is a strike, an outbreak of food-poisoning, or a public criticism of hygiene standards, journalists telephone the hospital, or take themselves down there. They talk to union officials, the doctors (who sometimes prefer not to be quoted by name) and the hospital administrators. Only in particularly awkward situations, or where the administrators are simply too busy, are calls referred to the regional administrations and there, as often as not, it is a positive help to find teams of professional information officers who see their job, partly at least, as a conduit for information, not as a stopper.

Governors do encounter the press on stage-managed trips around prisons. Even on these harmless occasions, the Home Office feels obliged to nanny its senior officials. The 1971 *Governors' Handbook,* obtained by Cohen and Taylor, enumerates 'golden rules for dealing with the press'.

> Don't make instant comment; don't believe anything said to a journalist is off the record — don't be rude or argumentative; and don't forget that behind the intelligent, knowledgeable and understanding reporter there is a headline-seeking sub-editor, who appears to be none of these things.[17]

The nervousness of the Home Office about allowing its staff to discuss prison matters is not, of course, merely a reflection of a wish to avoid disparaging allegations about physical discipline in our prisons. Civil servants perceive political difficulties in humane as well as inhumane administrative practices. A notorious murderess has only to be allowed out for an accompanied walk, or a swimming pool installed in a jail, for howls of execration to be heard in the 'pop' newspapers. 'Luxury for criminals', like sexual incontinence in vicars, is a reliable stereotype, always worth a few column inches. Decent civil servants come to believe it is only possible to do good by stealth and can thus point to 'liberal' grounds for stopping the mouths of, for example, reactionary prison officers. It is a horribly question-begging and corrupting procedure. Prison officers might not be so difficult if they themselves had fewer legitimate grievances; the public might be less inclined to take such complaints seriously if there was a tradition of sensible discourse about prison matters; the air of furtiveness generated by unpublicized experiments suggests in itself that there is something to be ashamed of; and concealment for good motives can slide, unchecked, into concealment for sinister ones.

Prison chaplains are supposed to be independent, professional (not to say godly) persons, working full time within the prison system. They are subject to the same bureaucratic hand across their mouths, although, as with surprisingly many applications of the Official Secrets Acts, it provides less of a tangible threat than a respectable rationale for a silence which may be attractive for other, institutional reasons; no one likes to be loathed as a Judas by his colleagues in a closed system. But the Home Office is perfectly prepared to bully priests if necessary. The Rev. John Cooper, a Bristol prison chaplain, wrote to the Franks Committee describing the way the Official Secrets Act turned him into an 'unchurched' member of a Home Office religious department responsible to the government before the Church.

> I find also that the repression of frank discussion with the outside world through the OSA has a parallel effect reflected in the hierarchical structure of the prison service, in that just as views cannot be expressed freely outside, neither are they expressed freely within the prison service.[18]

The Rev. Cooper fell foul of the system when the Home Office insisted on cutting about a third of a 'highly critical' paper he had written, before allowing its publication in a clerical magazine called *Contact*. The chaplain was upset, although his complaint showed what must have been to the Home Office a satisfactory confusion in his mind between the state of the law and the Home Office's own particular games with its employees: 'According to the Official Secrets Act, all papers to be published outside the service have to be vetted by the Public Relations Officer.' The Rev. Cooper became embattled; shortly afterwards he deliberately wrote a letter to the *Church Times* commenting on the prison system. The Home Office sent him a letter:

> Our attention has been drawn to your letter about prison security that was published in the 19 March issue of the *Church Times*. We have no record of permission having been given by the Department for this letter to be sent for publication, and we find this particularly puzzling since the Assistant Chaplain General wrote to you last year about the publication of articles and it is assumed you are aware of the procedure to be followed.

The Rev. Cooper wrote a spirited reply and after three months silence was told the matter had been referred to the Establishment Department — presumably a genteel way of indicating that the Home Office bluff had been called. One doubts, however, if the Rev. Cooper was ever subsequently considered for promotion to the higher reaches of the prison chaplaincy.

The prison doctors are secretive in a more alarming way. They are prevented from speaking out in the usual fashion, and they and their employers are rendered almost immune from criticism. The prison medical service is not a part of the National Health Service; it is isolated, under the control of the Home Office, which is not interested in health but in discipline; and it is staffed by inadequate numbers of doctors. May in passing recommended 'an urgent review ... to encourage more and better qualified doctors to join the prison medical service'.

How strong institutional pressures can be on the inhabitants of a closed system was recognized by Mr Justice Bridge before the trial of 14 prison officers (five of them hospital staff) for beating up IRA prisoners. Those charged were eventually acquitted, although the Home Office was eventually to concede that the prisoners had indeed been assaulted in prison.

The 1975 trial of the IRA men themselves had hinged on whether they had been assaulted by the police before arrival at the prison (in which case their confessions might have been worthless). Mr Justice Bridge drew attention to the evasive testimony of the prison medical officer that although he had found the men 'black, blue, battered and bleeding', the injuries were old ones, in effect, they had been sustained before arrival in prison. Of the prison doctor, the judge said, in dismissing his evidence:

> If this gentlemen has come to this court, deliberately to give false evidence to protect his cronies in the prison service, he is not fit to be a member of the honourable profession upon which, if he has perjured himself, he has brought terrible shame.[19]

The drugging of prisoners in order to sedate them — what has become known expressively as 'the liquid cosh' — is a topic about which frequent allegations are made by aggrieved or dazed prisoners. Prison doctors are not open to interview about such matters. They have a journal (the *Prison Medical Journal*) for private circulation only, which appears to give the lie to Home Office assertions on the subject. Shirley Summerskill, a junior Labour Home Office minister, announced from her brief on 15 December 1978 to sceptical MPs:

> Prison doctors have not and would not practice the use of drugs as an aid to discipline or to control behaviour. I am also convinced that none of the doctors who work in the prison medical service would respond to requests from prison staff to prescribe drugs for this purpose.

It is hard to reconcile these bland remarks with such accounts as that given by Dr O.H. MacCleery, medical officer at Parkhurst, in the *Prison Medical Journal*, which described how psychopaths who resorted to 'senseless aggression' were contained by being given drugs, to which they rapidly developed tolerance. 'Huge doses become necessary, which reduce the patient to a cabbage existence.'[20]

The other aspect of 'treatment' which is most alarming if we are to leave aside simple questions about the standard of routine medical care, is the matter of medical therapy for deviance. It was only in 1978, following an account by a recently retired psychiatrist in the *Prison Medical Journal*,[21] that it was publicly realized that experiments had been going on for ten years on dosing sex offenders with oestrogen. One of the side-effects was that the men thus treated grew female breasts which had to be amputated. Such experiments may be carried out from the best of motives and at the pleading of the inmates, but when the free choice of the 'patients' is so questionable, and the danger of experimenting on powerless persons so obvious, there should be maximum public discussion among doctors and the general public — not secrecy.

One favourite Home Office ploy is to assert to journalists and pressure-groups that it will not give details of drugs ordered, or treatment given, to preserve the confidentiality of the doctor-patient relationship. This happens if a prisoner indicates consent for the disclosure; and even in the case of figures of overall drug purchases for unnamed inmates. When a prisoner cannot choose his doctor, and the doctor is forbidden by his terms of employment from talking even generally to the public, it is, of course, mere hypocrisy to protest concern for a prisoner's 'privacy'. The doctors themselves are in the happy position that they are barely accountable to anyone, and if newspapers are incautious in printing allegations, they can sue. Three prison doctors obtained large sums in libel damages from the *Guardian* following an account it printed in November 1978 of the complaints that John Stonehouse, a jailed ex-Labour minister with a heart condition, was apparently making about conditions at Wormwood Scrubs. Prisoners may be biased and unreliable; doctors can retreat behind a wall of silence; and, as Robert Kilroy-Silk, a Labour MP put it in December 1979, 'It is no longer possible to believe statements from the Home Office.'[22] Under such circumstances, truth may suffer but secrecy rebounds. Far from acting as a buffer for the failures of the Civil Service, it gnaws away at public confidence.

People Allowed in Prisons

The Home Office does not limit attempts at sealing the information-flow to those who live or work full-time in prisons. There are (confusingly) three types of people known as 'visitors' — the friends and relatives of inmates, official visitors and the Boards of Visitors. Ordinary friends and relatives are controlled in straightforward ways — they are only allowed in with the approval of the prison administration, which can be arbitrarily limited or withdrawn; they do not have privacy for their conversation; visits may be suspended if prisoners have visible injuries after riots or disturbances, to prevent such evidence emerging; and visits may be cut short if the prisoner concerned appears to be talking out of turn. These habits are unsurprising, and well documented by civil liberties and prisoners' rights organizations. The Home Office does not seriously attempt to dispute the existence of such restrictions, which can be cloaked under a general concern for 'security'.

Official visitors are volunteers who have a certain marginal status within the prison system. They visit otherwise isolated prisoners, and the price exacted by the Home Office for allowing them in is a silence about what they see. They are appointed by the Home Office and pioneered voluntary social work in prisons. 'He is unpaid, and comes to the prison because he wants to and for no other reason.'[23]

The Home Office put the matter briskly in 1980, dismissing Mr Jonathan Pollitzer for describing to newspapers and television the injuries he had observed on an inmate after warders armed with staves had broken up an apparently peaceful demonstration which was originally described by the Home Office as a 'riot'.

> The view which you may have formed of the incident at Wormwood Scrubs on August 31st does not of itself affect the decision to terminate the apppointment. Whatever your views may have been, any evidence available to you as a prison visitor could and should have been offered to the governor or to the official enquiry into the incident. Your insistence on broadcasting your personal comments on these matters is however, not compatible with your retention as a prison visitor.[24]

Mr Pollitzer riposted indignantly: 'How can they justify sacking me over a technical breach in view of the fact that they have lied three times over the Wormwood Scrubs incident? It's a question of conscience. I've put public interest above prison visitors' rules.'

The third group known as 'visitors' are the local Board of Visitors of prisons. These rather ambiguous functionaries are local worthies appointed by the Home Office, and supposed to combine a concern for prisoners' welfare with the punishment of their

misdeeds at the private courts conducted within the prison. Their
ability to dispense justice in these intimate circumstances has been
long questioned, and so has their reluctance (with some exceptions)
to conduct themselves in an independent way. The May Report felt
bound to address itself to the question of secret justice, although
the committee members were in too much of a rush, as they
conceded, to go into the question thoroughly. Some of their
witnesses thought proper disciplinary tribunals should be set up
with lawyers and legal aid, on the grounds that 'whatever the
complications and additional expense, sooner or later prisons had
to be opened up to public knowledge and inspection'. But May
consoled itself with the thoughts that the Home Office had recently
(1977) circulated guidance to Boards 'to ensure that proceedings
were fair to all and the principles of natural justice were
observed'.[25]

Furthermore, two recent Appeal Court judgements had
established, the committee pointed out, that it was after all possible
for proper courts to review the decisions of Boards of Visitors; the
judgements, in 1979, were a consequence of growing concern
among lawyers and civil libertarians about secrecy in prison. To
instance them, as May did, as grounds for settling back peacefully,
was perhaps to miss the point. A number of punishments imposed
by Boards of Visitors after the riots and beatings at Hull were set
aside by the Appeal Court, which accepted complaints that
prisoners had not been allowed (among other restrictions) to call
witnesses. The witnesses had been 'ghosted' to other prisons. Until
then the courts had taken the view that 'domestic discipline' by the
Boards of Visitors was of no concern to judges.

The threat of the Official Secrets Acts as applied to Boards of
Visitors has been recently established to be a piece of bluster.
Islington Borough Council made an attempt to be represented on
local Boards of Visitors, which the Home Office predictably
spurned, in December 1976. The councillors had said that, if
allowed on Boards of Visitors, they wished to be allowed to report
back freely to their council. 'Authorized disclosure goes on all the
time', wrote back the Home Office 'and like others who receive
information from official sources, members of boards of visitors
may be authorized to disclose it.' This meant nothing more of
course than the usual Home Office claim to censor in advance all
statements made by others. When, however, the councillors went in
a deputation to Lord Harris, the then junior minister, he
announced that it was inconceivable there would be any

Form D

VISIT UNDER RULE 37 (1)

I, ... authorised clerk to Mr.

.... Solicitor, of ....

request permission to see No. .... Prisoner ....

on professional business, Mr. .... having

been instructed by Mr. .... of

....

The words inapplicable should be struck out	to*	(defend him (her)
		(enter an appeal on his (her) behalf
		(conduct on his (her) behalf legal
		(proceedings in which he (she) is a party

State relation-   the said Mr. .... being ....
ship to, or
connection with   Signature ....
the prisoner
Date ....

I hereby undertake that this interview and any subsequent interviews with the prisoner shall be used solely for that purpose named above, and that any information obtained as a result of such interviews, *shall not be communicated either directly or indirectly to the Press or to any person other than those to whom it may be my duty to communicate information for the purpose of the legal proceedings.*

Signature ....

Date .... 19..

No. 931 (23656-21-5-51)

[The italics are those of the Home Office.]

prosecutions under the Act in this respect. 'With regard to the Official Secrets Act, Lord Harris expressed surprise that it was felt that this inhibited members of the Boards of Visitors from disclosing information on prison conditions to outsiders. He did not think that the disclosure of such information came within the scope of the Act.'[26]

This catalogue of information control in prisons may be thought to be taking a symmetrical form; uncertain legalisms explained away by nonchalant disclaimers, and furtively shored up by the occasional brusque sacking. A few more examples will continue the demonstration of Home Office sealing mechanisms for visitors. Teachers are allowed into jails to give classes. They are employees of the local education authority, and so cannot be dismissed by the Home Office. Required to sign the Official Secrets Act, of course, and warned not to enter into discussion with inmates about their grievances or conditions, teachers who offend are simply barred from the prison. The Home Office banned one woman, Meg Howarth, after she helped take out of Wormwood Scrubs a petition from 175 inmates calling for an inquiry into the suicide of a prisoner. 'Access to prison is of course entirely at the Department's discretion', the Home Office wrote on 6 February 1975: 'It was in the exercise of that discretion that it was decided that you should not henceforth work at Wormwood Scrubs prison.'[27] Lawyers too, when permitted to visit inmates, are subject to restrictions of an entirely arbitrary kind. These extend even to the preparation of printed forms for solicitors' clerks, which make the direction of the Home Office's anxieties quite transparent: see Form D, p. 115.

Journalists and Public Representatives

To complete the *laager* drawn up around prisons (which only differs, we should remember, from control of other executive areas in its slightly crazy explicitness), one would expect the press to be carefully monitored. And so they are. The Official Secrets Act is a long way in the background here. The practical emphasis is on preventing journalists from slipping in to jails, controlling their contacts on official tours, and feeding them via single, Whitehall PR outlets with unsatisfactory information, much of it variants of the fine English phrase 'no comment'.

Standing orders, as furnished by Cohen and Taylor, deal with visits.

1. Visits to prisoners by journalists in their professional capacity will in general not be allowed and the Governor has authority to refuse them without reference to Head Office. Where the proposed visit presents special features, however, the Governor will report the facts to Head Office, if necessary by telephone and request instructions. Meanwhile the visitor will be informed that pending instructions from Head Office, the interview cannot be allowed.

2. Where a journalist claims to be a friend or relative and wishes to visit a prisoner in this capacity and not for professional purposes, the Governor will inform him that before the visit can take place he will be required to give a written undertaking that he will not use any material obtained at the interview for professional purposes and in particular for publication by himself or anyone else. Such visits will be reported to the Home Office.

Brief official tours of prisons by journalists with an acceptable background are now allowed by the Home Office ministers. Although it is possible to see some basic circumstances, such as the abominable overcrowding and poor physical condition of prisons (useful publicity for a cash starved department) these tours do not have much more of a probing nature than a guided tour of, say, the Soviet Union. It may be a cruel comparison; no starry-eyed journalist has ever come back like the Webbs from Russia, crying, 'I have seen the future and it works.' But the tours are explicitly manipulative.

Visits by journalists and authors to Prison Department establishments

The Prison Department of the Home Office gives facilities for journalists and authors to visit prisons, remand centres, borstals and detention centres on the following conditions:

Interviews with staff

1. Members of staff may not be quoted without their consent and the approval of the Governor or Warden; interviews should normally be unattributable.

2. Interviews with staff must be confined to eliciting factual information about their own work and the work and regime of the establishment; they must not involve discussion of individual

inmates, the merits or demerits of penal policy, or matters of political controversy. There must be no detailed reference to security matters.

Interviews with inmates

3. No inmates may be spoken to without the permission of the Governor or warden and the questions asked should have a specific purpose related to prison treatment generally; questions must not be about the inmate's personal affairs, his case or family background.

Two copies of the text and copies of the photographs and captions must be sent to the Press Office, Home Office, and no public use may be made of them until they have been cleared by the Prison Department. (Note: the material is examined by the Prison Department not to suppress facts or to inhibit editorial opinion, but to check accuracy and to prevent identification or embarrassment of prisoners or their relatives).[28]

It is rather tempting to take a deep breath at this point, and launch into a long denunciation of the futility of such prohibitions. What convict or junior prison officer is likely to court disaster in the first place by saying something gravely out of turn to a visitor who has the prison governor at his elbow? Not many. More important perhaps, is to note the semantics. Once again the question of privacy is woven into what is really an attempt to avoid any administrative embarrassment. In Sweden they have a very good way of protecting the privacy of prisoners. The equivalent of the Press Council does not allow individuals to be named. But you can go and talk to them as much as you please, and they can talk to you.

Ros Franey, who spent six months as a social administration student on a placement at Holloway prison, was allowed to write an article about it. She described the way in which she was allowed to interview prison officers, but only in the presence of a press officer. The press officer asked her to withdraw one question: 'From your considerable experience of looking after women in custody, do you think that most women benefit from prison or not?' He further told her to ignore the answer to another question, 'that in the opinion of one of the officers, the women ought to be allowed to do more interesting work'.[29]

The Home Office has now dropped the demand that copy must be submitted for advance 'checking for accuracy'. Given the tight control over who can be talked to about what, the practical difference has not been great. Another small restriction imposed by the Home Office is that civil servants are not allowed to appear on public platforms with organizations of which the Department disapproves, such as Preservation of the Rights of Prisoners (PROP). This is information control with a vengeance, and Cohen and Taylor quote three well-attested examples of it in different forms.

And finally, in this long list of border controls, we come to the question of official inspection. Outside inspectors are more of a threat to the calm of the Home Office Prison Department than any number of journalists on brief guided tours. The May Report, in a recommendation publicly accepted by the Home Secretary William Whitelaw in the summer of 1980, called bluntly enough for them:

> We have no doubt that the prison service would benefit from and that public sentiment requires that as many aspects of government, which includes the prison service, should be opened up to as wide an audience as possible ... there should be constituted within the Home Office an independent department to be called the Prisons Inspectorate, headed either by someone independent of the civil service entirely, or by a senior ex-governor ... HM Chief Inspector of Prisons and his staff should be available to make *ad hoc* inspections of any incidents which may occur at the request of the Home Secretary; they should be empowered to set out unannounced and make an inspection of a particular establishment or a particular part of an establishment as and when they think it necessary or desirable to do so ... we recommend that except where security considerations dictate otherwise the reports ... should be published and laid before Parliament ...[30]

Fine words. The Home Office fought against them with all the casuistry of which it is capable. Publication of reports was of course, it argued, an incorrect idea. 'They might well contain frank criticisms of personal performances which it would be better to keep within the sphere of management and not make available to a larger audience.' A number of hair-splitting constitutional arguments were produced to demonstrate that there could be no such thing in nature as a truly 'independent' inspectorate in the first place. The pinnacle of Home Office enterprise was to announce that if an outside inspector was allowed to make reports, a new bureaucratic department would have to be set up 'to advise the Permanent Under-Secretary of State whether the quasi-independent inspector's report should be accepted or not'. These chambers of infinite bureaucratic regress are a magnificent abstract feat, but the key to what Home Office attitudes are all about lies a few pages away in the same report. The Prison Department draws up ten-year forecasts of the prison population. Not only does it keep them secret from the public — in case they should cause misapprehension — it also attempted to keep them secret from the May Committee which was constituted precisely to inquire, as an outside inspection, into such matters. 'Exposing planning problems as frankly as possible would seem to be an essential part of the openness to which we refer elsewhere', noted the report tartly. (The ten-year forecast for average daily population, predicts about 48,000 by 1987 — obviously a figure prone to error, but more than 14 per cent over the 42,000 Roy Jenkins as Home Secretary predicted would be intolerable given the same size prison system as we have today.)

Policy-making in a Secret System: 'Control Units', 1972-5

In 1980, more than 100,000 words of Prison Department documents were released by a series of court orders. From them emerged the history of the way one piece of policy — the so-called 'control units' — took its course. The policy was a fiasco.

The story disclosed in rare detail the way the Home Office invented 'special control units'; launched them amid bureaucratic infighting, ruthlessly sweeping aside protest; hastily changed the regime when its apparently harsh and pointless nature was exposed; and finally abandoned the whole notion, admitting its uselessness.

It was a story of muddle and recriminations in which civil servants experimented with psychological techniques for punishing subversives; techniques which were quite different from those originally approved by ministers. They set up a system which was arguably illegal and led to a long and expensive High Court case five years afterwards. When publicly exposed, the system was widely criticized as inhumane, and was eventually admitted to be a waste of bureaucratic energy and public money. It was organized in secrecy which allowed one school of thought in the Home Office — that of the 'disciplinarians' — temporarily to triumph.

The documents were obtained, despite the ritual protests of ministers that disclosure, especially of 'policy advice' was not in the public interest, by the National Council for Civil Liberties. The NCCL's lawyers obtained disclosure in a case brought by one of the original inmates, Michael Williams, alleging the Home Office had behaved unlawfully. The minutes, reports and submissions to ministers documented many justifications for the public fears about the way the Prison Department is run behind the facade of official secrecy.

At the beginning of the 1970s, the Conservative Home Secretary, Robert Carr announced his general intention to do something about the wave of rooftop protests and demonstrations over prison conditions. Unannounced, he set up an internal inquiry with a brief to improve 'control' within prisons. The inquiry, carried out by an eleven-man commitee chaired by the Prison Department director W.R. Cox, produced a 20,000 word report. It was never published and even the governors themselves were refused permission to see it. The report claimed to have identified a rise in 'anarchist attitudes' in the prison system which had been helped along by the media. There were 72 particular troublemakers in the system, many of them young men serving long sentences, the report announced confidently. To handle them, it recommended a refinement of the existing dispersal system with 'special control units' which would perhaps eventually cost £1 million to construct from scratch.

Although possibly misguided, this document was thoughtful and relatively humane. In a later Home Office document on the control units, prison officers were quoted making remarks on the measures suggested by their superiors as being 'sheer panic and blue funk . . . due to pressure from do-gooders'. But the working party saw them as men who felt threatened and impotent, confronted by prisoners with little to lose. It recognized 'the deep-seated fears that prisoners have of staff brutality' and the acute danger of violent confrontations from 'any slight misuse or even threat of force on the staff side'. The report proposed a sort of specialist 'segregation unit' which would avoid confrontations and allow staff to be constructive and helpful. It seemed to be suggesting something comparable with the Barlinnie Special Unit in Scotland, which has had some success in handling long-term prisoners without attempting to destroy their personalities. Yet the reality, over the next year, turned into something very different. It became an attempt to force into final submission prisoners on whom punishment had already been tried and failed. What happened?

There was, it seemed, a persistent strand of belief within the Home Office that 'subversives' ought not only to be transferred, but also made to suffer until they changed their natures. Just after the riots report was composed, G.G.S. Chambers of P5 (the division in charge of security and control) was recording his own idea that the units should be 'short stay with only the essentials provided.' Dismissing fears that the ventilation envisaged for the control-unit cells was insufficient, he said that the prisoner would realize what 'normal delights he has forfeited by his bad behaviour'.

Carr, the Home Secretary, endorsed the original report at a meeting on 9 April 1973. P2 Division ('medium and long-term policy') immediately started thinking about the precise regime involved. 'P2 should take the lead on this', observed K.H. Dawson, going on to mention 'a relaxed and purposive regime' with 'communal activities of all kinds ... pitched to a standard just below that of the main prison'.

The head of the Home Office, Sir Arthur Petersen, shared these progressive ideas, recording that the units would be 'spare but not spartan', providing 'positive treatment and work' in an atmosphere 'sufficiently relaxed to encourage ... worthwhile relationships between staff and inmates'. He was anxious to avoid 'an oppressive bias' and wanted a constructive regime in which 'the staff can see the prisoners as individuals needing help and therefore deserving of some special tolerance'.

Chambers of P5 had a very different attitude. When submitting 'my own ideas on what I consider should be the regime' he called for 'realism', announcing that it was extremely unlikely that troublemakers would be in the least influenced by 'any kind of training or treatment, call it what you will ... I advocate that the regime should be extremely simple and based strictly on what a prisoner has to be legally provided with under the Prison Rules'. Advocating 'sterility ... seclusion and anonymity', Chambers outlines 'a barren existence more likely to persuade him [the prisoner] to behave ... largely ignored by the staff. Such a regime strictly followed would prove successful in most cases in a matter of months.' He added: 'No doubt it would arouse strong criticism from some quarters, and protests.' Chambers was not keen on over-exposure: 'We play down the setting up of the two units from the beginning ... drop the word "Special". We must not allow the units to become notorious.'

Carr told Parliament on 11 May (although the key details of the regime were still at issue) that he had a plan for 'a strict regime for the control of intractable troublemakers'. Between then and the year's end a bureaucratic battle raged between some members of P2, who were trying to implement the original scheme, and the authoritarians in P5 and elsewhere. As a later self-excusing minute tried to explain: 'P5 prevailed'. It was also later explained that P6 ('training') had been responsible for composing the actual staff instruction manual, though that responsibility was then further delegated to the prison staff college.

The disclosed documents do not show precisely how the novelties of would-be psychological manipulation which later caused so much embarrassment were arrived at. There are references to 'US experience' and B.A. Emes of P2 visited the USA during the course of 1973 to look at 'correctional' experiments. But the minutes of endless committee meetings, drafts and re-drafts, do show the outlines of the struggle:

> There is a fundamental dispute about the function of the control units ... who is to settle that?

> A genuine difference of approach ... 'confinement to cells' is too close to 'cellular confinement' which has a distinct disciplinary meaning. I suggest we refer instead to 'non-association'.

> ...the regime may be a shade more bleak than was originally intended ... it is only by cooperation and hard work that he will get himself out of the control unit. [Initialled by the Permanent Secretary and the junior Minister, Viscount Colville.]

By 12 September, the idea had already crystallized that the regime was to be 'very spartan' and based on isolation. Staff were not to talk to inmates but were to maintain a 'cool neutrality'.

On that date, P5 put in a successful submission that the total stay should be a minimum of six months, and crossed out their own figure of 'one month' for the basic initial regime and wrote in 'three'. At a meeting chaired by Miss G.M.B. Owen of P5, the six-month figure was accepted. It was to be 'a stronger deterrent for trouble-makers' who were now believed to face a 'powerful incentive', at least temporarily, to do as they were told. An original scheme of short, trial returns to the main prison was finally killed off, and the notion of 'reversion' was agreed upon: if a prisoner did anything wrong, he went back to the very beginning of his six-month punishment period. Emes was even heard arguing unsuccessfully that breaking the prisoner's spirit required him to take even his single hour's daily exercise without human company. This was dismissed as impractical.

The ambassador who had been held captive by the Tupamaro guerrillas, Sir Geoffrey Jackson, was commissioned to explain to trainees how deprivation affected prisoners: 'The regime ... will cause some deprivation ... the staff will need a keen appreciation of this.' Sir Geoffrey explained in his lecture that one indignity particularly hard to bear was to have to excrete without privacy; control-unit inmates subsquently complained that this happened to them.

It was regarded as 'rather tricky' within the Prison Department that statutory prison rules only envisaged either proper disciplinary proceedings or segregation on 'Rule 43' for good order and discipline reviewed at monthly intervals, as proper grounds for solitary confinement. Emes warned on 29 July 1974, just before the first unit at Wakefield opened: 'This is the kind of discrepancy which could be picked up by the prisoners, or for that matter, the Howard League or some other pressure-group.'

But the circular actually setting up the unit was kept secret even from MPs. An early draft of the circular warned prison governors there were 'bound to be pressures to modify its severities' and 'censorship must be rigid'. Governors had to be careful not to create martyrs if the regime was to be 'defensible to the public'. One official wondered whether it was wise to use the word 'defensible'. Another phrase, he wrote, would avoid 'making our position so clear'. Miss Owen of P5 reassured him: 'Only circular instructions which modify standing orders are sent to the House of Commons Library. This one will not therefore go to the House of Commons.'

Thus it was decided behind the public's back to take so-called 'subversives', without any trial or hearing, and subject them to virtual solitary confinement for at least three months, with deliberately impassive staff, in bare cells described by one prison doctor as 'dark and dismal'. No radios or belongings were allowed. If prisoners had caged birds, they were to be 'disposed of'. If during this experience the prisoner was 'civil and co-operative', he was allowed limited human contact over a further three months. If he offended in any way, he 'reverted' instantly to day one of the system with another six months to go. It was unclear whether this experience was supposed to encourage the recalcitrant to 'mend his ways' in the future. It did not have that effect.

The Home Office took a deliberate decision, endorsed by the new Labour Home Secretary, Roy Jenkins, to keep quiet about the pilot unit apart from announcing its planned opening. David Hewlings, controller of operations, advised Jenkins that, 'intense curiosity from the media ... could seriously handicap the smooth running of the units during their difficult initial stages'. They would have to perform in 'a blaze of publicity'. The Home Office believed in a policy of complete frankness and openness, of course, he explained. What it understood by openness was that when and if the regime of the units leaked, Jenkins would then respond to questions 'from any responsible source'. Advice to ministers about political tactics is the very information Whitehall most jealously wishes to keep secret. This was certainly a piece of dreadfully bad advice. When conditions in the units leaked out Jenkins and the Home Office found themselves at the centre of a highly embarrassing storm about control units.

But meanwhile, secrecy was also keeping the public in ignorance of protests already voiced and squashed. A chaplain, the Rev. P.L. Ashford, from the Institute of Professional Civil Servants trade-union section, protested on 30 April 1973 that there would be a 'strong temptation to regard the units as places of punishment'. He had 'important reservations', but feared consultation was 'a meaningless exercise'. When the circular instruction finally went out in 1974, the Chaplain-General, Canon Lloyd-Rees, protested about 'the basic terminology being used ... [and about] some of the theories about basic human behaviour implied in the regime'. He objected to 'a belief in the efficacy of deterrence I find almost naïve ... likely to deepen hostility'.

A regional principal medical officer, Dr D.O. Topp, also recorded his alarm. He feared that psychopathic people would end up by behaving worse under such conditions: 'Segregation in this way will rapidly become intolerable to them.' A crushing reply came to him from the Home Office saying: 'You are inevitably unaware of the arguments and reasoning which have preceded these decisions.'

A worse fate than receiving rude letters was inflicted on a priest who actually experienced the Wakefield unit at first hand. Fr John Gott protested indignantly to his religious superior that the unit was 'a scandal in a democratic and free society' and 'an affront to human dignity'. His superior, Mgr Anthony Cunningham accused him of 'hysteria' and when Gott refused to retract, had him declared 'emotionally unsuitable for prison work'.

Cunningham wrote to J.H.J. Beck of the Home Office Personnel Division: 'The Bishop of Leeds has promised to move Gott . . . as soon as possible . . . I am sure you will be as relieved as I am.' Beck replied: 'Dear Tony, Thank you for letting me know Fr Gott is on his way. I am grateful for the way you have steered this delicate matter to the right conclusion.'

However, on 6 October 1974, after the sister of one of the first three guinea-pigs (Michael Williams, serving 14 years) was allowed to visit him, the *Sunday Times* described the unit system for the first time. There was a public row. Jenkins was extremely unhappy as the minutes of a top-level meeting called by him make clear:

He felt most concerned about the fact that allocation to the control unit was an administrative matter, although it had many of the features of a punishment. He saw considerable force in the argument advanced by a number of critics that 'allocation' should be the result of disciplinary proceedings.

The most significant criticisms apart from this were objections to the length of time and the fixed nature of the 90-day period, the automatic reversion for the slightest offence and the adverse psychological effect. [Minutes, 16 October 1974.]

A report was commissioned by the Director General of prisons to explain how the original plans for the units had become so different. He was told: 'There were differences of emphasis and approach on the part of various interested divisions . . . compromise was inevitable.'

Jenkins ordered some immediate changes, but by December the total abandonment of the idea of units was being mooted. At a meeting of officials in July 1975, the mood was very different from that of two years previously: there was 'general recognition that the unit as it now operates is unsatisfactory in several respects'. Ministers hoped that the 'need for the unit would disappear by the end of the year'.

Dr Topp sent a prescient 'private and confidential' note that April to the joint ethical working party of the Royal College of Psychiatrists: 'the whole exercise so far has largely proved a non-viable proposition . . . of little practical use to the system and, besides which, a rather politically unacceptable concept . . . left alone, the whole situation will die a natural death'.

Only twelve 'subversives' had ever been recommended for the control units. Six had been considered unsuitable for behaviour modification attempts. Three were still inside the machine in August 1975. Only three men had graduated from the experiment: one was already back on 'segregation' in his own prison; one had been put on report for 'misconduct' and the third was causing more disruption at Parkhurst and had to be transferred again. As Hewlings was told in a memo from P2 on 18 September 1975: 'Control units are never likely to be a real help to the prison system.' Abandonment was awkward, of course: 'the snags are largely presentational ... how do we persuade staff that such a decision has been made on merit and not as a surrender to pressure groups?'

In these dying days of a secretive policy blunder, only one submission from within P3 ('sentenced adult male offenders') struck a fresh note: 'One of the ways out of our present situation may be to lay it all open, both to get public support ... and to persuade the staff that we will not get what we need by pretending we do not live in a democracy.'

On 23 October 1975, Jenkins announced the closure of the Wakefield 'control unit'. He said: 'It has not been used to the expected extent.' Nearly five years later, on 25 February 1980, the case of Williams *v.* the Home Office opened before Mr Justice Tudor Evans and, largely thanks to the tireless lawyers of the NCCL, the whole disreputable and futile experiment was thrown open to the public gaze.

This chapter has quoted extensively from the May Report, despite its limits as a quick inquiry designed to do something to deflect strikes and go-slows by prison officers before the Home Secretary had to call the troops in to man the jails. Its main purpose was to give the warders a pay rise. None the less, it is the most thorough analysis of the prison system in the 1970s and 1980s that we are likely to see, and the general picture it paints is of a bureaucratic disaster area. It is not the fault of one man that the number of prisoners has soared since the war from 18,000 to 44,000; that prisoners have to sleep three in a cell and excrete into a bucket; that the Victorian prisons are squalid and not replaced; or that prison brutalizes more people than it reforms. Nor even that 'many of those employed in the service feel a deep sense of dissatisfaction with the organization and management of it as a whole'.[31] It is, of course, the fault of a political system.

And it is quite possible that extravagant methods of secrecy and information control within the system are not the sole cause of its faults. The United States is a less secretive country than Britain and its prisons are notorious for neglect, injustice and violence. Perhaps the secrecy is an expression of deep political wisdom within the Home Office, and its servants know better than we know ourselves that we would rather forget about prisons and prisoners while we get on with our decent, industrious, lucky lives. It would at least be worth the experiment of abolishing prison secrecy in order to find out.

4
Secrecy and the Jury System: How to Silence a Jury

Some judges today may suppose that the rule of law means the rule of the people by any old codger in a wig. They confuse the law with their own persons and suppose that they (and the DPP) are those that rule, and who may instruct the BBC and Press as to what is an authorized view. [E.P. Thompson, *New Society*, 22 November 1979.]

Now for the question of what are unctuously known as 'the secrets of the jury room'.

This issue came to a head recently in the Thorpe case. After years of underground scandal which the newspapers judged too tasteless or dangerous to pursue, the prepossessing Old Etonian who led the Liberal Party was charged with conspiracy to murder the man who claimed to be his abandoned homosexual lover. Thorpe, his laconic and bespectacled Oxford friend David Holmes and two other men, were acquitted by the jury after all but one had refused to testify; after Thorpe had conceded his homosexuality; after unchallenged evidence that Thorpe had persuaded a Bahamas millionaire to give him £20,000 for the Liberals which he handed over secretly to Holmes; and after an admission from three of them that there had indeed been a conspiracy against the voluble Norman Scott — they said it was merely to 'frighten' him, and not to murder.

The jury were out for two-and-a-half days and their acquittal on 27 July 1979 caused a sensation. What did it mean? Why had they taken so long? Was Thorpe, who had always denied the charges, totally vindicated? Had the Director of Public Prosecutions made a mistake in this, the most sensitive and internationally famous Old Bailey trial for years? These were not simply academic questions; quite apart from several million Liberal voters who wanted to know what they were to think of their former leader, there was a good deal of excitement among the nation's legislators. In the House of

Lords it was debated whether steps should be taken against the press, whose belated activities in exposing the affair and buying-over witnesses appeared to have blown up in their faces. Contributions were being solicited to pay Mr Thorpe's defence costs, which he had, wisely perhaps, not attempted to recover from the court. (His friend, the industrialist Sir James Goldsmith, about to set up his own newspaper, gave him £5,000.)

Peter Chippindale of the *Guardian* and I had already spent an exhausting fortnight composing a number of optional accounts of the Thorpe affair according to how many of the defendants eventually found themselves convicted or acquitted. (This process of faking reality in order to stay on the right side of the law is described in the chapter on libel.) Now we were faced with a new dilemma. Would the law of contempt, such as it was, intimidate jurors from speaking about the case, and newspapers from printing what they said? The answer was to be, unusually enough, 'not entirely'. One juror was confident enough about his rights of free speech to want to talk to us, albeit with theatrical precautions against discovery on our part; and one magazine, the *New Statesman,* was bold enough to print what he said and to be followed into the water, once the ice had been broken, by others. We ended up the victims of a test prosecution brought by the new Tory Attorney-General, Sir Michael Havers, who turned out to take as dim a view of free speech as his Labour predecessor, the barrister Sam Silkin.

It will come as no surprise that the question of free speech for jurors turned out on inspection to be deeply obscure. The really valuable knowledge, possessed by the authorities alone, was whether jury deliberations were a secret or not. Although there are one or two quite sound arguments for limiting what jurors disclose, no one had ever taken the trouble to evaluate what precisely, in the words of the European Convention on Human Rights, might constitute restrictions on free speech 'necessary in a democratic society'. Instead wholesale intimidation was relied on as a method of keeping the mouths of jurors shut. The newspapers and their lawyers, faced with the threat of unspecified contempt, had cowered in an appropriately tradesmanlike way for more than fifty years, hardly ever overstepping a completely invisible line.

In 1922, the notorious murder case of Armstrong the poisoner had led a number of judges to say what they thought about jury secrecy. Chief Justice Hewart was confronted with newspaper accounts of events in the jury room.[1] He said:

In the opinion of this court nothing could be more improper, deplorable and dangerous. It may be that some jurymen are not aware that the inestimable value of their verdict is created only by its unanimity, and does not depend upon the process by which they believe that they arrived at it. It follows that every juryman ought to observe the obligation of secrecy which is comprised in and imposed by the oath of the grand juror.

If one juryman might communicate with the public upon the evidence and the verdict, so might his colleagues also, and if they all took this dangerous course, differences of individual opinion might be made manifest which, at the least, could not fail to diminish the confidence that the public rightly has in the general propriety of criminal verdicts.

These rather metaphysical statements did not explain whether talkative jurors were actually breaking the law. In the same year, the Court of Appeal heard a complaint; a juror disputed the unanimity of a verdict given by the jury foreman.[2] The court neatly solved the dilemma of whether to hear evidence from the jurymen, by declaring a retrial on the grounds that procedure had not been complied with: the verdict should always be given in the presence of all the twelve jurors, they pronounced. But, 'What passes in the juryroom during the discussion by the jury of what their verdict should be, ought to be treated as private and confidential.' The reason why courts should not enquire into it, said Lord Justice Atkin,

is both to secure the finality of decisions of fact arrived at by a jury and also, which is a matter of great importance, for the protection of jurymen themselves, to prevent their being exposed to pressure that might otherwise be put on them with a view to explaining the reasons which actuated them individually in arriving at their verdict.

Lord Justice Bankes left the press, as he no doubt intended, in a state of free-floating anxiety.

I may say that I saw the other day with astonishment and disgust, the publication in a newspaper of a statement by the foreman of the jury in an important criminal trial, as to what took place in the jury-room after the jury had retired. I do not think it necessary to express any opinion as to whether such a publication amounts to contempt of court, but I feel confident that anyone who read that statement will realize the importance of maintaining the rule.

Lord Justice Warrington, agreeing, spoke of the 'grave impropriety' of such a publication. Many years later, in 1951, the then Home Secretary, Lord Chancellor and Lord Chief Justice took it on themselves jointly to compose a notice, which the Home Office arranged to be posted in every jury-room. It read:

> Her Majesty's judges remind you of the solemn obligation upon you not to reveal, in any circumstances, to any person, either during the trial or after it is over, anything relating to it which has occurred in this room while you have been considering your verdict.[3]

This was mere eyewash, and in 1959 the legal correspondent of the *Observer* pointed out that such a notice had no legal force whatever.[4]

A Home Office committee under Lord Morris of Borth-y-Gest decided in 1965 that jurors needed even more vigorous bullying.[5] It inaugurated a pamphlet which deliberately omitted to tell jurors that they could take notes during the proceedings and ask questions whenever they felt like it. 'It would be unwise to give any positive encouragement to jurors to embark upon note-taking. The process of note-taking is one that requires a good deal of experience and skill', the committee urbanely remarked.

> Rather similar considerations apply to the problem whether jurors should be told they can ask questions. We think there is some peril in encouraging them to do so ... it is better if jurors do not intervene too readily, though it can undoubtedly happen that some point that seems to the jury to be important may not have been sufficiently probed, and it would be unfortunate if a jury thought they could never ask a question. Much must be left to the handling of proceedings by the judge.

The important thing was to add yet another printed warning about keeping quiet. 'It should emphasize the confidential nature of their duties, and the fact that even after a trial is over they must not make disclosures about what went on in the jury-room'.

The committee recognized that some people might think this

slightly obsessive, 'and even that the requirement shows a lack of confidence in the jury-system and implies that the system would break down if it were generally known what happens when a jury retires to consider its verdict'. They produced an explanation, which has a deeply familiar ring, on behalf of the flocks of unconsulted jurors: 'If such disclosures were to be made, particularly to the Press, jurors would no longer feel free to express their opinions frankly when the verdict was under discussion for fear that what they said later might be made public.' The committee added: 'In fact they might even fear reprisals from criminals for whose convictions they were responsible, and who had heard about their deliberations.'

Once again, a vague and unstatutory threat was flourished: 'Gross breaches of the obligation to preserve secrecy might be treated as a contempt of court, especially if the judge in a particular case had expressly told the jury that they must not make any disclosure.'

The Home Secretary to whom the committee reported, Henry Brooke, found himself a peer when majority verdicts were brought in under the 1967 Criminal Justice Act. It worried him that majority verdicts, invented to get more convictions despite the possibility of 'nobbled' jurors, might over-excite the newspapers. The peers debated the dangerous possibility that the press might decide to write about what happened in jury-rooms, despite the threats and notices. Perhaps there had better be a law against it. Lord Gardiner, Labour Lord Chancellor, thought so too, and the criminal law revision committee under Lord Justice Sellers was asked by the Home Secretary, Roy Jenkins, to consider the question.

The committee[6] of sixteen was replete with senior judges, barristers, academics and prosecutors — Sellers L.J.; Edmund Davies L.J.; Winn L.J.; Lawton J.; James J.; the Common Sergeant, Mervyn Griffith-Jones; Professor Glanville Williams; and the Director of Public Prosecutions, Sir Norman Skelhorn. They concluded that the emperor had no clothes and there was no real legal backing for jury secrecy. But it did not matter very much.

The gentlemanly conduct of the press was proving more or less reliable. What the committee did not say was that it was only the residual uncertainty of the law which kept the press in line. It was fear, not sportsmanship which wiped juries off the map of things Britons were prepared to discuss in public. The committee airily implied once more, in the course of explaining how the criminal law had no place in the jury question, that behind the velvet glove might lurk a rusty mailed first; 'In our opinion, the conduct referred to ... is not a criminal offence, at present, except that possibly in some circumstances it might be contempt of court.'

But the general tone of their brief report was relaxed. There was no judicial authority on the issue, and little judicial comment; the Lord Chancellor himself said, during the Lords debate, that there was no law against disclosure. Secrecy, the committee reported, 'has been generally accepted by the public as a rule of conduct ... such breaches or attempts to breach it as have become known so far have not established a mischief so extensive or serious that it calls for legislation and punishment'. The rule should remain as long as possible, 'one of conduct — a solemn obligation', the committee breezed on, 'rather than one to be enforced by criminal sanctions'.

People might say that this public announcement that there was no law on secrecy and no intention to pass one, would give the game away. But:

> We do not fear this because the absence of sanctions has been well-known ... and yet the press and public generally has respected the rule. Should any newspaper be tempted to take advantage of the freedom which at present exists to approach jurors for information in order to prolong the sensationalism of a criminal trial, we would hope ... intervention by the Press Council ... would be effectual to check any such abuse.

In the same magnanimous tone the committee allowed that jurors often found their experiences interesting. There was clearly no objection to them talking about their experiences in a general way, without identifying cases, 'and in any event, there will inevitably be minor disclosures of a kind which, although they ought not to be encouraged, few people would regard as deserving of punishment'.

Obviously the same principle is at work here as that which keeps jurors ignorant of their right to ask questions — that is, don't quite tell the truth and jurors won't make too much of a nuisance of themselves. The committee also realized that it would be tricky to formulate a legal principle, because in the drafting it would become clear there was not one available. Jurors would have to be allowed to break their silence to the authorities, as had become plain in a couple of recent cases, if the authorities themselves considered it a good thing. The committee quoted a 1968 appeal case in which the court had considered an affidavit from a juror who realized halfway through a trial that he knew the defendant to have a previous conviction. It is a problem we see perplexing the power-holders time and again in their efforts to make the public behave as they would not behave themselves. 'What I do is briefing, what you do is leaking'; 'authorized disclosures'; 'jury vetting ... in the public interest' — the attitude spawns a crop of unattractive paradoxes.

The committee gave two reasons which occurred to them, why blanket jury secrecy was in the public interest — both are familiar. First, jurors had to be protected from pressure so they could speak freely without fear of it being laid at their individual door; and so they would not be harassed afterwards to talk. Secondly, there was a variant of Chief Justice Hewart's 1922 metaphysics about 'public confidence' — which still only appeared to make sense in the case of conviction. A public 'retrial' might well give a false impression of the reasons for the verdict, and this 'might lead to unjustifiable dissatisfaction with the results of the trial'.

After these pronouncements, the authorities slumbered for eleven years. Jurors, harassed and nervous, rarely spoke to journalists. Journalists, told by their office lawyers that their ambitions were probably illegal, rarely tried to have their stories printed. There was a fair stream of reminiscences from jurors about unnamed cases, some of which had the undoubted effect of 'diminishing the confidence the public rightly has in the general propriety of criminal verdicts'. The *Sun*,[7] enquiring 'What really goes on behind the locked doors of the jury room?', printed a full page of readers' reminiscences, along the lines of:

One juror said, 'It's near Christmas — we'll find him not guilty.'

He was barely sober ... he told me he had not heard half the twaddle by counsel but it was obvious the bloke in the dock was a rotter.

I told the usher I was deaf and would not be able to hear anything. He told me not to worry ... all I was required to do was to sit on the jury bench and look intelligent.

These anecdotes included some cheering accounts of democracy in action as well. One Cornish juror described, for example, how his jury had acquitted a man of dangerous driving because he had killed his wife in the crash and spent six months in hospital himself:

'We knew this man was guilty, but we took the view he had suffered enough.'

In exceptional cases, when there were apparently abuses in the jury-room, or when the authorities might be gratified rather than displeased at disclosures, newspapers printed what identifiable jurors said about identifiable cases. The hapless Miss Joan Hamilton Lawford complained in 1967 that she was browbeaten into agreeing to convict a man of assaulting the police. Newspapers printed her alarming account of two hours in the jury-room in great detail. Ten jurors thought the man was so obviously guilty as to make a verdict a mere formality. One man was persuaded to go along with the majority, and the others, Miss Lawford said, anxious to get home, shouted at her until she gave in. The case went to appeal[8] and the Lord Chief Justice made it clear that they would not hear evidence from jurors because it could lead to attempts to interfere with jurors after trials, and their evidence might finish up endlessly being used to upset cases. No one suggested that Miss Lawford's conduct or that of the newspapers amounted to contempt of court; it was well understood that the threat was only useful to intimidate jurors in advance. Miss Lawford's affidavit, which the court refused to hear, contained a key explanation. She had really been a victim of legal hocus-pocus which far from protecting her, had done her out of her right to insist on a disagreement and a retrial (this was just before majority verdicts were introduced). 'When the foreman . . . was asked whether it was the verdict of them all, she wanted to stand up and say it was not, but was too frightened to say so because she thought she would have been in contempt of court.'

Ten jurors signed a protest letter to the *Daily Telegraph* in 1978[9] after Judge Crichton directed them to acquit in a Manchester rape case, saying he 'had seemed unsympathetic from the start', to the raped woman. The jury unhesitatingly felt there was a case to answer; over two days, the prosecution had presented, what was in their opinion, 'a substantial case'. The judge, who had just retired from the bench, riposted to them in public that there had been too little corroborative evidence to identify the two brothers on trial as the perpetrators. One of the jurors, Mrs Kathleen Baker, undaunted, wrote to the Lord Chancellor complaining that juries, at the bottom of the hierarchical pyramid, tended to adopt an attitude of humility. The affair constituted a rare dialogue.

More characteristic of the strangled approach to debate was the way one jury's views emerged about allegations of 'planted' police evidence in IRA trials. After a bombing trial at Winchester in 1974, the *Guardian* nerved itself to print, with some fear that it might be illegal, an anonymous juryman's views. He said that he, along with six of his colleagues, believed it was a bad thing defence counsel should be allowed to make such allegations against the police without the jury having the opportunity to comment. When convicting the defendants, they had felt cheated of the opportunity to add a rider deprecating these allegations. The *Guardian's* boldness in printing this one anecdote had gratifying results; far from being proceeded against, the newspaper found itself congratulated by the Police Federation magazine.[10] If the newspapers' lawyers took one lesson from the episode, it was that the law might be mysteriously flexible in its operations. By 1976, Michael Zander, the *Guardian's* legal correspondent, had been sufficiently mystified to assert that journalistic attempts to investigate important public-policy questions about the criminal process were 'almost unthinkable in this country'. He maintained, in a choice of legal language characteristic of an enfeebled press: 'there is a general feeling it would be contempt of court ... interviews with journalists for publication would be regarded as unacceptable'. The 1967 committee report, which was clear enough in its statements that journalists were free to approach jurors and that contempt was a remote and restricted possibility, had apparently been incorporated into the lawyers' received wisdom and undergone a sea-change. 'It did not actually commit itself as to whether ... contempt ... already covered jurors disclosing their deliberations', said Zander.[11]

Zander was bemoaning the mystery over the case of Peter Hain, a well-known South African exile and libertarian who had become the *bête noire* of many prejudiced people for his campaign against apartheid in sport. He had been arrested by his local police on a ludicrous charge of bank robbery on the distinctly unreliable identity evidence of two small boys. It was his case which, with some others, was to lead to a general recognition of how dangerous identity evidence might be, and to its consequent devaluing by the courts. What was strange was the jury's behaviour. Despite a thin Crown case, lack of obvious motive and Hain's patent innocence to all who knew him, the jurors took five hours and only acquitted by a majority verdict. For a country which professes it is better for ten guilty men to go free than one innocent to be convicted, such a close shave deserved close examination. Were some jurors too bigoted to acquit on the evidence? Or did they cling to the view that those whom the police arrest must be guilty? Or did they simply overvalue identity evidence? I do not know, Peter Hain does not know, and legal journalists, instead of finding out, wrote newspaper articles about 'general feeling' and 'unthinkability'.

Freedom of information has two virtues in civil society. The first is that it encourages fertile debate. Lack of this can be seen in the jury question: occasional low-key disclosures in a climate of fear and obfuscation have not been enough to generate a lively and rational debate in this very important area of social control. The second virtue of free expression follows from this, and is a negative one: it keeps down the weeds of misinformation. As no one has had any clear knowledge about juries other than anecdotal, the way has been open for vested interests to propagandize.

In 1974, Sir Robert Mark, Commissioner of the Metropolitan Police, launched an attack on the jury system for failing to convict enough people. He based this partly on anecdotes. Courts refused to take evidence of the incompetence and perversities displayed by juries in certain cases. 'If exposing the truth about the jury would destroy the public's belief in its value, then surely it's high time the belief was destroyed', he said.[12]

Also he presented statistics to suggest the amateurs had the wool pulled too easily over their eyes; they acquitted half of those they tried, he said. Put in perspective, his statistics were not very worrying for a country committed to a deliberate policy of not putting people in gaol without overwhelming proof. Ninety-two per cent of offences are disposed of without any democratic nonsense by magistrates. Of all the remainder, only a margin of 12 per cent get themselves acquitted by juries. The rest either plead guilty, are acquitted on the direction of the judge, or are convicted by the jury. Often too, juries can be seen to acquit on a large number of charges, perhaps convicting only on the least serious as a mark of the degree of severity they think proper (the judge being allowed the sole pleasure of passing sentence). As no one knows a jury's line of reasoning in cases where one acquits against expectation, 'the secrets of the jury-room' merely allow men like Sir Robert to argue into a vacuum.

After the Thorpe trial when we heard, in the haphazard way newspapers learn things, that one of the jurors was apparently willing to talk, we were thus the inheritors of a particularly muddled tradition of secrecy. There had been perhaps a dozen occasions in the previous decade when the press had openly interviewed jurors. The *Sunday Times* had been the most recent, in the notorious ABC secrets case which had managed to put administrative secrecy on trial wholesale. Elaine Potter wrote: 'Just how relevant this information would have been ... was revealed to the *Sunday Times* by one of the jurors.'[13] (The case is discussed in its inglorious detail in Chapter 5.) No thunderbolts fell.

I start being secretive myself at this point because I believe in protecting sources from reprisals. A former colleague ran across the Thorpe juror in the course of his work. They chatted about the trial. Our former colleague rang up one of his acquaintances in the *Guardian* who was rather at a loss to know what to do with the knowledge, but solemnly burned the details he had committed to paper in his office ashtray. Peter Chippindale and I decided to try to talk to the juror, and in this legal no-man's-land, made up our own ethics. Justice would suffer if future jurors imagined they were likely to be harassed by outsiders; this was one of the points judges and commentators stressed. Therefore, we would be fanatically careful not to put him under any pressure to talk to us. Similarly, it would be wrong to offer him any inducements; journalists commonly pay informants, from a few pounds for an early 'tip' of a train crash to five- or six-figure sums for the memoirs of ex-Prime Ministers. No one would be able to say we were tempting this or future jurors to sensationalize or even distort their experiences in the hope of making money. (It was as well we took this firm attitude; when it was decided to make an example of our impertienence, lawyers could be heard saying, apparently seriously, that we were opening the way to corrupting jurors who would dishonestly convict in order to have a better story to sell afterwards.) The third key point was anonymity. If we offered our juror absolute anonymity, and made sure he did not identify the individual stances of his fellow jurors, no one could accuse us of making future jurymen unwilling to speak out in the jury-room; this seemed the only other point of substance in the various expostulations about jury secrecy.

So we passed a message back along this chain of acquaintances. If he wanted to talk to us, the juror should give his telephone number for transmission back to us. Back came the number. One of us rang, the other carefully witnessing the phone call, and we asked him to suggest a convenient time for us to meet.

We each witnessed every move the other made. It was we who were tense and the juror who was relaxed when we finally called at his house, were introduced to his family and, as none of us had eaten after work, adjourned to the Venus Steak House in the

London suburbs. The juror was untroubled by the threatening notices about secrecy in the jury-room and the general air of legal bullying that infests courts. As a matter of fact, he explained, one of the jurors had sent off in the course of the trial for copies of the leaflet recently published for jurors by the National Council for Civil Liberties.[14] This leaflet remedied certain omissions in what jurors are told, pointing out they could ask questions, had a constitutional right to acquit and could ignore any notices forbidding them to talk to the press after the case. At the time we were interviewing the juror, the NCCL were following up their campaign by complaining to the Lord Chancellor, Lord Hailsham, that his own leaflet urging secrecy on jurors was misleading. Lord Hailsham was to write back, two days before we eventually published, saying the leaflet 'does not purport to lay down the law'. It was an 'instruction', he said, which anyone who knew anything about the matter would support.[15]

'The usher was furious when he saw the leaflets', our juror said. 'He demanded to know who was responsible, and the juror concerned told him she had collected them from the NCCL.' It was a bad omen for us all; the letters NCCL are to the average court official what a red rag is to a bull. They think of the NCCL as a subversive, anti-police organization almost certainly run from the Kremlin. Judges can be provoked into the most extraordinary tirades, behind which there often seems to run some underlying notion of property rights, against the NCCL and its libertarian lawyers. Like the press, the NCCL are seen as loiterers and potential burglars, preventing the proprietors of the legal machine from sleeping easily in their beds.

We had a long talk with our juror and I must confess that as Peter Chippindale and I had invited him to eat, we picked up the bill. Lawyers concerned about 'inducements' may be horrified to learn that on the top of his steak the juror treated himself to a fried egg. It seemed fair: we spent three hours with him, making him repeat what he had said from different angles, seeking to eliminate possible bias and embroidery from what he told us. On a 'one-source' story such as this, one has to take particular care in interviewing. We were eventually satisfied he was giving us a fair account. What was particularly interesting from the point of view of public education was that, precisely because the trial had been so lavishly written about, the evidence of the witnesses was already familiar. It was an unusual chance to analyse the course of a trial alongside an informed public.

There were, of course, many other constraints; critics of jury disclosures seem not to realize how the laws of contempt and libel mesh into a seamless robe which can destroy free speech and can certainly prevent even the most reckless journalist from merely writing down what a juror says and printing it. First of all, we would have faced a serious problem had Thorpe and his co-defendants not been acquitted. There would have been appeals. We would have faced a charge that we were interfering in the course of justice by providing possible material for appeal (such as, that a bit of evidence had been misunderstood, or that a juror had misbehaved). Or it might even have been said that we were prejudicing an appeal by clouding the judge's mind with comments about the accused's guilt. Or even that people might think such material was clouding a judge's mind. (This too, can sometimes apparently be regarded as contempt of court.) There would have been legal defences to all these accusations, but they would certainly have provided added complications.

Because the quartet had been acquitted, we faced different restrictions. What is said in open court has 'absolute privilege' against libel, if fairly reported. Allegations do not have to be proved to be true. But what was said in the jury-room has no such privilege if publicly reported. A man who is acquitted has an important status in the eyes of a newspaper lawyer; he is somebody whose reputation has suddenly become worth money again. So, we would have to be exquisitely careful not to print anything rude the jurors said about Jeremy Thorpe and his friends — or any of the witnesses come to that, or any of the barristers, or indeed anybody at all — which lowered their reputations below the pitch they could be fairly said to have reached already. Had the juror said, 'We decided to acquit because we thought the chief crown witness was a homosexual himself', this news would have had to be kept from the public. The chief witness had admitted to a number of damaging things in court, but not to being a homosexual. He could have sued us for printing such an allegation (which I hasten to add, is not suggested is really the case).

Even more restrictive is the protection the laws of libel offer the jurors themselves. Were we to print anything which suggested that any of the jurors, including the one we were speaking to, had not behaved and thought with the utmost high mindedness, he could have sued. Not naming the jurors is only a partial protection. We would have been sued by the lot of them.

As we all munched away in the Steak House, however, it became clear that we were in luck. The jury seemed to have been sensible and thoughtful. Because of the peculiar circumstances of the trial, in which so much had gone admitted or unchallenged in order to escape the single charge laid, we could report their thoughts more or less freely.

The acquittal turned out to be perfectly comprehensible; because of the lack of conclusive proof of what was intended when a pistol was waved at Norman Scott, the jury decided they could not convict on conspiracy to 'murder'. Other, lesser charges had not been laid against anyone and the suspicious circumstances suggesting that a conspiracy of some kind existed became irrelevant.

Many important issues were thus cleared up. Thorpe had not been let off because he was an important person, nor as a mark of hostility to the witness Norman Scott, his alleged victim. The chief Crown witness, Peter Bessell, had his evidence rejected because he had used it to buy immunity from prosecution for other offences, and because the defence had made a great impact with their complaints of a 'double-your-money' contract he had signed for his memoirs with the *Sunday Telegraph*. The pre-trial publicity at the committal had not affected the jury's minds in the least. The 'right to silence' claimed by three of the accused turned out to work considerably in their favour, the jury accepting their duty not to draw adverse conclusions from it. The jury's verdict was not designed to exonerate Thorpe from all taint of wrongdoing, but to express their rigid and wholly proper view of the solitary charge before them. Sir Tony Hetherington, the Director of Public Prosecutions, should have been fascinated by these discoveries and used them to draw lessons for the future (indeed, in fairness to him, there is reason to believe he did not want to take a punitive attitude to the disclosures).

The *Guardian* declined to print this dangerous tale after receiving a legal opinion from Geoffrey Grimes of Lovell White & King opining correctly that such an open challenge to the authorities might lead to a test case, and pointing out that it was a very different matter from disclosures for which the DPP might want to pat the newspapers on the back. There was also an understandable reluctance on the part of the *Guardian* to take pointless risks over the rather distasteful Thorpe affair in the absence of any truly sensational discovery from the juryman. One of the side-effects of secrecy in Britain is, of course, that newspapers, magazines and television companies become playgrounds for lawyers. When conduct that displeases judges becomes 'contempt of court'; conduct that displeases the rich and famous becomes 'libel'; and conduct that displeases the government becomes 'an Official Secrets Act breach', then there is no certainty in law but only a maze of guesses. Lawyers get paid for the guesses; if they guess too cautiously, no one ever proves them wrong.

Bruce Page, Editor of the *New Statesman*, took a more confrontationist view. The barrister Geoffrey Robertson pointed out (free of charge) that not only was our action not contempt, but that the Government was currently in breach with Strasbourg until it rewrote the law of contempt. Arthur Davidson QC, Parliamentary Secretary to the Labour Attorney-General Sam Silkin, told us later that his advice would have been identical. Page cheerfully printed, as one of a series of pieces analysing the Thorpe case, the following article:

Thorpe's Trial: How the Jury Saw It (from the *New Statesman*)

The outcome of the Thorpe trial looked remarkably like a débâcle for Britain's official prosecutors. After elaborate proceedings, men went scott-free whose counsel had indicated that they might well have pleaded guilty to crimes of considerable magnitude. One defendant, John le Messurier, plans a profitable book in which he will boast about his role as author of a criminal conspiracy. And anyone sifting the Old Bailey record can find evidence of sins as various as electoral fraud and application of persuasion to witnesses.

Traditionally the Director of Public Prosecutions is a mysterious fellow, protecting himself, if at all, not by public debate but by letting things discreetly be known. Discreetly, he and his minions are letting it be known that they justify their conduct of the Thorpe case by reference to the jury's having taken more than two days to reach a verdict. Does not this show it was a serious case, seriously considered?

The same line of argument applies also to supporters of Mr Jeremy Thorpe. His conduct was exhaustively examined, and in the end adjudged innocent. His name is therefore clear.

These arguments have been advanced so far, into a vacuum; gaining force from the fact that convention (though not law) treats jury decision-making as a kind of holy secret. What are the facts? We have conducted a detailed interview with one of the jurors involved, and his evidence suggests that the DPP's self-justification is hopelessly wide of the mark.

The Crown's main charge, conspiracy to murder, never made any serious impression on the jury; the juror interviewed said that after little more than an hour's deliberation on the first day, there was a clear majority in favour of throwing it out. Questioned further, he was emphatic on the point:

Q: So you never got around to considering who was involved in the conspiracy ... what you basically came down to saying was it's not proved there was a conspiracy to murder in the first place?
A: Yes.
Q: So you basically only reached Square One ... if you decided there was not a conspiracy to murder there [was] no point in going on to consider who was in it and who was out of it?
A: Yes.

If the centrepiece of the Crown's case assembled so painfully — amid almost unprecedented sensations — collapsed so abruptly, what was it that occupied the jury's time for the remaining two suspenseful days? The answer, according to our interview, is that the time was consumed in trying to persuade a single juror, who had held out for conviction, to accept the view of the other eleven. The jury did not think that a majority verdict would be acceptable, and strove hard — and successfully to achieve unanimity.

It was always going for an acquittal ... [but] we got it on good authority that he [the judge] wasn't going to accept a majority — we kept saying: 'Do you think he'll call us in today for a majority.' But one chap ... he kept saying: 'No, I'm certain beyond reasonable doubt of conspiracy to murder.' We kept on saying: 'But why? What sways you that way? And he'd say: 'Oh well, look at this ...'' And we'd say yeah ... we've looked at the evidence and agreed that it's irrelevant or that's uncorroborated.

A contributory reason for the drawn-out nature of the discussion was that the majority of the jury — while dismissing the Crown's main charge — felt troubled that so much evidence of wrongdoing should not lead to censure of any sort.

What we were all agreed on was there was definitely a conspiracy of some sort. They were definitely guilty of something. All of them.

And towards the end there was some discussion of the possibility of adding a critical rider to the verdict:

> The foreman wanted to . . . she was going to bring it up, the fact that we're all agreed they're guilty of something and we're certain there was at least a frightening . . . it just didn't seem the thing at the time — you can add a rider by rights, but the fact is you've got to come to a decision . . . I thought about it afterwards; with hindsight, we should have said something.

Essentially, what emerges from this juror's account is that the Thorpe trial — one of the most complex, long-drawn-out State trials in recent British history — was misconceived almost from the first. The picture which appears is one of an intelligent, conscientious cross-section of citizens confronted with a mass of scarcely comprehensible evidence, in circumstances where a sensible judgement about its value was nearly impossible to make. Given that the issues involved are very different, the same basic question is raised as was raised by last year's massively expensive, abortive Official Secrets trial; what is the competence of the DPP and his staff, and what, if any, are the principles on which they work when deciding how cases shall be laid?

In part, the jury seem to have felt the case was obscure. Lawyers and journalists observing the trial felt doubtful whether the Crown had succeeded in making clear the role that money played in the case; particularly, the £20,000 which Jeremy Thorpe raised from 'Union Jack' Hayward, and which was passed through Nadir Dinshaw's unsuspecting hands into the bank account of David Holmes. Only two days were spent on the issue out of a six-week trial. Our juror's account tends to corroborate these doubts:

> The money? I found it baffling — everybody was definitely of one mind — they [the defendants] were definitely worse off when the money was brought up.

But it did not crystallize as an issue. What did crystallize was the issue of large payments offered by newspapers to witnesses in the case. Peter Bessell — just as many observers calculated he must be — was by this means almost wholly destroyed as a credible witness:

> He had a sweeping immunity, plus the difference of twenty-five grand on a conviction. This was very important. I wrote in big-

letters on one page — half-price acquittal.

Q: That really impressed everybody on the jury then?

A: It impressed me a great deal. I think it must have impressed the others.

Q: Obviously Scott and Newton were going to make money, if there was a conviction and not much if there was an acquittal, but it was the Bessell contract that crystallized that side of it?

A: Yes.

The fact that Peter Bessell's publishing arrangements had such profound effects inside the jury-room must add fuel to the controversy over the degree to which the DPP's office was aware of what this major witness was up to. Lord Wigoder QC said in the House of Lords last week that Bessell's conduct with the *Sunday Telegraph* was not quite as simple as 'half-price for acquittal' because:

> the lawyers who drew [it] up did not indulge in any crude language of that kind. It was disguised very simply in this way. In clause 1 of the contract it was stated that in consideration of the sum of £50,000 ... the licensor [Bessell] granted to the publisher [the *Telegraph*] exclusive world rights to publish extracts from his book. Then in clause 4 it was stated: If on the advice of his legal advisers, the publisher is not able to publish the extracts, then instead the publisher will pay £25,000 for up to six articles. What that meant ... was that Mr Bessell stood to gain handsomely from a conviction.

Lord Wigoder, a senior criminal lawyer, said that one evil of such an arrangement was that witnesses were bound to press to ensure that a conviction should result, and another was that: 'once this web of contracts came to light ... doubt was cast upon the whole of the evidence of those witnesses as to whether it was truthful.'

Our juror interview confirms Lord Wigoder's assessment precisely. But in the same House of Lords debate Lord Hartwell, Editor-in-chief of the *Sunday Telegraph* defended the Bessell deal by saying that it had been made with the consent of the DPP's office. Before any contract was signed, he said, Bessell's London solicitor

> spoke to a senior official of the Director of Public Prosecutions and explained to him the nature of the proposed agreement.

Would the DPP's Department he asked see anything objectionable in the precise financial terms outlined? The answer was that the Department would raise no objection . . . it is not what Mr Bessell said; it was his London solicitor . . . who if necessary, is prepared to swear an affidavit.

The Attorney-General Sir Michael Havers, at once issued a denial — which he has since had to retract. Bessell's solicitor, Mr Lionel Phillips, 'remains confident' that he spoke to the DPP's office on 2 October 1978, writing immediately afterwards to Bessell:

I have told the DPP that a contract of this kind was in the offing, and he did not seem unduly concerned, mainly, if I understood him right, because you would be attacked on so many grounds that one more really would not make much difference.

In the mind of one juror at least, it clearly did.

The jury appears to have been a reasonable cross-section of working-class and middle-class Londoners — a teacher, a young welder, two elderly office workers, a civil servant, secretaries and housewives. But the man we interviewed felt that he and his colleagues got little help from the Crown, although the prosecution lawyers in court did 'a very good case . . . with the little they had'. But as a case of attempted murder, 'it didn't hold water'.

In run-of-the-mill work, policemen and lawyers apply a rule of practice which says that if a murder charge can be laid, then it should be — and no lesser offences, such as manslaughter, ought to cloud the issue. In this complex case, with only shaky evidence of lethal intent, but with considerable evidence of other and disparate offences, some with political implications (Jack Hayward's £20,000, to repeat, was solicited as an improper electoral contribution), a more sophisticated judgement might have been appropriate. And the DPP supposedly exists to provide just that.

But available evidence suggests it was never forthcoming. The case which finally reached the Old Bailey was planned while Sam Silkin, as Labour's Attorney-General, was responsible for the DPP: the brief, according to report, was sent for advice to Sir Peter Rawlinson — better known as a Tory parliamentarian than as an active criminal lawyer. As put, eventually, to the jury the case seemed to rely heavily on the gamble that some of the accused men would abandon their 'right to silence' and go into the witness-box, to their own prospective embarrassment. Our interview showed this working-out in particular detail on the question of whether there had been incitement to murder.

> We came to a decision on that almost immediately ... you've only got Bessell and Holmes to say that. Holmes didn't get in the box, so you've only got Bessell's uncorroborated word which ... all twelve of us agreed you couldn't take.

So extensive has been the propaganda by senior policemen against the 'right to silence' that prosecutions may have begun to think that the option is a dangerous one for defendants. Our evidence from the Thorpe jury suggests that a prosecution operating on such principles is not likely to succeed in any important case:

> I suppose we were a bit disappointed as well [at the defendants' not testifying] although the judge says 'it's not an admission of guilt ...'
>
> Q: Did you think they had something to hide?
> A: We all thought of it, but none of us actually brought it up, because as the judge says ... it would have been dangerous to take it into consideration.

Simply because the Crown's attempts to prove a conspiracy to murder came so rapidly to grief, there was little or no concrete deliberation in the jury-room on the question of Jeremy Thorpe's alleged connection:

> When you look over the evidence as a whole there wasn't a great deal, apart from the verbal stuff [see above] against Thorpe ... [The money] convinced me he was involved ... but we don't know exactly how the money went to Holmes ... we don't know what was actually going on between Holmes and Thorpe ...

But this is not the same thing as an acquittal on the charge laid, counting as a clean bill of health:

> Q: If the charge had been conspiracy to intimidate, or something like that, would you have convicted?
> A: Oh, undoubtedly, yeah. We was all certain of that. The only thing that stopped you obviously was that you can only convict him as charged.

Clearly, the Crown's ill-judged decision to put the dramatic word 'murder' on the charge-sheet added terrible weight to the ordeal that Jeremy Thorpe and his co-defendants had to endure. But at the end of the day this piece of over-kill produced a sort of bitter benefit for them; at the cost of doing some harm to Britain's name for humane and sensible administration of justice.[16]

People were quite interested in these disclosures. The *Daily Mail,* often establishment minded but always highly professional in its tough approach to press rights, reminded the world that what we had done had never been illegal in the first place. Gerald Adams, an official in the Attorney-General's office, remarked to the *Observer* that the interview was not contempt although he took a dim view of the accuracy of some criticisms of his department we had made in passing. In an affable conversation I had with him, he pointed out that the law officers would want now to go over the question of juries as they set about drafting a reformed contempt law for that session of Parliament. The *Sunday Times*, then writing a book about the Thorpe affair, was emboldened to publish its own more elaborate account of events in the jury-room. Harold Evans, its campaigning Editor and victor of Strasbourg said handsomely that he envied our initiative. Sam Silkin went on the radio to say that what we had done amounted in his view to contempt of court.

Two months of the summer passed peacefully, the authorities apparently occupying themselves with their own attempts to interfere with jurors in the case of some anarchists due to come on in the autumn. Suddenly, from nowhere, Sir Michael Havers stirred, and wrote to the *New Statesman* announcing his intention to prosecute them for a 'serious contempt'. It was to be a head-on attempt, bypassing the forum of Parliament, to ask the judges to extend an already archaic and discredited branch of the law in order to bring about a wholly new curb on the press. In any other democracy there would have been an outcry. In Britain there was very faint unease.

Havers wrote to us (or rather, the DPP acting as the government's solicitor wrote) in mid September:

This article contained a report of an interview with one of the jurors at that trial and included the juror's account of significant parts of the jury's deliberation in the course of arriving at their verdict. It is the Attorney-General's view that such publication involves an interference with the due administration of justice as a continuing process, and accordingly constitutes a contempt of court. The Attorney-General regards the contempt as a serious one, particularly in the light of the widespread publicity which inevitably attended the publication of this juror's revelations.

Havers was not going to be so foolish as to try to make martyrs of us. He would not try to have the authors and the Editor jailed, but was merely going to bring a test case against the *New Statesman* publishing company, which might of course have the effect of bankrupting it. Fines can be unlimited in cases of contempt and — ironically enough — there is no right to trial by jury. The letter went on:

[Havers] recognizes that the position in law has been considered by some to be unclear. He therefore desires me to indicate that his essential object in bringing contempt proceedings is to seek to clarify the law on this matter of grave public importance.

This then was to be a test case along the lines of the *Sunday Times* thalidomide affair. Havers appeared unwilling to take on the *Sunday Times* once again, although they had done just the same as us. He also brusquely refused to pay our costs for this excursion into the invention of law by others; he appeared unembarrassed by the recommendation lying on his desk and shortly to be published in the report of the Royal Commission on Legal Services, that all costs to determine a point of law of public importance should be paid from public funds.[17] Sam Silkin joined in again. 'I am sure he is doing the right thing', he told the BBC. 'In any future case a similar revelation might have been made without any penalty at all.'[18]

He took the view that a decision by the courts might well be sufficient to make new law. 'I personally, if the matter came before Parliament, would wish to see specific provision to make it illegal.' Taxed that October at a Society of Labour Lawyers meeting in Brighton[19] with his illiberality, Silkin produced an apparently novel reason for silencing the press: 'If a juror knows he is at risk that another juror is going to report what he says they said, there may end up being a battle over who said what ... the whole system of secrecy may be in danger.' It was in fact a faint echo of Chief Justice Hewart's paternal metaphysics in 1922: 'Differences of individual opinion might be made manifest which at the least, could not fail to diminish the confidence that the public rightly has in the general propriety of criminal verdicts.'

It was also an exact echo of Silkin's failed High Court plea in 1975 that the law of confidence should be extended in a novel fashion to silence government ministers themselves in the Crossman *Diaries* case:

> Each member of the Cabinet or each minister or each official, of course ... would be in a position to give to the press his own account of what he and each other member of the Cabinet or minister or official said, as soon as the meeting ended; and what happens then? ... What of those to whom the information has been given who may not be liable to penalties? ... You would have set in motion what I, I think, have described as the snowball process.

So we set off to fight the massed ranks of lawyers, as Lord Chief Justice Widgery granted the Attorney leave to bring this wholly novel proposition before him by Christmas. On the face of it, Havers's claim was nonsense. The test of contempt was not supposed to be mere 'interference', whatever that was. The Phillimore Committee five years before had recommended 'a risk of seriously impeding or prejudicing the course of justice' as a narrower test.[20] Lord Scarman the previous year in the 'Colonel B' case had ruled that 'the court must be satisfied beyond reasonable doubt that the interference is of such a character ... as to render impracticable the administration of justice or to frustrate the attainment of justice'.[21] He had even made reference to the phrase 'freedom of speech'. Should we lose before Lord Widgery, we had a right of appeal direct to the House of Lords. Were that to fail, we would appeal to the Court of Human Rights at Strasbourg. We were confident that the exact circumstances of what we had done threatened no danger to jurymen, even if others thereafter did the same. The Human Rights Convention ought to protect us on two grounds. Restrictions on free speech are only allowed if 'necessary to a democratic society' for the protection of the legal system, and if they were 'prescribed by law'. Surely only a madman would regard a total ban on jury interviews as 'prescribed by law', let alone 'necessary'?

Meanwhile we set out to persuade MPs and lawyers, many of whom plainly thought our conduct was not cricket. My own view is that the only good grounds there are for secrecy are to protect people from reprisals who are acting in the public interest. Some simple legislation would allay anxiety about the welfare and outspokenness of jurors, and help take free speech issues away from judges obsessed with the seditious nature of the press. The courts, after all, are supposed to belong to us, not to people who decide to become barristers and find themselves appointed to the bench (perhaps it is needless to add, by secret processes). The problem with the 'independence of the judiciary' like the Northcote-Trevelyan moves to achieve the independence of the Civil Service from political pressure, is that the lawyers end up independent of everything except their own sociology. They cease to be accountable, and stifling information about the courts is a key agent in the process.

If we want laws to protect jurors, I suggest these:

1. It shall be a criminal offence to hold out any prospect of personal gain to a juror as an inducement to disclose the deliberations of the jury room.
2. Any complaint by a juror that he has been subjected to harassment or intimidation to disclose the deliberations of the jury room may be treated as *prima facie* evidence of an attempt to pervert the course of justice.
3. It shall be a criminal offence to publish information capable of identifying any juror, without the written consent of that juror.

It is perhaps worth pointing out that the US manages to run a jury system perfectly well without any secrecy at all. British television viewers in 1979 could watch interviews with Miami jurors, after following their televized cases, explaining how they reached their conclusions. They did not seem to be particularly intimidated.

On receiving a thick file from us including a sample of fourteen previously published jury disclosures, Sir Michael Havers decided not to make his personal debut in court with us after all. Simon Brown, employed instead by the DPP, asserted that there had been 'an apparent change of gear' by the media in recent years; the convention of silence had thus become 'enfeebled' and needed 'bolstering' by what he described as a developing branch of the law: that of contempt. The *New Statesman* article was, he told Lord Widgery, 'the thin end of the wedge'. Sitting in the High Court, it was hard to avoid the feeling that these notions of gear-changing wedges lacked a certain legal precision. The Lord Chief Justice himself seemed to have difficulty in making the leap from undesirability to illegality, although we fully expected to be convicted.

Lord Widgery, a conservative judge, decided to take an impeccably conservative line, accepting every point we made, dismissing the case and awarding costs against the Attorney-General and the government. To the surprise of many commentators and to our relief, he appeared to heed the dangers of judges inventing law on free speech issues, and declined to lay down general rules about jury interviews.

We appeared, in a modest way, to have called the authorities' bluff. Until the government's lawyers were prepared to put proper contempt laws openly before Parliament, one fact was now established Common Law: to publish 'the secrets of the jury room' was not, in itself, contempt of court. Jury disclosures in future could still be of a kind that actually was contempt of court, of course, but only if they imperilled the finality of verdicts or upset future jurors.

> Each case of disclosure has to be considered in the light of the circumstances in which the publication took place. In the instant case, the sole ground on which the allegation of contempt is based is the publication of some of the secrets of the jury room in the Thorpe trial. Apart from that, there are no special circumstances which, it is suggested, call for condemnation.

Lord Widgery, sitting with Mr Justice Park, noted flatteringly that we were 'two reputable and experienced journalists', and that Bruce Page, Editor of the *New Statesman* had acted with the 'best intention'. The words we had published were unexceptionable since they: 'demonstrated that the jury had approached its task in a sensible and responsible manner'. There had been, he agreed, many disclosures over the years.

> Looking at the case as a whole, we conclude that the article in the *New Statesman* does not justify the title of contempt of court. That does not mean we would not wish to see restrictions on the publication of such an article. We would. But our duty is to say what the law is today, and to see today whether the activity in question is a contempt of court. We are unable to say that it is.[22]

The courts, it seemed, were in a cautious mood — and free speech, on the ground on which we had chosen to turn and fight, had quite simply, won. The next step was for Parliament.

How to Interfere with Juries

The criminal and legal field in Britain works in much the same way
as other central social institutions: showy, democratic and public
on the surface; subterranean in its real decisions. The public is
encouraged to stare at the democratic glory of barristers arguing in
open court before a random jury of ordinary people who — cricketers
all — raise a solemn umpire's finger by which the issue is decided.

The secret parts, however, tend to be about rather important
questions, and not only about the arguments behind locked doors
in the jury-room. Who is arrested under what circumstances? Why
are they charged with one offence and not another? When can a
defendant do a deal to avoid some charges by admitting others?
Can you get bail by bribing a policeman? How can evidence be
hidden from a jury by private deals between prosecution and
defence? What sort of person is the judge? How did he get himself
appointed? What sort of person is it who is about to be sentenced
by the judge? What is the nature of the Crown case on which
somebody is being sent for trial?

The most powerful machine for obscuring daylight on all these
issues is usually the notion of contempt of court. Newspapers are
very frightened of investigating the legal process because no one
knows exactly what contempt of court is. It is therefore almost
impossible, as has been outlined earlier, to know whether you are
committing it in advance. The only safe rule of thumb is to do
nothing that might be remotely interpreted as contempt. This has
the classic consequence for the public that they are never allowed to
know what is being kept secret from them. No blank spaces appear
in the newspapers and on the television screens; issues are merely
never discussed. The combination of boasts about our public legal
flummery and a nervous silence about the machinery in the
basement is a classic kind of mystification. It is an insult, as usual,
to any workable idea of the freedom of the press. We have seen
how the notion of the secrecy of the jury-room is used simply to
shield legal administrators from comment about the imperfect
processes over which they preside. To see how policy-making
actually takes place in the system, it is worth staying with that
democratic irritant: the jury.

One of the fundamental principles of State secrecy operates in
relation to the jury system as it does elsewhere. It is that, in an ideal
world of administrators, the citizen should find his rulers opaque,
misty, shielded; while his rulers, for their part, do their best to

make the citizen transparent. The furtive history of jury vetting shows the process at work very neatly, and it is another field in which disclosures have led to shouts of protest from the authorities. My own newspaper contribution to the debate led to an investigation by the then head of the Fraud Squad, Commander Peter Westley, not, of course, into the abuses disclosed, but into me and my sources. This is the sort of 'investigation' journalists in this country bear with amused resignation time and again; it may be morally contemptible, but at least it rates as small beer in the international habit of persecuting writers.

Enough has emerged about post-war jury vetting for the interplay between democratic rhetoric and secret policy-making in the legal system to be seen in unusually clear outline, like the bones in a kipper — a pretty rancid kipper at that. Jurors have not, throughout English history, been universally democratic as we now understand the word, but they have often stood outside the current establishment. In the eighteenth century they stood against the Crown and the court as members of the radical middle classes. In the nineteenth century, the enfranchised male, property-owning, middle-class juror probably acted as antagonistically towards Chartists, trade unionists and suffragettes as any judge, but in post-war Britain we once again find ourselves at a moment where jurors have become more democratic than jurists. Anybody, since 1972, can sit on a jury, provided they are of voting age and not exempt for miscellaneous reasons from service.[23]

You can be a woman, a black immigrant, out of work, a trade unionist, the owner of a stately home or the inmate of a Salvation Army hostel. Since the Criminal Justice Act of 1972 abolished the hangover from the days of partial suffrage allowing only the heads of households of a certain value to hear cases, all voters are allowed to join in, the victims as well as the victors of society. The 'special jury', drawn from a selected group of solid citizens and long discredited, had almost died out well before that, too, was finally abolished. Curiously, the one remaining piece of paternalism is to prohibit old-age pensioners from jury service, presumably on the grounds that their addled brains, while good enough for the ritual activity of voting, might be unable to cope with the weighing of evidence. Judges, on the other hand had, until recently, no retiring age at all. They are now allowed to continue to the age of 75 and those septuagenarians appointed before it occurred to anyone to retire judges are allowed to continue as they please. The reasoning behind this laxity is, one imagines, that old age does not addle the brains of judges, but steeps them in a special virtue, like brandy. It may also have to do with the difference in access to decision-making in their own lives between the judges, with their elite, informal, coherent and discreet networks, and the pensioner forced to depend on the public power structure for the exercise of influence. The private exercise of power is frequently rich and rewarding in Britain; use of the public system is frequently as threadbare.

The public has however, been allowed to watch, over the last fifteen years, a series of open efforts by prosecutors and officials to 'improve' the jury system in order to convict more people, more smoothly. As the authorities could not very well present it so baldly, various reasons have been put on public display: jurors are corruptible; IRA scares justify unusual steps; cases take too long to come to trial; juries cost a fortune and — a sanctimonious idea — the defence lawyers must not be allowed to undermine the randomness of the jury.

Thus, in 1967, the centuries old requirement that juries must be unanimous was abolished. Police and prosecutors argued that professional criminals, becoming more dangerous by the hour (as they have no doubt always been considered) only had to 'nobble' a single juror by threats or bribes to ensure a hung jury and a retrial. It was scarcely an argument of principle, or even one of overwhelming necessity, to be set against Chief Justice Hewart's ringing discovery of a grand principle in 1922 which he might use in order to abuse newspapers: 'The inestimable value of their verdict is only created by its unanimity, and does not depend on the process by which they believe they arrived at it.'[24]

Acting on a different principle (presumably that of 'horses for courses') the Criminal Justice Act 1967 invented the majority verdict. Only ten of the twelve jurors need to be sure 'beyond reasonable doubt'. The other two could think what they liked. At least this went before Parliament.

So also did Parliament have to approve a scheme hatched by judges, magistrates, magistrates' clerks and Conservative ministers, which whizzed from conception to execution in four years, and deprived about 8,000 people a year of the right to trial by jury. (It is rare for laws to come to birth so fast, especially when they require analysis by some kind of committee, but if executive officials actually want something to happen, as distinct from merely affecting to respond to public pressure, then the government machine suddenly discloses a silky turn of speed.) The

James Committee, established by Lord Hailsham, was set up after his public expression of concern in 1973 that poor souls were piled up in goal awaiting their jury trials. At the end of 1975 the Committee published its view that the answer was to deprive people of their right to jury trial in a wide range of 'trivial' cases. They could be dealt with by magistrates. This frequently meant, not the traditional trio of country worthies, but a single fifth-rank judge who might have spent his life as a barrister in the shallows of prosecutors' offices — the stipendiary magistrate.[25]

Parliament, which is capable of some response when at least given the chance, heard the complaint of civil libertarians that people charged with stealing small amounts should not lose their right to demand jury trial. Convictions for minor dishonesty can be quite serious in their effects, as any respectable reader can test for himself by going and pinching a pound of butter from his nearest supermarket. But the rest of the James plans stayed intact in the Criminal Law Act 1977.

Those affected included people arrested during political demonstrations — providing the police are acute enough to charge them with public order offences, such as 'threatening behaviour'. And there are hundreds of such people, who leave the public arena of justice spiritedly described by Lord Devlin:

> What makes juries worthwhile is that they see things differently from judges, that they can water the law, and that the function which they filled two centuries ago as a corrective to the corruption and partiality of judges requires essentially the same qualities as the function they perform today as an organ of the disestablishment.[26]

The demonstrators who supported a group of Asian strikers in North London at the Grunwick factory in 1977, and those who protested against a National Front invasion of an immigrant community in West London at Southall in 1979, were deported from this noble arena to a danker, more discreet place, with an East European flavour, and to Magistrates' Courts little frequented by journalists. In a further refinement at Southall, more than 300 cases, many of which rested on unsupported police assertions, were tried 20 miles away in Barnet by a drafted team of stipendiaries in a place inaccessible to the community from which the demonstrators came.

In Northern Ireland, the whole community was in the 1970s

considered too politically unreliable to bring in verdicts against warring IRA men and guerrilla 'loyalists'. Jury trials were brusquely abolished in 1973 for terrorist trials, on the grounds that jurors were not safe from threats. This appeared plausible to many, as unwholesome ideas emanating from the failure of British politics in Ireland frequently have, such as the invention of the Special Branch or the passing of the Prevention of Terrorism Act. But had the integrity of the jury been the real issue, trials could have been removed to neutral ground in England and steps taken to protect the identity of jurors. As was later to be discovered in the jury-vetting uproar, there were covert pressures to abolish juries in 'political' cases in England as well.

Three sets of changes took place in the 1970s to make it easier to get convictions by interfering with the customary composition of the jury. Only one went before Parliament while the other two were carried out by executive action — the government and its judges holding hands. But at least all three took place unavoidably in the open. It was said, for public consumption, that all were designed to uphold the random nature of the jury — which once again appeared plausible to many.

In 1973, the senior judges issued a practice direction to all the judges, putting a stop to defence questioning of jurors about their attitudes. There had been a 'political' case in which some young English revolutionaries had constituted themselves 'The Angry Brigade', and let off a number of bombs, some at the homes of ruling Tories. The trial judge had allowed defence lawyers to ask questions of potential jurors, such as which newspapers they read, and whether they belonged to the Tory Party — the questioning being in public view, of course. The defendants imagined they would be better off without jurors (to borrow a later phrase of the government's) 'antagonistic to their cause'. The judge declared: 'A jury consists of 12 individuals chosen at random ... it is contrary to established practice for jurors to be excused on more general grounds such as race, religion, or political beliefs or occupation.'[27]

In the same year, Lord Hailsham, then Conservative Lord Chancellor, after consulting with the Home Secretary, the Attorney-General and what he described as 'a number of judges', arbitrarily removed the list of occupations which appeared beside the name of each juror. He said the knowledge was being abused by the defence in, among others 'cases with political overtones'.[28] He was referring to the mythology of the Bar, always proud of its tricks of the trade, that defence lawyers try to manipulate their right to 'challenge' jurors in order to get a box-full of citizens who might be either sympathetic towards their client, ignorant, or at any rate unenthusiastic about the police. It was made clear that, as neither the defence nor the prosecution knew jurors' occupations now, the whole thing was perfectly fair.

The third ploy was equally sanctimonious, although at least it was put before Parliament as an obscure clause in the 1977 Criminal Law Bill. As custom stood, defendants could challenge up to seven jurors each 'peremptorily' without having to say why. The prosecution had the same right to challenge, in practice, an unlimited number of jurors. It was seen to be done in obscenity trials in the early 1970s, when unconventional young men with long hair were 'stood by';[29] in cases involving close-knit communities, when East Enders might for example be excluded; and in such 'political' cases as those of the Angry Brigade or the Shrewsbury pickets, charged under the Heath Government with conspiracy to intimidate other building workers. In this case six jurors were challenged.

No one appears to have displayed much public interest in the precise source of the prosecutors' information although Lord Dilhorne, former Lord Chancellor, had disclosed on television in 1966 that in a spy trial: 'I had to ask for one juror to stand by for the very reason that he was an active member of the Communist Party and therefore I thought unsuitable to be a member of the jury in that case.'[30]

The defence would use its ancient right of challenge as well, in the usual ill-informed, superstitious way. Every time I have been at the Old Bailey, I have watched grey-haired ladies challenged by defence barristers off jury after jury; is it some theory the Bar has about the menopause? Sometimes lawyers will try to get women, young people or blacks present in great numbers.

I once heard Judge Alan King-Hamilton deliver rather well at the Old Bailey the received wisdom of the Bar on defence challenges:

King Hamilton: It was being abused. I once tried 7 defendants. There were 49 challenges in order to get off the jury anybody who looked respectable and sensible.
Michael Mansfield: That's your Lordship's view ...
King-Hamilton: It's a common view of the Bar, and you know it!
Michael Mansfield: It's not an abuse for a defendant to exercise his legal right.[31]

The legal right was lopped down in 1977. The number of challenges allowed to the defence was cut by a clause in the Criminal Law Act from seven to three. The prosecution's unlimited right remained. While the defendant's rights were thus diminished, no one realized that the prosecution had been engaged for many years, possibly since before the war, in the ancient and secret practice of jury rigging.

In particularly sensitive cases, precisely those where a jury performs its most important role, it is the prosecutor's habit to slip to the police a list of potential jurors for the trial. The police can then check those named and let the prosecution know which jurors they do not care to see try the case. It is an echo of the notion of the 'special jury' used in the early nineteenth century when random jurors insisted on acquitting reformers accused of treasonable and seditious publications, and which led Bentham in 1821 to describe the packing of juries as a 'regular, quietly established and quietly suffered system'.[32]

We do not know to this day precisely which cases since the war have been brought to a conviction with a rigged, vetted or sanitized jury. Spy cases, professional gang cases, such as those involving the Krays and the Richardsons, Irish cases and anything with a political flavour — these are certain candidates, and their common thread is that they make the authorities feel insecure and consequentially anxious to see the 'right verdict'.

What we can trace is the way the authorities have stalled, fudged and blustered over the last five years as details of this abuse have been slowly brought to light. It is a sad story for those who believe in an independent judiciary, the power of elected representatives, and the strong-mindedness of ministers. I am afraid it demonstrates what the history of the Official Secrets Act already teaches: that the press does not get anywhere by whining. It only puts the authorities on the spot when it is prepared to call their bluff. And that is something very hard to do without a sense of oneself as a servant of democracy, professionally opposed to all secrecy.

Jury vetting appears to have begun to get rather out of hand during the panic in the early 1970s about IRA bombing campaigns on the British mainland. A certain loss of nerve among an aging elite after the university radicalism of the late 1960s might also have been expected; how could one trust these youthful, dope-smoking, over-educated persons on juries? How could one trust the Irish community clustered in Kilburn, and probably collecting funds for the IRA round the pubs every night? How could one trust the Communists who were everywhere, the trade unionists slugging it out so unscrupulously with the Heath Government, the East Enders who lived by driving minicabs and buying goods off the back of lorries, the blacks who rioted and bag-snatched in their ghettoes and who seemed to hate the London police?

As the Chief Constables' lobby put it, calling for universal vetting: 'the juryman is the personification of the reasonable man'.

The qualifications on property holding meant that, prior to 1974:

> juries were predominantly male and middle class, with a responsible outlook and middle-class standards ... the Juries Act 1974 completely altered the picture ... It is quite possible for a person who has numerous convictions for crimes, and not necessarily petty ones, to be sitting on a jury ... [Society] would welcome the concept that juries should be comprised of people who are not shown to have been *irresponsible* or criminally dishonest. (My emphasis.)[33]

One PC Acworth who was caught up in scandals involving the Drug Squad, mentioned in his memoirs that policemen did their colleagues a favour at those trials by carrying out checks on the jury lists. This might have raised an eyebrow or two among lawyers who read paperback books,[34] but the authorities are impervious to mere anecdotes about their activities.

The Old Bailey prosecutors overreached themselves in 1972, when they stood down six skilled labourers from a trial (which was eventually dropped) involving suspected IRA members. The Special Branch officer in the case was cross-examined by John Platts-Mills QC:

Officer: There was written information from records against a number of the names of the jurors. Information from Special Branch and other police records.

Platts-Mills: Did they include such things as belonging to the Labour Party?

Judge: There is no question of any political party being listed against any name. Where is this leading?

Platts-Mills: I intend to show that this whole case has been engineered by the Special Branch through a man, Parker, to plant these guns on my clients. (To the officer) Your objection has nothing to do with politics?

Officer: I didn't say 'nothing to do with politics'. The word 'object'
that I put against these jurors signified doubt about their political
activities and their criminal activities.
Platt-Mills: It is the right of the defence to have a jury that is not
picked by the Special Branch.
Officer: I was asked to take these steps, sir.[35]

Word of this exchange eventually reached a Labour MP and
barrister, Brian Sedgemore, in 1974. He put down a parliamentary
question in 1974 to the new Labour Government. Roy Jenkins, the
Home Secretary, and Sam Silkin, the new Attorney-General, were
quite unaware of what had been going on at the Old Bailey and
elsewhere for at least 25 years according to Mr Silkin's later
testimony.

What appeared on the public record, in Hansard, was the
genuine, and apparently routine dismissal by Alex Lyon, a junior
Home Office minister, of some mad allegation by an over-excitable
MP: 'I am not aware that there is any such practice. If my
honourable friend has evidence of it, perhaps he will send it to
me.'[36]

Sedgemore was bothered about the case, about which he
submitted evidence, but his efforts to drum up public interest with
his newspaper and television contacts made no headway. An MP's
world is a busy one, and it was more than a year later that Silkin
suggested he might like to ask another question on the topic
because he had an answer he wanted to give. The answer was bland
enough,[37] and a promise to write to Sedgemore explaining exactly
what was going on was never honoured. Silkin said, five years later,
that Jenkins was supposed to write the letter; Sedgemore swears he
never got one.[38] All the time, like a journalist, an MP has to push
and pester; it is an endless trudge up a glassy Whitehall gradient,
and if you slow down or stop, down you slither again to the
bottom. One might be tempted to conclude that the truth of
Sedgemore's situation was that no one really wanted to tell him
what the government was doing. It might lead to embarrassment.
But at the same time, the authorities must affect honesty. We are
watching well tried Whitehall techniques at work.

So much for Parliament, guardian of our liberties. Meanwhile,
there had been something of a storm over the disclosure within
Whitehall. Silkin was startled to discover what, as senior Labour
barrister and newly appointed chief law officer of the Crown with
direct responsibility for prosecutions, no one had apparently

mentioned to him over the years — that Crown prosecutors, on behalf of the DPP, on behalf of a minister of the Crown, on behalf of Parliament, on behalf of us, were getting the police to vet juries. They used police records, computerized or soon to be computerized, of convictions, associates, political activities, and anything else local police station 'collators' might have by way of tittle-tattle.

Silkin's first impulse, according to Alex Lyon who studied the papers, was to put a stop to the whole furtive practice. (This assertion by Lyon presumably constitutes a breach of the Official Secrets Act, by the way.) But he was talked out of it by Sir Norman Skelhorn, the DPP, and the civil servants in the Home Office. They painted a picture of the series of pending IRA trials, and the dangers of communistic jurymen being entrusted with 'official secrets' in spy trials. (What was meant by this was to become clearer in the ensuing ABC case against journalists.) They dangled before him the even more alarming prospect of the total abolition of juries in 'terrorist' cases, as had just been brought about in Northern Ireland.[39] They no doubt pointed out what some of the judges knew, if the Bar in general did not: that jury vetting had been going on for many years. One would rather like to see the papers that were put before Jenkins and Silkin, two anxious liberal ministers, but they are not considered to be our business.

Silkin gave in, and agreed to allow vetting to continue, but he insisted, good liberal that he was, on certain reforms. He said:

> It was decided that the practice should be allowed to continue, but only subject to firm safeguards, the object of which was to ensure it operated in the interests of justice, fairly, without abuse.

It took more than a year of leisurely meetings and arguments to draft an elaborate Code of Practice, which Sir Melford Stevenson, then one of Britain's more reactionary judges, was later to describe contemptuously as 'like a Salvation Army tract'.[40] This literary exercise in squaring the circle was very long, confused and imprecise. It was a disgrace to a lawyer, and the kind of document for which there might well be a case for secrecy, out of mere kindness. Its existence was eventually to get Mr Silkin himself, and those prosecutors charged with operating an essentially unfair system in a disingenuous way, into a terrible mess.[41]

What did Silkin do with his Code of Practice, his own personal contribution to the government of Britain, good or bad? He kept it secret. Other ministers, 635 MPs, the entire legal profession, and the general public who were actually to have the Silkin code of practice practised on them, were not informed. He handed it over to the DPP who sent a circular round his staff. When the DPP's office hired prosecutors for 'vetting' cases, they were handed a copy along with their brief. Apparently as an afterthought, the Home Office circulated this guidance on what was theoretically expected of them to Chief Constables up and down the country. This was five months later, on 10 October 1975.[42]

The circular was classified 'confidential' (prejudicial to the interests of the nation), and in 1980 the Home Office was still refusing to publish it. This was not surprising in view of events. Listing the guidelines, the circular had called up the personal authority of Roy Jenkins: 'In order to ensure consistency of practice and avoid any danger of abuse ... the Home Secretary asks chief officers of police for their part to ensure jury panels are only investigated with the authority of the DPP or his deputy.'

Provincial prosecuting solicitors were unenthusiastic about this limitation and complained; the Home Office told them firmly that, 'the procedure is only to apply in the context of exceptional cases'. Northamptonshire decided to ignore the guidelines, their solicitor assuring the Chief Constable that they had no legal force. Having done its duty by two fussy ministers, the Home Office passed into a non-accountable slumber, broken in early 1979 by a magazine article about Northampton's apparently shameless practices. Sam Silkin 'expressed grave concern at the failure to follow the guidelines' and the Home Office sent off another confidential letter to Northampton: 'We anticipate some correspondence ... let us know in detail what your practice is.' The county solicitor thought the freelance way they had always done things in Northampton was nothing to trouble about (the vetting was relatively limited, being confined to minor conviction records), and wrote back to the Home Office saying so. In July of that year, the Association of Chief Police Officers privately assured an anxious Home Office that Northampton had now 'reviewed their arrangements' and the guidelines were being adhered to by all forces. When Northampton's deed finally hit the headlines, the new Attorney-General, Sir Michael Havers, expressed his alarm and astonishment to Parliament at what had been going on there.

Another letter was despatched from the Home Office, and the Home Secretary shortly afterwards announced, tactfully letting bygones be bygones, that Northamptonshire had once again given 'an assurance' they would put a stop to vetting. The Chief Constable of Northamptonshire, Frederick Cutting, maintained a dogged public silence about these events which had lasted behind the public's back, from 1975 to 1980.

As far as the guidelines were concerned, Silkin's main reform was to order prosecution counsels to let the defence know if they came up with any information which might appear to bias a juror the other way — against the men in the dock. After all, the most obvious inequity in the whole business was that the defendant was blindfolded, and the State armed with a vast array of police dossiers. Naturally, defence lawyers could not be told exactly what the Special Branch knew; that might let far too many cats out of the bag. But, 'wherever possible, the principle of equality of information should be observed'.[43]

He defined the type of case where vetting was to be carried on 'broadly speaking', and put the final decision whether to vet in the hands of the DPP, a powerful and non-elected permanent official, who is supposed in constitutional fiction to be merely the agent of the minister, acting as his solicitor in the preparation of cases. The guidelines make several shots at defining what precisely the vetting is supposed to be for. The linguistic unease reflects the impossibility, under the new 'fair' dispensation, of telling the coarse truth: that vetting is to chuck out jurors in an important case whom the authorities don't think they like. The nearest Silkin gets to a definition is 'might be influenced . . . by extreme political, racial, or other convictions'. One imagines that 'racial' was a sop to the Attorney's sincere wish to prosecute vigorously the National Front when they broke the law. There are no sanctions for any breach of the 'guidelines'.

The respected barristers who are hired to prosecute for the Crown at the Old Bailey — John Leonard, Michael Coombe, Michael Worsley, for example — carried on for three years or so tossing baffled jurors out of court on the suggestions of officials and policemen. Only in the the course of what became known as the ABC Official Secrets trial did a series of explosions take place which forced vetting into the open. It involved journalists taking risks.

Lord Hutchinson, defending the left-wing trio who stood accused of spying on their own government, discovered by accident on the morning the trial opened at the Old Bailey that the police had been handed the jury panel list from which the trial jury would be selected and had been working away having them investigated for five weeks. He complained in court. He was 'extremely unhappy that a panel of jurors should be examined to make some decision about their loyalty'. John Leonard, QC, for the Crown said: 'Anyone who is known to be disloyal would obviously be disqualified.'

The public were a trifle startled by these assertions. On the principle of 'sauce for the goose', the defence did their own investigations on the sworn jury. They discovered that three of them had actually signed a version of the Official Secrets Act, and that the man who had come to be made foreman was a former SAS security officer. 'He was going around', said one of the other jurors, 'saying they knew how to deal with people like that in the army. March them in, give them 14 years, march them out again.'[44] All those journalists, lawyers and political activists who had suspected a sinister plot by the security services against decency and liberty, had their darkest suspicions instantly confirmed. M15 were packing the jury! This is the kind of belief which is immensely damaging to public confidence, and matters were not helped when Mr Justice Willis not only refused to discharge the jury, but turned the whole topic into wild rumour by suggesting (or ordering — he used the phrase 'I am sure the press will use their discretion') that the courtroom discussion in the absence of the jury should not be reported in the newspapers.

Of all unlikely people, it was the ITV chat-show 'Saturday Night People' hosted by the engaging Russell Harty, which brought the trial to a dramatic halt. Barry Cox, the producer and an investigative journalist in his own right, had the SAS affair described on the air by another journalist, Christopher Hitchens. The jury foreman was furious, and complained.

Mr Justice Willis, angrily ringing down the curtain and discharging the jury after ten days, on 18 September 1978, launched into the kind of tirade that the Old Bailey hears again and again against journalism and its interfering ways.

Last week I gave instructions in words which could not be misunderstood by any responsible journalist, that there should be no publication during this trial of the subject matter which had just been discussed and decided in your absence. This was in accordance with time-honoured custom under which the press do not publish matters which arise in the absence of the jury for reasons which are obvious.

Nevertheless, last Saturday night on a programme on LWT a journalist named Hitchens, said to be on the staff of the *New Statesman*, was invited by the chairman of the panel, someone called Russell Harty, to give news items which he did not choose to disclose in his own publication. Hitchens then proceeded to disclose fully matters which have happened in your absence.[45]

It was a 'piece of gratuitous journalistic gossip' he said, and he would tell the Attorney-General about it. The Attorney, the hard pressed Sam Silkin, did not show any disposition to embark on a full-scale contempt prosecution against Hitchens. London Weekend Television who said the judge had not made it clear in the first place that he was ordering the press to silence, delivered themselves of a grovelling apology, and promised never to report anything said in the absence of any jury ever again. The rest of Fleet Street had decided in the first place it was too dangerous to print such information, but they were now becoming visibly uneasy about the subject of jury vetting.

The trial recommenced under Mr Justice Mars-Jones (Mr Justice Willis had fallen ill) and a new jury. This time the defence were rather pathetically conducting its own jury investigations. Duncan Campbell pedalled around on a bicycle to inspect addresses. The Crown ran the new jury-panel names through its computers.

Lord Hutchinson made a passionate appeal to the judge:

Your Lordship will remember that Blackstone in his commentaries wrote 'the liberties of England depended on the jury remaining secret and inviolate, not only from open attacks, which none would be so hardy as to make, but from all secret machinations', and to subject citizens to surveillance, to run their names through an M15 computer and then on undisclosed criteria via hidden methods pronounce upon their loyalty is, in my submission, to strike at the very heart of the jury system and does indeed amount to a secret machination.

The jury knew they were being vetted because of the publicity, he said. They thought the Crown regarded them as safe and if the defence complained about vetting '[they] would be put in the position of apparently wanting disloyal members of public on the jury and would therefore be looked upon with suspicion from the start'.[46]

Mr Justice Mars-Jones said briskly: 'We'll get around that. I direct the press not to report these discussions about jury vetting.' One more secret process was being imposed. He refused the application to know on what authority the vetting was being done. The defence had been told they could not see the vetting regulations as they were in a 'restricted document'. Bizarrely enough, the eggs were broken this time by the Attorney-General himself. Failing to read in his newspapers of the prohibition on discussions of jury vetting by the new judge, because no one was allowed to report it, and obviously irritated by the tide of rumour, he published, for the first time, his secret guidelines on jury vetting. It seemed they were not 'restricted' after all, nor even *sub judice*. The judge could barely stop the trial and report the Attorney-General to himself for contempt, so the whole *sub judice* issue was allowed to drop.

Publication of the guidelines, far from exonerating Silkin, caused a terrible row. Why had he kept them secret? Was he then, the furtive architect of jury vetting? Libertarians, politicians and lawyers were suspicious and appalled that a minister should legislate behind everyone's back. Juries are a sensitive nerve in the British body politic, and rightly so.

Michael Foot, leader of the House and nominally deputy head of the Labour Government, was stung by a savage article written by the distinguished historian and author of *The Making of the English Working Class,* E.P. Thompson:

> All is passed over now to a neutral public office, a Director of Public Prosecutions. This is a great personage indeed and the microchip is still on the drawing board that will take his place. (The DPP should not be confused with the DPM or Deputy Prime Minister, whose office is the writing of essays on Hazlitt and the making of speeches on Tom Paine, as a screen behind which the DPP may go about his work.)[47]

Foot felt the government should perhaps investigate this issue of jury vetting and went to Silkin to raise the topic of an inquiry. According to Foot, Silkin reassured him that everything was all right, and there was nothing wrong with the system. Unfortunately, the following autumn was to prove his complacency wrong. The public found out just what part of the information the police went trawling for — and it did not seem to fit Mr Silkin's tortuous guidelines at all.

Even before that, the uselessness of the guidelines as they stood had emerged. Some Welsh language activists charged at

Carmarthen with trying to blow up a transmitter were mortified to discover that, although 75 per cent of the local population were Welsh, most of the jury had English surnames and only two spoke Welsh. It was denied that the jury was packed or officially vetted, although the basic 'pricking' of jurors from voters' rolls seems not to have proper safeguards. The local MP, Dafydd Ellis Thomas, persisted, and the new Tory minister, Lord Belstead, finally admitted 'a police officer of junior rank, acting without authority, did in fact obtain a copy of the jury list an hour before ... and undertook a limited check'. He had been 'admonished, and reminded of the need to abide by the guidelines'.[48]

The prosecutors were being forced into a corner as radical defence lawyers showed every sign of making a row when juries were vetted. But the legal machine still had formidable reserves of secrecy. The police urged the vetting of the jury for the trial of six anarchists in autumn 1978; this group had been dramatically arrested, held in 'Category A' top security conditions in prison, and accused of attempting to overthrow the state by kidnapping members of the Royal family and blowing up nuclear power stations. In a high state of excitement, police were linking the youthful group with the IRA, the remnants of the 1960s Angry Brigade and the German Baader-Meinhof gang. This picture of a seething threat to all that Englishmen hold dear was rather deflated by the time they came to trial. Not only had bail been granted, but the charges had been reduced on Silkin's instructions to a mere set of conspiracies to rob shops, in order to get cash and guns. The number of dedicated anarchists, let alone members of the Baader-Meinhof gang, in the average Old Bailey jury is probably quite small, but vetting had to be persisted with. In order to be fair (did not the guidelines stress 'equality of information'?), the Crown told the defence in advance they were going to ask the judge for the jury list.

This hearing took place in what are known as 'Chambers'. This is when the judge orders the public and press to clear the court and a notice is placed on the door saying 'In Chambers'. The status of such proceedings is vague. Judges do not like to see what goes on reported; it is too near the meat of the legal process for comfort, although this unease is often dressed up as concern not to prejudice the defendants and their eventual jury in criminal cases. The phrase 'contempt of court' hangs around the proceedings like some vague buzzard, although curiously, the press has a little piece of statutory protection. Under the Criminal Justice Act 1960, certain classes of

Chambers proceedings such as civil wardship cases, are specified as private, and it is automatically contempt to find out what has been happening. This means it is not automatically contempt to find out what went on about other, unspecified types of hearing, such as a 'pre-trial review'. The problems for journalists, with what the Press Association wire service describes worriedly as 'non-public hearings', are practical ones: the fear of lawyers and others that they will get into trouble for telling you what is going on; and the nervousness of newspapers over printing it.

The *Guardian* and I were the ones who took up the torch in this case. We found out about the pre-trial review, and decided to put the subject on the public agenda. Some of the things said behind closed doors were really rather alarming. Michael Worsley, for the Crown, held forth about the Royal family and nuclear power stations, and described one defendant as a former member of the IRA and an inmate of Long Kesh (his conviction for killing a policeman had been quashed and none of the current charges related to Ireland).

It was, said Worsley:

> vital to secure that any jury empanelled is independent-minded ... we must be careful therefore for example, that no members of the jury have relatives in Long Kesh ... a substantial proportion of the male population of London have criminal records. And the number of persons with connections through close relatives with criminals or other undesirable elements is wider still ... were there to be one, two or three jurors who have connections with violent organizations, they might be more open to pressure.

Judge Gibbens, embolded by the privacy in which he spoke, said vetting would be necessary, 'if, for example, the jury panel came from Kilburn where there is a high content of Irish people and most of them go round to pubs collecting money for the IRA, which is a proscribed organization'. It would be impossible for any anarchist-minded person to try the case dispassionately, he asserted.

We decided to print a guarded piece, merely saying that vetting was going on in the forthcoming trial, it would involve the Special Branch, and the case concerned a number of anarchists. It demonstrates the burdens under which journalists labour, that to print this simple piece of information involved five quite subtle legal dangers: (a) Was it contempt because it prejudiced the pending trial by casting doubt on jury-vetting? (b) Was it contempt because it was material gleaned from a hearing in chambers? (c) Was it contempt because it discussed allegations made at committal hearings, which are hedged with special restrictions? (d) Was it libel because the references to the original committal proceedings were no longer protected by privilege as 'contemporaneous reports'? (e) Was it libel because proceedings in chambers are not (unlike those in open court) covered by privilege at all?

Meanwhile defence lawyers were engaged in their own gambits. Failing to stop vetting, they demanded and got the right to do the same. They even at one point spent £5,000 worth of legal aid on private detectives, who inspected the 90-strong panel and made a few banal discoveries about their jobs and houses. To carry out full 'status reports' on the panel, including embarrassing inquiries about their political, sexual and financial habits, would have cost between £14,000 and £25,000. While Judge Gibbens found himself unable to prohibit such activity when allowing the prosecution to do what they liked, he could put a stop to the mounting legal aid bill; why didn't the Crown share its computerized discoveries with the defence, he said? That would be fair. The defence complained that they were not allowed to see the contents of the police and Special Branch files. The Crown said they would show them what they could, and apparently by way of compensating for the obvious editing-out of all political material from the Special Branch computer, handed over a good deal of police tittle-tattle.

This is the list that the prosecuting barrister produced, from which we extracted an analysis in the *Guardian* the morning the trial opened, written in quite a dispassionate way, but pointing out that all these people were perfectly entitled to serve on a jury, and had not actually asked anyone to go behind their backs and dredge up information the police might think made them 'undesirable' for one reason or another:

2	Marion O.	Victim of crime (burglary).
13	Sharon D.	Association with criminal (drugs theft, handling).
21	Alec H.	Probably identical with CRO 62808/65. 9.7.65 Larceny Servant — two counts Fined £5. Cond. disch. for 12 months.
22	Jean R.	Complaint against Police later withdrawn.

23	Peter P.	Victim of crime (26.6.76 TDA by employee).
39	Isobel K.	CRO 3098/70. 12.5.70 Handling (39 boxes of razor blades) 6 mths imprisonment susp. 3 yrs.
42	Randolph P.	Address believed to be a squat.
51	Harold E.	Thought to be identical with J.M. (see Form 609 att.).
53	David P.	Believed identical with CRO 11831/74. Pre-cons. for theft, ABH, TDA, Crim. Damage, Handling. Last offence 1978.
54	Geraldine Y.	Victim of crime (GBH).
69	Albert S.	Victim of crime (TDA & theft of contents 16.5.71).
71	Brian R.	CRO 20053/61. Pre-cons. for robbery firearms, prison escaping, assisting prisoner to escape, handling. Longest term of imprisonment is 2 years.
77	Olwen P.	Victim of crime (Theft of handbag & £700 cash — 5.1.79).
78	Rosemary J.	Son was charged with murder, but convicted of affray and sentenced to 6 mths Detention Centre.
79	James J.	Alias Stephen M—— CRO 48957/69. 15.5.69 Wasting police time, permitting no insurance. Fined £20 & £15. Licence endorsed, Disq. 6 mths.
80	Michael J.	May be identical with CRO 133243/70. 15.12.70 2 counts theft. Cond. disch. 3 yrs on each count.
84	Peter C.	CRO 31741/43. Pre-cons. for 4 counts theft, ABH, malicious damage. Last offence 1969. 4 mths imp. sus. 2 yrs.
85	Angela S.	Close member of family has criminal record.
91	Aileen A.	Close member of family has criminal record.

The numbers on the left-hand side are the listings in the jury-panel, so that crosses could be put against the names if the prosecution or the defence wanted to have them kept off the case. The names have been changed to protect their privacy. The police reference numbers are those of the Criminal Records Office computer, with the final pair of digits marking the year their convictions file was opened. The document is not reproduced in its original typescript to protect its source. Some of the police abbreviations may be unfamiliar: 'TDA' means 'taking and driving away'; 'ABH' means 'actual bodily harm' (e.g. bruising); GBH means 'grevious bodily harm' (e.g. breaking bones); 'conc' means 'concurrent'; 'susp' means 'suspended'.

The *Guardian* piece, the culmination of a series on these pre-trial manoeuvrings, said:

What the Police Computer said about 19 Jurors [from the *Guardian*]

A list showing the results of the jury vetting carried out by police on 93 potential jurors without their knowledge in preparation for an Old Bailey trial which begins today, has been obtained by the *Guardian*.

The prosecution authorities claim that the trial of six people, facing conspiracy to rob charges, constitutes a case with political overtones. They therefore wish to vet the jury for possible sympathisers. The 93 reported for jury duty this week.

Not only people with minor criminal records are listed, but those whose family or friends have records. People who live in 'squats'; complain about the police; who have children the police have charged but failed to convict; have expired convictions under the Rehabilitation of Offenders Act; or people who have been the victims of crime — all these have been logged on police computers, and the information passed on to barristers and the defence.

Of the 93, police found something out about 19 men and women which might be useful to challenge a juror (without the public or the jurors themselves being given any reason why). The ostensible reason for the searches is to find those with extremist political sympathies.

The Lindop committee on data protection recently recommended that information collected for one purpose should not be used for another without the consent of the person concerned.

It also criticized the police and the Home Office for refusing to accept that their files should come under a comprehensive system of safeguards.

It was also made clear during recent legal arguments about the extent of jury vetting in the present case, that the Crown would keep strictly to themselves such discoveries as that a juror had terminal cancer, or an illegitimate child.

One individual on the jury panel Randolph P. (the *Guardian* has changed names in order not to further invade the juror's privacy) is recorded thus: 'Address believed to be a squat.' Jean R. is listed as having made a complaint against the police, which was later withdrawn.

Five of the panel were listed because they had reported crimes committed against them. Marion O. was burgled; one of Peter P.'s employees stole his car; three years ago Geraldine Y. suffered grievous bodily harm; Albert S.'s car was robbed more than eight years ago; and Olwen P. had £700 stolen from her handbag.

Such information could be useful to a lawyer. The Crown might not challenge a juror in a 'mugging' case if he had suffered such an attack himself. The defence, on the other hand, might well fear such a juror was prejudiced against them.

In the courtroom itself, no questioning of jurors is allowed. Lord Hailsham when previously Lord Chancellor, ordered that jurors' occupations should be struck off the panel list so that no one should know them.

Four of the potential jurors for the current trial have police records although they have never been convicted of a crime. But in two cases a 'close member of their family' has been convicted. Sharon D. ... is listed as associating with a 'criminal', who, to judge by other entries, is not necessarily a person with an actual criminal record.

Rosemary J.'s son spent six months in a detention centre after being convicted of affray. But the information supplied by the computer shows that he was originally charged with murder.

Eight potential jurors have records of criminal conviction. Under the Rehabilitation of Offenders Act, at least four of the eight, and probably two others, have 'spent' convictions. Alec H. may imagine his solitary theft from work 14 years ago, for which he was fined £5, had been expunged from the records.

Isobel K. had something to do with 39 boxes of stolen razor blades nine years ago; nine years ago Michael J. received a conditional discharge on two counts of stealing; and 10 years ago James J. was disqualified from driving for six months and fined

£35 for allowing someone to use his car without insurance, and wasting police time.

Michael J. and Alec H. may even be stigmatized incorrectly. The police record lacks the date of birth so the print-out says they 'may' or 'probably' are the people in their files.

A person who has his old offences retrieved in this way might be able to sue prosecuting barristers.

Of the jurymen listed by the police whose convictions may still be 'live', none appear to be definitely disqualified from jury service under the 1974 Act. Peter C.'s four months suspended sentence for malicious damage would have disqualified him until recently, when it became ten years old.

David P. who has been convicted over the last five years for stealing, hitting people, taking cars, damaging property and handling stolen goods, does not seem to have been imprisoned.

Brian R. whose listed record numbers 'robbery', firearms, prison escapes, assisting prisoners to escape, and handling, was once goaled for two years. Only if it was after 1965 would he be disqualified from jury service.

Out of 93 Londoners, more than a fifth turn out to be on police files, although not all of them would realize it.

Some 8 per cent have criminal records, most of them minor; only one might probably find himself, statistically, on a 12-man jury, which is empowered to reach a 10-2 majority verdict. More than 5 per cent have, on the other hand, been victims of crimes which might be argued to bias them the other way.

None apparently, are members of professional gangs; Irish republican sympathisers; or dangerous revolutionaries.

There was consternation. Michael Worsley, the prosecutor, complained bitterly to his masters in the DPP's office and to the judge. Judge King-Hamilton, a rather erratic figure at the end of his days on the bench, appeared to be enraged with this impertinence, and obsessed with the idea that it was a ploy by defence lawyers to postpone the trial. (It is a mark of how introverted and protected from scrutiny British lawyers become, that they can only think in terms of legal gamesmanship.) Sitting in the Old Bailey press benches the next morning, I listened to a long harangue against the *Guardian* which culminated in the ritual reference to the DPP. Although the DPP dutifully appointed the head of the Fraud Squad, no less, to investigate the so-called leak, he did not appear minded to overspend the public purse. It was five months before Commander Westley even bothered to come and ask from where I got the information. Journalists are very frightened of the wrath of judges, partly because it can have unpredictable practical consequences, and partly because regular court reporters tend to become infected by the authoritarianism and deference of the courts; all those 'my lords' and that leaping to one's feet, lead them to fancy they too, are servants of the court.

I must admit, I half expected to be hauled to my own feet and ordered to explain my conduct, as I have watched happen to demonstrators, the occasional reporter, and others whom it is decided are interfering with the smooth conduct of a trial. But my small speech to say that I was not a servant of the court, I was not answerable to the trial judge for so-called contempt outside the courtroom, and that please could I have a lawyer, was not required. The bluff had been successfully called on this backstairs work, by simply making it public. The jury were discharged and recycled to other cases, although one of them, Dr Chris Bottom, was sufficiently indignant at having been spied on to make a public protest, twice, as he was being sworn in at other cases, and was hastily stood down by the Crown. The trial of the anarchists was postponed.

Worsley complained of 'a series of breaches of confidence by this newspaper', and King-Hamilton fulminated 'the whole thing is an outrageous intrusion into confidential matters, not in the public interest'. In a master-stroke of logic, he declared that it was not the prosecutors who had invaded the jurors' privacy, but the *Guardian*. Telling the truth, it seemed, was 'material calculated to prejudice a jury'. The freedom of the press he said 'does not imply an unbridled license if it is obvious that such publication involves prejudicing a fair trial. Freedom of the press involves retaining a sense of responsibility.' For good measure King-Hamilton referred a political protester's leaflet to the DPP as well, saying it was ignorant and 'highly inflammatory'. (It was certainly picturesque in phrase: 'Its powerlust never satisfied, the State now aims to vet juries, using information and files its police are secretly building up on the whole population. This strengthens the POLICE STATE.' But I am not sure that the defence campaign's propaganda was all that wide of the mark.)

These bursts of indignation finally put jury-vetting on the map. Over the next couple of days, virtually every paper in Fleet Street and the regions carried an editorial expressing its disgust at some aspect of secret vetting. Labour and Liberal politicians professed themselves appalled, and Lord Wigoder QC made it clear, roundly condemning vetting at the Liberal Party conference, that many barristers shared his outrage.

The DPP Sir Tony Hetherington ploughed stubbornly on, summoning a new jury, and vetting them all over again. This time the jurors knew, of course, what was happening to them. They were ordered not to believe what they read in the papers, and, having achieved only partial success in censoring a BBC television programme on vetting, the judge further lectured them not to believe what critics such as the NCCL said on the programme. There were ten-minute rule Bills, calls for debate in Parliament and other protests from affronted jurors. One, Charlotte Atkins, made a protest speech three times at Inner London Crown Court, and was each time stood down by the Crown. The Crown made matters worse by ostentatiously 'standing by' one juror in the new anarchists trial, saying he would be biassed *against* the defendants and it was their duty to be fair. Interviewed afterwards, the rejected juror turned out to be a highly respectable right-wing economist; what precisely the Special Branch fancied they had on him was the subject of interested debate. There were victories for secrecy in a small way; some newspapers did not dare interview the rejected juror for fear of 'contempt'; the BBC were prevailed on not to put either Dr Bottom or the rejected juror on their programme ('He cannot have the least idea', said King-Hamilton loftily, 'why he was stood down') and the *Guardian,* not wishing to cause a nuclear explosion, wrote about the affair in a muted fashion from then on.

But vetting had taken a bad knock. Sam Silkin, the former Attorney, found his colleagues more than uneasy; three weeks after the disclosures, when Parliament resumed, the Conservative Home Secretary, William Whitelaw announced: 'The guidelines laid down by the then Attorney-General last year sought to restrict this practice to certain exceptional cases. The Attorney-General and I are, however, considering whether any changes are required.' Sir Michael, the Attorney, took official vetting out of the DPP's hands and into his own. The whole mediocre, unprincipled, furtive business, seemed to be slightly decomposing in the daylight.

And King-Hamilton's last case came to a spectacular conclusion. The jury refused to convict in December 1979 on any of the charges put before it. Judge King-Hamilton exploded with rage, ordered the jury to return the next day to hear the detailed confessions of the one man who had pleaded guilty, and harangued them to the effect that their verdict was wrong. They had been 'remarkably merciful in the face of the evidence'. 'Nobody ever criticises a judge when he says that he agrees with the verdict', he said, 'I do not see why anyone should criticise a judge if he happens to indicate that he does not agree with it.' About 10 per cent of juries 'sometimes seem to refuse to act upon unchallenged and undisputed evidence which I must respectfully say could not confuse a child'. Turning to the jurors in their box, (who had been vetted supposedly to ensure their independence) he announced 'You can see what you have done. I hope to God that none of you will ever have occasion to regret it.' He jailed Stewart Carr, the anarchist who had made a confession, for nine years, and as the jury were trooping out of court, hoping no doubt to be allowed at last to go home, he ordered them back in and issued one final command, also to be rightly ignored. They were not, he said, to allow themselves to be interviewed by the press.[50]

5
National Security:
Last Refuge of the Patriot

Most of the information ostensibly relating to the policy of the government or to defence matters, and I can say with absolute assurance that information about my own affairs which appears in the newspapers ... is 90 per cent inaccurate. [Sir Martin Furnival-Jones, Director-General of MI5.[1]]

It has been reassuring to find — this will strike you as funny — conscientious people outside the agency. We were such a religious order and so convinced that all journalists are devious and that all Congressmen are corrupt, and only the agency knows what national security interests are. To get out and find people who have a lot more integrity than agency officers did in terms of making personal sacrifices to work for a better world was reassuring. [John Stockwell, in charge of 1975 covert CIA intervention in the Angolan civil war.[2]]

There are enthusiastic supporters of the freedom of information lobby in Britain, who think it an extremely poor plan to demand reforms in the secret service side of government (the overtly covert arm of the State as distinct from the covertly covert). They suspect that bitching about MI5 and the rest is to play into the hands of Whitehall, because officials become free to present the whole open government campaign as a left-wing plot to undermine national security.

This is a weak argument, both from what one might term the John Le Carré perspective — that the secret services represent the soul of Whitehall — and from a practical standpoint. The love of indirection, the cosiness of a tight personal elite, and the sheer self-importance of government servants, find their clearest expression in the intelligence community — among the spooks, secret policemen, wiretappers, black propagandists, electronic eavesdroppers, professional patriots and those they purport to serve. Many of the arguments that civil servants put forward for administrative secrecy are watery echoes of what the security men tell them: that all bits of information are potentially dangerous; that one is surrounded by omnivorous enemies; and that careless talk costs lives. I remember once wandering around the bowels of the Foreign Office in 1978, on my way to talk to Roy Hattersley, then a junior minister and I swear I saw an old wartime poster about 'careless talk' still up on an office wall.

In the quotation at the beginning of this chapter, Sir Martin, the taciturn ex-solicitor who ran MI5 between 1965 and 1972, was not only relishing the fact that information about MI5, which is deliberately mystified, is always wrong. He was also saying that virtually everything the public reads about government policy in general is wrong. Somewhere along the spectrum between this unwholesome pleasure at the ignorance of *hoi polloi* and an insincere enthusiasm for democracy, lie the attitudes of most public officials, and too many of our politicians.

The secret world is worth inspection for another reason. If we are to mount a critique of administrative secrecy, it is worth looking at its purest forms — bureaucratic totalitarianism in the Home Office Prison Department; ostentatious news management in the justice system; and proudly self conscious secrecy among the spooks.

The covert arm of government consists of half a dozen large organizations all ostensibly aimed mainly at foreigners. There is a spying agency, MI6; an anti-spying agency, MI5; a political police, the Special Branch; a covert propaganda agency, IRD; a telephone-tapping system; a foreign radio surveillance organization, SIGINT; a system of emergency government, largely underground; and various psychological warfare, interrogation, propaganda and covert commando units under direct military control and used largely at the moment in Northern Ireland. This list leaves out of account straightforward development of weaponry, location of missile sites, etc. which are traditional military matters. (There are one or two question-marks, none the less, over the secretive way in which we handle the purchase of expensive weapons from our allies, and sell our own to any small country our officials can separate successfully from its money). Most of these organizations are not in fact secret; they are merely not talked about in front of the public.

MI5 and MI6 do not officially exist; it is a bizarre assertion to make about bodies which are the subject of reports and debates in

Parliament when things go wrong, but it is an assertion to which Whitehall clings with tiresome persistence. They have no legal status, no parliamentary questions are answered about them on principle, and their senior personnel have their status disguised, although not abandoned entirely, in such publications as *Who's Who* and the Diplomatic List.

There is no mention of either of these bodies in any official reference book, and the Thatcher Government, or its officials, were on the point of making any reference to them whatever a criminal offence in the small print in their Bill to modify the Official Secrets Acts, before it was suddenly dropped. All documents in government archives, even after the expiry of 30 years, are held back by 'weeders' if they contain reference to either MI5 or MI6. One might think this a bit odd; it is reasonable enough to keep quiet what precisely a secret service is doing at any particular moment, but an affectation that it does not exist at all must have other justifications. There must have been, one imagines, a time when it was considered indecent and ungentlemanly to admit one kept spies and secret agents. It can still be embarrassing to admit precisely whom one is spying against, or interfering with, of course.

The only official reference to MI6 outside Whitehall, for example, is in the D-notices issued to newspapers. D-notice No. 10 (marked 'Private and Confidential') says:

> British Intelligence Services ... the broad functions of the Security Service and the Secret Service (often referred to as MI5 and MI6) are of course widely known. The Security Service is responsible for countering threats to the realm arising from espionage, subversion and sabotage, and the Secret Service exists to provide HM Government with secret intelligence concerning foreign powers. Both services must operate as far as possible in conditions of secrecy.[3]

Harold Wilson wrote a notorious chapter on MI5 and MI6 in his prime ministerial primer, *The Governance of Britain.* Less than one page long, and not worth the trouble of quoting here, it said in effect that there was no information at all that could properly be given about the working of the two services.[4] But later Wilson was to complain loudly to more than one journalist that MI5 were persecuting him, and keeping information from him. The journalist Chapman Pincher records that in 1961, George Brown, then shadow Defence Minister, wanted to ring up MI6 but had no idea where they might be found, and asked Pincher to tell him.[5]

MI5, the domestic security service, is rather better-known than MI6 largely because it has been the focus of criticism or praise in a number of spy scandals. But the identities of the men who head both spy organizations are kept secret to this day. 'Secret' in this context is again a relative word. Most senior civil servants in Whitehall, and most respectable newspapermen, know who they are. The Russians, if they are sufficiently interested and prepared to devote modest resources to the task (such as buying a couple of gin and tonics here and there) know who they are. The people who don't know are the more artless groups of domestic terrorists (who are scarcely short of establishment targets), and the general public who pay these officials' wages and, from time to time, as the more lurid rumours fly around about their activities, must wonder mildly what kind of men they might be.

The mumbo-jumbo about basic facts rests partly on the principle that all information is useful to an enemy; there are some security men who would not print on maps the location of London on these grounds. Pincher, describing this reflex 'muddying of the waters' says he once asked a senior MI5 official why confusion had been allowed to grow around the idea that MI5 and MI6 had been somehow rechristened DI5 and DI6 (D for defence). 'He said: "Why not leave it alone. It helps us to keep the issue confused." '

It also rests partly on a love of secrecy for its own sake, demonstrable when bureaucrats give successive justifications which are in fact quite inconsistent. In 1971, Sir Martin said:

> There has been some erosion of what was an extremely rigid position. This has not been a matter of policy, it has not been a conscious decision by myself or any of my predecessors that their identities should be disclosed, but the identity of my predecessor was disclosed, and my own identity was disclosed in some newspapers, and to that extent there has been a change, it is no good pursuing a policy that flies in the face of facts ... I have no direct relations with the press. Where does one stop? If my name is published, why not my deputy's name. If my deputy's name is published, why not my directors? And before you know where you are, you are publishing the name of someone who is running agents, and his photograph appears in the press ... the position in a number of other countries ... is that while they do not operate in the full glare of publicity,

nevertheless they do not adopt quite so restrictive an attitude to these matters as I and my predecessors have done. I doubt whether they benefit ...

Q:Broadly therefore, is it fair to say that your instinct is that for the efficiency of your service, the present state of public knowledge is sufficient and ideally ought not to be increased?

A:Yes, I do think that.[6]

But five years later, the IRA proved something of a godsend for secrecy and a little of it returned. The D-notices ask newspapers not to identity the heads of MI5 and MI6 unless the names have been already published in foreign magazines, which the Russians presumably read. In early 1976, the police found clippings naming Maurice Oldfield, then head of MI6, in an IRA hideout. A bomb had been left at Lockett's restaurant in Westminster, the previous October. Oldfield had a flat over the restaurant.

The D-notice Committee sent out a confidential letter (all their letters are stamped confidential). 'Domestic terrorist activities' were not exactly covered by a D-notice, it explained. But the IRA would read a name in British newspapers, and probably try to blow the individual up. It would be a great nuisance if the secret service heads had to be given bodyguards. Two years later, in January 1978, Tom McCaffrey, the press secretary to James Callaghan, the Prime Minister, told editors that the IRA threat 'continues to be a matter of major concern'. Callaghan was going to appoint new heads of both MI6 and MI5, but he was not going to tell anybody that the changes were being made. 'He and his colleagues have had in mind not just considerations of national security ... but also, and especially, the personal security of the individuals concerned.'

It was not the same reason as Sir Martin had originally given, which was that naming would lead to a kind of domino effect. And were every member of the IRA to surrender tomorrow, it is hard to imagine that names and changes at the head of MI5 and MI6 would suddenly start to be given. No doubt the anarchists would still be a threat, or the Cornish nationalists, or the Basques. For a while, the erosion has stopped, or even a little reversed.

MI6

MI6, the spies and secret agents' organization, has a certain corrupted glamour absent from MI5. Its present head is Sir Arthur Franks, appointed in 1978. His predecessors were Sir Maurice

Oldfield, who was pulled out of retirement in 1979 to handle security, under his own name, in Northern Ireland; Sir John Rennie; Sir Dick White, who went on to coordinate intelligence within the Cabinet Office; Sir John Sinclair; and Sir Stewart Menzies, who retired in 1953. The 'K' goes with the job, although the man at the top is known romantically as 'C', and MI6 is also known as SIS, the Secret Intelligence Service. In the Foreign Office, they are referred to as 'the Friends'.

Its London headquarters are at Century House, a modern 20-storey block adjoining Lambeth North tube station and represented to be the 'Government Communications Bureau'. The service is answerable to the Foreign Secretary and its spies are controlled, like every other country's, via officers working under diplomatic cover through embassies abroad. This fact is considered by the Foreign Office to be a great secret. MI6 has drawn in its horns, of course, with the end of empire, and functions very much as a junior partner to the CIA. Released State Department archives in the US show Sir John Sinclair, then deputy head of MI6 arriving in Washington in December 1950 to object to CIA plans for a multinational Western intelligence system. If institutionalized, he said, this meant the British might have to receive instructions from a steering committee 'probably including French and Turkish members; in which event there are implications on which the British Secret Service is not prepared to commit itself'. The British preferred, and obtained, arrangements made directly with the CIA, as part of the 'special relationship'.[7] All Western intelligence agencies have relations of a kind with each other, doing their best, like journalists, to gather in somewhat more information than they give out. MI6 trades information, for example, with the supposedly neutral Swedes, with the Israeli secret service, with the South African BOSS (now DONS), and, until its demise, with SAVAK, the unattractive secret police of the Shah of Iran. It also trains Nato countries' spies for them and those of organizations such as SAVAK. Some of its agents are full time, while others work on an intermittent *ad hoc* basis; they may be travelling businessmen or occasionally journalists (the Russians are often reviled, as are the more naïve Third World countries, for treating journalists as spies. Sometimes journalists are spies. Sometimes spies pretend to be journalists, which is not quite the same thing.) The worst that can happen to a high-level MI6 agent, as distinct from the native malcontents recruited to run local errands, is not necessarily to be caught; it is to be named. It is possible to negotiate the return and recycling of a captured agent to another unsuspecting country, but if he is publicly identified, he simply turns into a drain on the pay-roll.

It is a great mistake to think MI6 operates exclusively or mainly against those countries considered to threaten our safety — the Communist bloc. As Ray Whitney, the former head of Foreign Office covert propaganda turned Tory MP puts it: 'We need our intelligence services operating overseas. These services need to operate in many parts of the world. Our interests for example in oil and raw materials are worldwide and our services cannot be limited to countries behind a particular curtain. We cannot rely on our allies.'[8] So MI6 covert operations are no longer the traditional ones — parachuting emigrés into Albania; nosing up the fog-shrouded Bosphorus in a fast boat to land agents in Russia; sending frogmen to inspect the keels of Soviet cruisers in Portsmouth harbour. (Not that those particular operations in the 1950s appear to have been entirely satisfactory; the first two were betrayed, and the third killed the frogman and caused a diplomatic incident.)

Nowadays, we are at war in Ireland and with the Third World. There was post-war gossip that MI6 was ordered to sabotage Jewish refugee ships in ports bound for Palestine (in the archives concerning postwar Palestine, all papers mentioning MI6 are suppressed for 75 years), and that it connived at plans to have Nasser assassinated. It is certain that, more recently, MI6 was involved in the 1953 'destabilizing' of Iran which placed the Shah back on the throne for many years and in the despatch of British mercenaries and arms to Angola to fight on the side of the CIA's anti-socialist client Holden Roberto. The anxieties about MI6 are identical to those about MI5 — that in its airless self-recruiting way, it mimics in exaggerated form both the incompetence and the sociological tunnel vision of the most autocratic official departments of State — the Foreign Office and the Home Office. MI6 has, like MI5, been extensively penetrated by Soviet agents; Kim Philby, head of the anti-Soviet section, was one of the two most notorious, and George Blake, sentenced to 42 years and 'sprung' by the Russians is the other. If there is a consistent *raison d'état* behind MI6's secrecy about its mistakes, it is not that they alert the Russians, but that they upset the Americans; some of the truth about Philby was the subject of a D-notice in 1967; and the facts about Blake's career as an MI6 agent were leaked to Chapman Pincher by George Brown, then in Opposition, who was only informed himself on a secret 'Privy Councillor basis'.

The most systematic attempt to dig up the buried bodies of the Philby affair had been made in a 1967 book by three journalists from the *Sunday Times,* Bruce Page, David Leitch and Phillip Knightley.[9] They observed:

> When it became obvious that the *Sunday Times* planned to make some major disclosures about the Philby case, two D-notices were delivered simultaneously to all national newspapers. They said no reference should be made to the names of British secret departments, their responsibilities or past actions. Further, no mention should be made even of the names of people who had worked for such departments ... No self-respecting newspaper could have accepted them as they stood.

They rejected the D-notices: 'Virtually nothing had been revealed by the British government. After the disappearance of the two diplomats Burgess and Maclean in 1951, the Labour Government of the day made a few embarrassed and uninformative remarks ... it was not until 1955 that the White Paper was produced. It was almost unbelievably uninformative'. Not only was Burgess's secret work ignored, but so was Maclean's involvement in Anglo-American nuclear exchanges. When Philby defected in 1963, eight years after the White Paper and Macmillan's public defence of him, Heath said Philby had worked for the Soviet Union 'before 1946'; he did not even concede that the 'temporary first secretary' at Washington had been a spy, let alone the head of Britain's major espionage section. For Parliament, SIS did not exist.

Page, Leitch and Knightley ruminated:

> The affair tells us a good deal about the role of privilege in our society, and the degree to which irrelevant insignia of social and economic status can be fatally mistaken for evidence of political acceptability and wisdom. It also gives us an idea of how much our bureaucracy is prepared to hide; the White Paper on Burgess and Maclean and the tightly circumscribed official accounts of the role Kim Philby played in British affairs are classic warnings to those who are tempted to believe the official versions without powerful supporting evidence.

The fog covers ground both high and low. Pincher tells a ludicrous story of two MI6 trainees in 1956, deputed to trail another trainee and 'interrogate' him for vital information. They mistakenly abducted a clerk from the Stationery Office, took him to a safe flat in the Brompton Road, and removed his trousers. The police became involved in the fracas and so did a neighbour in the flat below; the *Daily Express* were tipped off and acquired the whole story.

> Shortly afterwards I was telephoned at my home by Admiral Thomson (secretary of the D-notices Committee) on behalf of security. He had heard that the *Express* were going to print the whole story and begged me to stop it, 'it will make MI6 look so stupid that it is bound to have a bad effect on their relations with America', he pleaded. It was an old ploy, but for his sake I agreed.[10]

The political attitudes of senior MI6 men are hard to test in the absence of any knowledge of their identities. One former deputy director, George Young, became prominent in the Monday Club and right-wing anti-immigrant circles; Pincher quotes a 1977 letter of his saying:

> At one point under Wilson there were five ministers of the Crown whose membership of the Communist Party of Great Britain is not known to have been renounced, and overlapping with them other ministers whose allegiance is outside Britain.

This attitude may represent an obsessional fear of the KGB, rather than loathing of Socialism; who can tell? Pincher himself asserts nonchalantly:

> I can quote from a 1978 Intelligence report in my possession which states that 'at least 59 serving Labour MPs — 19 per cent of the parliamentary Labour Party, have current or recent connections with Communist, Trotskyist or other Marxist organizations. The incidence of such activities has increased enormously over the past five years'.[11]

What is quite plain to see is that the 'secrecy' in which this most secret arm of government operates is not really secrecy at all. Elaborate intimidation of outsiders and those low in the hierarchy is accompanied by extensive leaking, briefing and otherwise propagandizing in the usual way. Pincher's series of anecdotes are sprinkled with references to intelligence sources, and although he makes much of attempts over the years to suppress him or bug him, it is clear that, as a protégé of Beaverbrook and the *Express,* he was regarded fundamentally as a club member. There was no attempt 'after very full study' to prosecute him for breach of the Official Secrets Act on publication of his memoirs — although this reflects less significantly on Pincher's attitudes than at first might appear. The Acts are primarily of use as a bluff, and if a powerful journalist is prepared to call the bluff, little will happen. Whitehall will occupy itself trying to trace his sources.

The art of information control by any government body is to pick on those targets which are not only hostile, but relatively small and defenceless, and will be susceptible to a campaign not merely to prosecute, but to discredit them. This was the pattern MI6 followed when it seemed that the cluster of disenchanted CIA 'whistleblowers' in the 1970s would turn their attention to Britain. The CIA operates in force in England, with at least two headquarters, aiming extensively at Third World countries; and MI6 helps it.[12] Phillip Agee, whose book, *Inside the Company* went into great detail about the CIA's efforts to keep Latin America safe for private enterprise, arrived in London in 1972 to finish his research.

> The British service was well prepared for my arrival. My name was on the immigration check-list, which caused me a long interview and then a longer wait ... I tried to live under an assumed name, more or less secretly, as I had done in Paris. But each night as I left the Museum, I was trailed by surveillance teams, and fatigue led me to give up the effort to conceal where I was living. My mail is again being opened, quite obviously, and meetings arranged by telephone have generated immediate surveillance once more. At times I wonder if the surveillance is mainly for harrassment, as it is so clumsy and indiscreet, but if the British service does nothing more serious, I shall be able to finish in calm.[13]

After the book's publication in 1975, the Labour Home Secretary was persuaded to deport Agee and another American, refusing to state the evidence and demanding that uneasy MPs should trust his secret judgement. Deportations, like immigration cases, are entirely secret administrative procedures except where ministers decide to bolster their decisions by selective release of material. Reginald Maudling, who as Tory Home Secretary, had in 1971 deported the ailing German student revolutionary, Rudi Dutschke, at the request of MI5 or MI6, made his own views clear in the bars of the House of Commons: 'It's quite simple. If a chap's a foreigner and you don't like him — kick him out.' MI6 were eventually to overreach themselves in the pursuit of Agee and his friends, and to put up two journalists on unconvincing spying charges in the ABC affair, which is dealt with later in this chapter.

All intelligence services naturally try to protect themselves. There was a rather similar *furor* in Sweden when two journalists were jailed after working to name names with a whistleblower in the Swedish service, the IB. But this did not mean the Swedes regarded espionage services as something to be complacent about. I asked the then Swedish Prime Minister, Olaf Palme in 1978, about the IB; he was irritated with the two journalists for falsely accusing him of bad faith in having the organization set up. 'Of course we knew that they would run around with the CIA', he said. 'But we avoided the dangers by keeping the IB very small.' The British government makes no public recognition that there are any dangers in having a secret service at all.

One has only to read the official apologies made for the CIA in the US to see spelt out the dangers of a secret, amoral, unaccountable arm of government. Richard Helms, who headed the CIA for seven years, describes the postwar drift thus:

> There was nothing about this organization that had to do with clandestine work such as espionage, counter-espionage or covert action. But there was one sentence put in the law stating that the agency was to perform certain 'functions of common concern'. Now, under this particular dispensation, the National Security Council (which in effect means the President) issued a series of highly classified directives which pushed the agency into secret activities, such as espionage, counter-espionage and later covert action, and paramilitary operations. This was done over a time, it wasn't done all at once. It was intended that these activities should be relatively small, that they would be decently 'covered' in the CIA. Along came the Korean war however and the expansion of the covert apparatus of the CIA. From then on, the covert part of the agency began to be the tail that wagged the dog. People forgot that the agency had been set up for an analytic purpose, and began to see it as an activist agency. It was involved in various kinds of clandestine manipulation, cloak and dagger if you like, dirty tricks if you like ...[14]

The success of MI6 in its prime role, the provision of accurate secret intelligence, must also be open to question. All Soviet information was made worse than worthless by Philby for a decade. After the declaration of UDI by Rhodesia in 1965, the Prime Minister, Harold Wilson, was allowed to say that sanctions would cripple the rebel regime in 'weeks rather than months'. Only with the 1978 Bingham inquiry was it publicly realized that British State-controlled oil companies and others had been making a mockery of international sanctions for years. While tiny firms were prosecuted for selling bits and pieces to Rhodesia, and bored sailors mounted the so-called Beira patrol at the tax-payers' expense, secret 'swap' arrangements were fulfilling the multinational oil companies' ambition to keep on selling. MI6 were certainly not alone in a vast infection of ineffectiveness and duplicity, among ministers and civil servants. It was decided in 1979 to abandon further investigations into the affair. There were to be no prosecutions and no further inquiry.

SIGINT

The British government's prime source of real international intelligence is by radio eavesdropping — a topic which was successfully kept secret for more than my own lifespan. (I am 34.) It is run by a large, international organization, once again dominated by the US and operated in Britain's sphere of influence by a complex of military and Foreign Office employees reporting up to the Cabinet Secretariat, the political influence of which is hard to assess. The whistleblowing achievement of the last few years has been to establish that they exist at all.

The object of this [D-notice] is to draw attention to the need for careful handling of information about HMG's ... interception of communications as a method of obtaining secret intelligence concerning foreign powers ... publication of any information about our interception arrangements tends to stimulate other countries into taking measures which could make the work of our security and intelligence services more difficult. In these matters, many of the security interests of our allies are identical to our own. You are requested not to publish anything about: ... details of duties and numbers of employees in defence and diplomatic communications establishments ... c) the nature and extent of interception by HMG of any form of communications or of transmissions such as radar, for the purposes of national security; this includes the establishments and the personnel, methods and arrangements involved.[15]

It was through Signals Intelligence, or SIGINT as it is called, for example, that Britain established, during one crisis over Cyprus, that the Turkish fleet was on the point of mounting an invasion. It was through SIGINT that Iraq's claim to be sending a division of troops to assist Syria in fighting Israel was discovered to be bogus — a discovery passed on to Israel. Both these successes of the 1960s were not achieved through code-breaking as such, but through sophisticated 'traffic analysis' of the weight and direction of radio traffic in the areas. One was directed against a nominal NATO ally; and one against a small middle-eastern country which, although presented as a Soviet client, is not, as such, a threat to our safety. In recent years, at any rate, code-breaking against Russia is a game not considered to be worth the candle; while the large computers possessed by Britain and the US can break Soviet codes, it takes them weeks to decrypt a message — by which time its relevance has probably evaporated.

The prime mover in SIGINT is the US National Security Agency based at Ford Meade, Maryland. Britain signed in 1947, the secret UKUSA pact by which universal international radio monitoring was to be carried out by the US, Britain, Canada and Australia, with the US, as the senior partner and paymaster, to receive the entire intelligence product of the joint effort. Other NATO allies and Japan later joined in. With the publication of recent books of memoirs about British wartime code-breaking triumphs and the cracking of the Enigma machine, some reasons for the elaborate secrecy about postwar code-breaking may have become visible.

After all, it was not always thus. Between the wars, the Government Code and Cypher School (GC&CS) circulated its intercepts to all senior ministers, and some to the entire Cabinet prior to 1924. This was the way the notorious Zinoviev letter, allegedly from the Comintern, was leaked as a stick to beat Labour at the polls, by dichard secret servicemen. Dr Christopher Andrew, a Cambridge historian, traced some of the subsequent political escapades in 1978, despite Whitehall refusal to allow GC&CS material into the archives. The Prime Minister Baldwin, and other ministers actually read out intercepted and decoded Russian telegrams to the House of Commons in 1927, in order to make stick charges that the Russians were interfering with British politics and conducting military espionage.[16]

It may be the case that the truth was suppressed about the code-breaking triumphs at Bletchley during the 1939-45 War because the Enigma machine continued to be sold to Third World countries such as China, who bought in all innocence. Or it may be that facts about Enigma were suppressed because it was important to demonstrate to the Germans that they had been defeated fairly and squarely by force of arms. At all events code-breaking was swept up in the great tide of Western Cold War activity between 1945 and 1950 — in total secrecy.

In 1958, SIGINT's operations led to one of the few Official Secrets prosecutions for simple journalism since the war. Two Oxford students wrote an article in a special issue of the undergraduate magazine *Isis,* devoted to the H-bomb. That May, Paul Thompson and William Miller were served with summonses under the Official Secrets Act on four counts. Both undergraduates had specialized in Signal Intelligence as National Servicemen in the Royal Navy.

Their article said:

The doctrine of Western Sincerity and the good fight against Russian wickedness is fostered in many little ways and not the least of these is the misreporting of news. We wish to expose one variety of this. Frontier incidents are almost invariably reported as ferocious and unjust attacks by Russian fighters on innocent Western aircraft peacefully cruising well within their own frontiers. All along the frontier between east and west from Iraq to the Baltic, perhaps further, are monitoring stations, manned largely by National Servicemen trained in morse and Russian, avidly recording the last squeak from Russian transmitters.

In order to get information the West has been willing to go to extraordinary lengths of deception. British embassies usually contain monitoring spies. When the Fleet paid a 'goodwill' visit to Danzig in 1955 they were on board. And since the Russians do not always provide the required messages, they are sometimes provoked. A plane 'loses its way'. There is no controlling the appetite of the statistical analysers at Cheltenham. Perhaps the best example of their activities is in the Baltic. After the war a fleet of half a dozen exceedingly fast Mercedes-Benz torpedo-type boats were built and manned by sailors from Hitler's navy, and were sent out under English captains to provoke and listen to the Russians. They would head straight for the Russian fleet at exercise and circle round a battleship, taking photos.

The case at the Old Bailey ended when the defendants pleaded guilty to the charge of communicating secret information to an unauthorized person and the other charges were withdrawn. Each received a sentence of three months' imprisonment.

The British part of the system operates from the so-called Government Communications Headquarters at Cheltenham. The fieldwork of monitoring and low-level analysis is done by the military (although they wear civilian clothes at Cheltenham) who have a chain of overseas bases manned largely by 'radio' soldiers of No. 9 and No. 13 Signals Regiments (originally the 1st and 2nd Special Wireless Regiments). Its cost was asserted to be in the region of £100m per annum by the MP Robin Cook, and its Cheltenham staff to number 4,000.[17] Cheltenham recruits linguists and code-breakers in the traditional way of the Civil Service; it even had entries in the commercial career directories put out for undergraduates, full of enigmatic references to 'certain tasks' and 'duties' which are the unmistakable trademarks of secret work. (Other key words are 'attached to' as in 'attached to Foreign Office', which means MI6; and 'special'; the propaganda department of the Foreign Office was often described as having 'special functions'.) The Russians are aware of SIGINT; an RAF technician Ronald Britten, passed a great deal of information about the Cyprus base in the 1960s.

Signals intelligence bases can probably be found wherever there is a residual British military presence; known units are in West Germany and West Berlin, where they have an obvious task intercepting Eastern block communications; in Turkey; originally in Palestine and now in Ayos Nikolaos in the British sovereign base on Cyprus, where they intercept all Middle-East communications and those of Russian ships in the Mediterranean; in Botswana; in Hong Kong, Ascension Island and Australia; and reportedly in Oman, Singapore and St Helena. The art includes analysis of radar (RADINT) and weaponry (ELINT) signals, which has an obvious military value. Many of the communications interceptions, however are likely to have political significance, especially if commercial traffic is monitored.

The NSA maintains its own bases in Britain, as part of the vast filigree of radars, early-warning systems, microwave towers, air control networks and command structures which make up an aircraft-carrier. Britain is a large supply base and aircraft-carrier for NATO. The NSA has bases at Edzell in Scotland; Chicksands, in Bedfordshire; Haverfordwest and Bude; and Menwith Hill near Harrogate. An experimental over-the-horizon radar at Orfordness was closed down when satellite surveillance became cheap and successful. One presumes that, as well as listening to *them,* they also eavesdrop on *us.* US computers are reportedly now able to store international telephone calls and retrieve those which mention key words; this would be a great technological advance, because the sheer weight of pointless and trivial material gathered by intercepts is a bigger bar to electronic surveillance than considerations of cost or morality.

All British-originating communications are swept up whatever their form by British undercover operations, as well as by the US and the USSR. Radio transmissions from foreign embassies; all outgoing cables; selected foreign mail and international telephone calls; the domestic mail and phone calls of those of interest to the authorities; the dinner-table conversations of those considered subversive. We are not concerned here with the ethical implications of a situation where the State turns itself into one vast ear — merely with the fact that it shrouds this aspect of its self-assumed functions in an extraordinary degree of secrecy. The attitudes of mind displayed about SIGINT emerge rather strikingly in the 1978 ABC trial, which is dealt with shortly.

A look at the SIGINT hierarchy is also instructive. The field operators are regular soldiers, particularly indoctrinated to secrecy, their tasks buried in the public role of Royal Corps of Signals. The analysts at Cheltenham are civil servants, similarly trained. The material is passed to other countries, such as Israel and formerly Iran, and most of all the US, by treaties and private arrangements. The Foreign Office and Ministry of Defence officials control the system, which they do not admit exists, and it reports ultimately to the Cabinet Secretariat, one of whose deputy secretaries always has an unacknowledged security and intelligence coordination task. Sir Dick White, a former head of both MI5 and MI6 was thus installed in the Cabinet Secretariat, and so until 1978 was Sir Leonard Hooper, who was actually the former head of GCHQ itself.

MI5

MI5 is at present run by the former ambassador to Moscow, Sir Howard Smith, who was appointed by the Labour Prime Minister,

Mr Callaghan, in 1978. His predecessors since the war have been Sir Michael Hanley, Sir Martin Furnival-Hones (who became an adviser to ICI on retirement), Sir Roger Hollis and Sir Dick White. The knighthood goes with the job.

MI5 was founded in 1909 by the Imperial Defence Committee to battle against the Germans and the French. Its London headquarters are a massive office-block, Curzon Street House, 1-11 Curzon Street, just round the corner from Berkeley Square. The organization moved in there in 1975. Its postal address is 'Box 500, London'. Previous smaller offices were further down Curzon Street in Leconfield House. Curzon Street House was one of a number of government buildings erected during the war with bomb-proof cellars, and was previously occupied by the Department of Education. The policy of pretending it does not exist makes for certain curiosities; there is no name on the door, although police at the desk inside check passes and the car-park barrier at the rear mews is manned by a policeman. Wall-mounted cameras conspicuously scan the surrounding pavement, and the whole of the ground floor has blank cement walls topped with a curious concrete verandah which makes the building look rather like a concert hall; it is in fact a blast deflector screen, to give protection against car-bombs. Registration numbers of the cars MI5 use are specially flagged on the vehicle licensing computer at Swansea to ensure no information is ever given out about them. The service was described officially in 1963 as a relatively small professional organization, with specialized agents in the field and advanced technical resources. MI5 men have, in theory, no executive powers but rely on police from the Special Branch to make arrests and carry out searches, on MI5 instructions. Their domestic sources of information are via the police (who keep their own political files and have their own phone-lines to them) and range through interception of mail, cables and phones, break-ins, and sophisticated 'bugging devices'. By 1976 they had access to 'bugs' sufficiently sophisticated to pick up conversations through closed doors.[18] Customs and Immigration officers pass on information about visitors to Eastern Europe and names listed as 'of interest' at ports and airports.

Much material about Soviet espionage reaches MI5 through defectors, either direct, or passed on from such friendly countries as the US and Australia. According to Sir Martin's 1971 testimony, a surprisingly small amount of effort goes into counter-espionage, the trailing of diplomats and the nailing of British renegades.

'Protective security' by way of vetting would-be officials, and having documents locked up, occupies more time.

Recruiting during the 1939-45 war on a class basis, from Old Etonians and debutantes, MI5 was badly infiltrated with Soviet sympathizers, to an extent only publicly realized in 1979 with the confession of Sir Anthony Blunt that he fed details of MI5's inadequate anti-Russian section and many of its other operations, straight to the Soviet embassy.[19] Soviet agents like Guy Burgess were part of a cluster of MI5 personalities, MI6 men and those who later became high-ranking diplomats.

Habits of secrecy were ingrained in Britain's postwar ruling class by the experiences of the 1939-45 war. It was a psychologically powerful experience for many of its members at an impressionable age, and they later continued to believe that they were at war — not all with the same enemy. With the end of the German war and the development of MI5 as a Cold War agency hand in glove with and largely subordinate to the US, none of the public were, of course, aware just how uncertain were the loyalties of the frequently homosexual public-school network who assigned to themselves on a self-recruiting basis the secret defence of the realm.

MI5 acquired a large measure of autonomy after the war. Sir Findlater Stewart successfully proposed in 1945 that the Prime Minister should take merely nominal charge:

> From the very nature of the work, need for direction except on the very broadest lines can never arise above the level of Director-General. That appointment is one of very great responsibility, calling for unusual experience and a rare combination of qualities; but having got the right man there is no alternative to giving him the widest discretion in the means he uses and the direction in which he applies them — always provided he does not step outside the law.[20]

After the traumatic flight of Burgess and Maclean from the Foreign Office to Russia in 1951 a panic wave of interrogations and purges took place in government. The Cabinet Secretary, Sir Norman Brook, mounted a coup which was designed to ensure that the security service was better supervised. 'I believe that Sir Findlater Stewart exaggerated the "defence" aspects of the Security Service' he said in March 1951 in a carefully composed statement:

and the arrangement by which the Security Service is directly responsible to the Prime Minister is now justified mainly by the fact that it enhances the status of the service ... I believe that it would be helpful to the Director-General of the Security Service to be able to turn to a senior permanent secretary for advice and assistance on the policy of his work, and on his relations with other government departments; and that he would receive from the permanent head of the Home Office support and guidance which the Prime Minister's secretariat is not in a position to give. The Prime Minister's personal contact ... need not be wholly interrupted ... on matters of supreme importance and delicacy, the head of the service should always be able, at his initiation, to arrange a personal interview with the Prime Minister.[21]

Translated from the veiled language of bureaucratic infighting, this means 'MI5 cannot be allowed to carry on doing as it likes'. The Home Secretary was put personally in charge of MI5, although the control was still rather blurred and nominal. The Home Secretary, Sir David Maxwell Fyfe, finally issued a detailed directive to MI5, which governs and limits it, in theory at least, today. 'This is a very un-English thing to have', Sir Martin revealingly remarked in 1971, 'and certainly it is unusual in the Government service for an organization to be given a specific directive as to what its functions are and what the limitations of its powers are.'[22] It may be noted that MI5 is not explicitly required to operate within the law, and that ministers are still only to be briefed on a 'need to know' basis:

1. In your appointment as Director-General of the Security Service you will be responsible to the Home Secretary personally. The Security Service is not, however, a part of the Home Office. On appropriate occasion you will have right of direct access to the Prime Minister.
2. The Security Service is part of the Defence Forces of the country. Its task is the Defence of the Realm as a whole, from external and internal dangers arising from attempts at espionage and sabotage, or from actions of persons and organizations whether directed from within or without the country, which may be judged to be subversive of the State.
3. You will take special care to see that the work of the Security

Service is strictly limited to what is necessary for the purposes of this task.

4. It is essential that the Security Service should be kept absolutely free from any political bias or influence and nothing should be done that might lend colour to any suggestion that it is concerned with the interests of any particular section of the community, or with any other matter than the Defence of the Realm as a whole.

5. No enquiry is to be carried out on behalf of any Government Department unless you are satisfied that an important public interest bearing on the Defence of the Realm, as defined in paragraph 2, is at stake.

6. You and your staff will maintain the well-established convention whereby Ministers do not concern themselves with the detailed information which may be obtained by the Security Service in particular cases, but are furnished with such information only as may be necessary for the determination of any issue on which guidance is sought.

Lord Denning said, rather pointedly 'There has been considerable misapprehension about the ministerial responsibility for the security service; and this misapprehension seems to me to be the cause of some of the troubles that have arisen. The relevant documents are so little available that it may be helpful if I give considerable extracts.'[23] There was not a soul in Whitehall, who would have dreamed of making public any part of these documents even to a Cabinet Minister. They were an official secret, and no doubt carried a high security classification. The general public, and indeed most politicians, were deeply confused as to what MI5 was meant to do, and how it was supposed to be controlled, if at all. Lord Denning gave chapter and verse in order to demonstrate that MI5 behaved more or less correctly during the Profumo scandal of 1963, when Sir Roger Hollis decided fastidiously it was no part of his duties to brief the Prime Minister on the sex life of the Secretary of State for War, or indeed to investigate it with any thoroughness.

The year following the Profumo scandal, in 1964, Sir Roger's men finally persuaded Anthony Blunt, former office colleague and wartime dinner-guest of the Hollises, to confess that he was a Russian spy, and the 'fourth man' in the notorious Foreign Office -MI6 Burgess-Philby-Maclean axis (Philby had fled to Russia the previous year). The confession was made in return for a promise that no one would ever be told and that Blunt, a knight and surveyor of the Queen's pictures, would not be prosecuted.[24]

The episode shows how the 'need to know' principle continued to be manipulated so as to leave an internal security service great freedom of manoeuvre, especially over skeletons in its own cupboard. The caretaker Prime Minister, Sir Alec Douglas Home, never got to hear what happened and Sir Harold Wilson, when he came to power, was told nothing of this *fait accompli* for three years, and then in so veiled a way that his memory had to be jogged in the eventual scandal of 1979. To put an obscure piece of paper at the bottom of an overflowing weekend red box is not the kind of accountability which should appeal very much to citizens of a democracy. As Merlyn Rees, a former Home Secretary, puts it 'Any [security] issue requiring guidance demands a great deal of information.'

Hollis and his men, having failed to nail Blunt over the years with a series of what Blunt describes as 'comfortable conversations', had decided to offer him legal immunity — it was a ploy tried several times in those rather panicky days — in return for a confession. They gave a sketchy account of what was needed to another official, the acting DPP, who gave an even sketchier version to the Attorney who could authorize it, Sir John Hobson. Hollis also gave Henry Brooke, the Home Secretary at the time, some sort of account of what was going on. Brooke said that the Queen had better know. What followed was an indication of MI5's state of anxiety; normally they interpret their duties (dubiously) as including the protection of the Queen and her family from embarrassing or insecure contacts.

Hollis and Charles Cunningham, the Home Office permanent secretary, summoned Michael Adeane, the Queen's private secretary. What was the Queen supposed to do if Blunt did confess? Adeane wanted to know. 'Nothing', they told him; it would alert the Russians and all the other suspect 'moles' in the establishment. By a curious and typical piece of British prudery, the Queen refuses to say to this day what or indeed whether she was told about the man she knighted, and who derived considerable cachet from superintending the Royal paintings. Mrs Thatcher was prepared to be blunt about the Queen's role in the end: 'The Palace duly followed the advice that had already been given', she said in 1979. (When it leaked after a full fifteen years the Queen hastily stripped Sir Anthony of his knighthood.)

The Blunt project had thus been 'sold' to those with technical responsibility for MI5. Hobson apparently failed to see the long-term implications of the scheme and mentioned it to no one. Brooke was of so little use to the public he supposedly represented in this secret world, that he apparently forgot the whole subject.

It worked, after a fashion. At Blunt's London flat 'he was told of the new information ... he maintained his denial. He was offered immunity from prosecution. He sat in silence for a while. He got up looked out of the window, poured himself a drink and after a few minutes confessed.'[25] It was almost two months before Hollis and Cunningham formally reported their great coup to Henry Brooke, again apparently in such terms that he forgot all about it. It is possible that, with an election pending, and the Macmillan-Home Conservative Government already reeling from the Profumo and Vassall scandals, it was not the kind of thing about which a minister could easily bear to think.

Wilson and the Labour Government were told nothing when they took over the reigns of power that year. Future ministers, as years dragged into decades, found their hands tied. At some point between 1973, when Blunt teetered on the edge of death from cancer, and 1978, when it looked as though a journalist's book would name him, the received wisdom in MI5 modulated from 'the secret is still worth keeping on security grounds' to 'it would put others off if the government was tasteless enough deliberately to expose his name'. The Cabinet Office drew up a statement, and waited quietly to be forced into pressing it into some pained Prime Minister's hand.

Had a journalist, Andrew Boyle, not written his book, and had the government's Protection of Official Information Bill slipped into law instead of running aground on the 1979 scandal, that prepared statement in the Cabinet Office would have peacefully yellowed. Someone might have leaked it on Blunt's death (with the key witness to what had actually occurred silent for ever) or it might have stayed in the archives for good. Documents mentioning MI5 are not released after 30 years.

On his death bed, Goronwy Rees, one of the Burgess-Blunt Cambridge circle who found his academic career blighted by gossip while that of Blunt flourished, claimed bitterly that there were half a dozen others involved in the affair whose names he would not mention. He said:

Our obsession with secrecy in Britain makes for twisted values and double standards when traitors or their accomplices, witting or unwittingly are found. The rich and powerful can hide away behind secret regulations and procedures which appear to be manipulated in their favour and against the rest of us.

If only there were a way of bridging the generation gap that keeps the young in blissful ignorance of traitors and treachery committed before their time, there'd be a better chance of a more open and healthier public life in future.[26]

Apart from questions of its competence in a dangerous world, the main political source of anxiety about MI5 is whether it is, directives notwithstanding, crudely polarized. These fears arise from excessive secrecy, the class basis of recruitment, and MI5's role as junior partner to the US. Successive spy scandals have given the security men great control over the careers of civil servants, through 'positive vetting'. As many academics are rather disconcerted to find, middle-aged colonels from MI5 will come knocking at their doors, asking about their students' politics, habits and sexual orientation. It is a pervasive atmosphere but a clumsy one. I know personally some young homosexuals and Marxists who have passed painlessly into the Foreign Office within the last few years. A vast compost of gossip grew in the latter days of the 1974-6 Wilson Government that Labour MPs, Cabinet Ministers and even Sir Harold himself, were communistic, or in thrall to the reds. Some of this gossip must have emanated from MI5 sources, and Sir Harold himself became convinced he was being 'bugged'. Sincere left-wingers in government like Judith Hart were presented to Labour Prime Ministers as potential security risks.[27]

Partly these rumours are a consequence of the paranoid conviction that no one in Whitehall can be trusted because the prewar Cambridge Soviet spy-ring was never really destroyed, but merely dented; partly they must arise because rumour is the faithful bedfellow of excessive secrecy, and partly, one must assume a tunnel vision in MI5 and elsewhere in Whitehall, in which Labour politicians are seen as hostile to defence, far too friendly with 'subversives', and hence almost axiomatically, hand in glove with the Kremlin. The efforts of the Russians and Czechs to pick up tit-bits by bribery and blackmail may also occasionally lead security men, by a kind of mental somersault, to believe that what they collect this way is important.

Sir Martin Furnival-Jones, for example, took a view of this sort, in his classic defence of every last comma in the Official Secrets Act:

A great deal of information is available to the press which never appears in the newspapers, and I think this is what [the Russians] are after. It may be material derived from confidential briefings, and it may be material which is being leaked on purpose, by a senior official or a minister ... if it is passed on either by the backbench MP or by the lobby correspondent ... this may be ... espionage by inadvertence, and it may be therefore just as damaging ...

A great deal of the information which journalists acquire is information about individuals, and a great deal of the effort of the Russian intelligence service is devoted to the acquisition of what generally one might describe as operational information.

Q: How would that sort of information be involved with the Official Secrets Act in any sense?
A: Oh, very readily. Every Government department, I presume, I am sure, maintains a personal file in respect of its employees.
Q: But is it an official secret?
A: It is an official secret if it is in an official file.[28]

Matters are not helped by the British government's definition of 'subversion', which it is the further task of MI5 to neutralize. Lord Denning defined it briskly and acceptably in 1963: a man's political opinions were subversive in so far as 'they would contemplate the overthrow of the Government by unlawful means'.[29] But subsequent governments have defined it as 'wishing to undermine parliamentary democracy by' (among other things) 'political means'. This conjures up dreadful visions of all kinds of harmless radicals and journalists among the two million names reputed to be on file in Curzon Street. As there is no independent check on the contents of MI5's registries (unlike in Sweden) and as parallel organizations such as the FBI in the US have been caught out persecuting such 'undesirable' persons as the late Martin Luther King, this picture may perfectly well be true.

A rare glimpse of MI5 going about its political work came in the diaries of one of Harold Wilson's Cabinet ministers, Barbara Castle (she presumably felt herself 'authorized' under the Official Secrets Act to divulge it). It dealt with the attitude of the new president of the Engineering Union, Hugh Scanlon, a former Communist party member:

October 31 1968: Another glorious document has been circulated to me by our Security boys on the attitude of the CP during the engineering negotiations. Scanlon, it says, did not seek the advice of the Party and had departed from the advice of the Party in the past by agreeing to talks about productivity before pay. Scanlon, had consolidated his position as president, and had to some extent freed himself from party direction. Interesting.[30]

Tony Benn, that much maligned would-be workers' friend and ex-Labour Cabinet minister, began pressing in the late 1970s to see an inquiry into the security services. Although there is still a knee-jerk reaction among Conservatives that to complain about MI5 is somehow unpatriotic — the opposite of the 'less government' attitude of US conservatives — it is a demand that is beginning to find its way on to the political agenda. Benn asserted, at the time of the debate on the Blunt affair:

> We need a Freedom of Information Act (which will exclude operational secrecy). We want to know the budget and the staffing. We are entitled to know the names of those who are in charge of MI5 and MI6. We need to know the policy, the number of dossiers and the names of countries with which we have intelligence links ... the House of Commons is entitled to know with which foreign intelligence agencies our intelligence officers exchange information. We are entitled to a Select Committee which would look at these policy matters. What is important here is the issue of accountability. We cannot entrust our liberties to a State within a State, with its own policies, its own prejudices, its own friends and its own enemies; with unlimited powers of surveillance, of scrutiny, of blacklisting or of granting immunity. The freedoms that we are trying to defend are too important to be left to the security chiefs or the secretaries to the Cabinet, however high principled they may be ... they were not elected to run the system that safeguards our liberties. They cannot be removed for what they do, because everything they do is behind the tightest secrecy that covers their failings, their successes, their friendships and their prejudices.[31]

Meanwhile, what reforms there may be in MI5 take place behind the curtain. The Prime Minister alone is shown the MI5 budget — a real document as distinct from the Secret Vote, which is a phoney public document announcing a modest cosmetic figure which bears no particular relation to the scale of Britain's secret operations, but which is none the less, treated with solemnity as part of the estimates; MPs are forbidden to debate it because it is secret.

In 1978, when Sir Michael Hanley retired, James Callaghan did bring in new blood from the rival service at the Foreign Office. Sir Howard Smith is an intelligence oriented diplomat, like Christopher Ewart-Biggs who, when assassinated as ambassador to Dublin to cries of 'foul' from the British press, was probably as near to a 'legitimate target' as any guerrilla organization the IRA could find. We were not told of the Smith move, which could be as significant in its way as the reverse move in 1956, after the spy scandals in MI6, when the secret policeman Sir Dick White was moved over to take charge of the swashbuckling secret agents.

At the same time as he made this appointment, Callaghan and his Home Secretary Merlyn Rees did make a number of reforms in MI5. They tried to change the basis of recruitment and it is a fair inference from similar moves which took place at the Foreign Office at the end of the previous year under David Owen, that some modest attempts at cutbacks and the removal of political bias were tried. There were a number of early retirements; one, Pamela Lamble, appeared to have been sufficiently mortified to try a little whistleblowing on her own account, and was suddenly thrown into prison on a spying charge, in the middle of the Blunt affair. She had been deliberately writing letters to Communist embassies criticizing the administration of MI5's secretariat, knowing these would be routinely steamed open by M15.

On Christmas Eve 1979, in a move bereft of political logic, the dramatic charges under Section 1 of the Official Secrets Act were suddenly dropped by the Attorney-General. Miss Lamble was allowed to go home to Staines in Middlesex after promising solemnly never to disclose why she had been charged in the first place. MI5 had been putting out feelers about the PR impact of the arrest through their former operatives in Fleet Street and visions of headlines about Christmas gruel for Miss Lamble and pheasant for the traitor Blunt, were floating before their eyes.[32]

Callaghan gave a guarded picture to MPs in 1979[33] of the regal audience he held to brief the two new heads of the intelligence services, although he glossed over the fact it was such a briefing. Sir Howard, Sir Arthur Franks, Sir Robert Armstrong the Cabinet Secretary and Callaghan's Private Secretary sat down at No. 10:

> I reminded them there was no room for complacency in view of what was going on — the attempted Soviet penetration which

still exists — and I reminded them of their past record, which is at the forefront of their minds all the time. Although I said the matter that weighed constantly on their minds had originated several years earlier nevertheless I wanted to go over the ground again. They confirmed to me ... that in their view those who might have been concerned with acts of treachery had, for the most greater part reached the end of their active life. They had either resigned or retired ... secondly we discussed once again the nature of the procedures for positive vetting. We discussed their thoroughness and whether they were adequate. These procedures had been changed since the time of the earliest incidents in 1964 ... we then went on to the question of the management and recruitment of the two services. I can tell the House there is no reason why it should not have been said earlier [this was because of the caution of the former Home Secretary, Merlyn Rees] — that the Home Secretary did change the nature of recruitment into the security service and the way in which it was conducted. I think it was necessary to do so.

We discussed to what extent the method should be applied to MI6 and whether we should make certain changes there in order to achieve a better balance [this must have been an interesting dispute]. We discussed the question whether any of the recent Soviet defectors who had come across had been planted, and what we thought happened to various people. Finally, we went over once more the most important question of all, which was whether grounds existed for continued suspicion in the security service, and if so, what should we do ... I believe that there are people who have remained undiscovered and unknown so far, who are still alive, though probably inactive.

The point to bear in mind about this description is that it was not given to inform the public. It was given because in the wake of a monstrous scandal, Mr Callaghan wished to show himself in a good light, as a man who took a profound and careful interest in the operations of MI5, and could not be blamed for anything. Had this rather generalized account of his meeting appeared in the press the day after it occurred, there would have been a great uproar, and threats of jail for all concerned.

Similarly, Mrs Thatcher's crisp announcements of yet further reforms to make MI5 decently accountable to her, were a political gesture. If MI5 heard that any minister, ex-minister or senior civil servant might have been a security risk, it was ordered to tell the

Home Secretary at once. The Home Secretary was instructed to tell the Prime Minister, and if MI5 asked the Attorney for any more immunities, he too was ordered to tell the Home Secretary. These gestures were no doubt made to satisfy the House of Commons; this is precisely why the House of Commons exists. Mr Benn put it succinctly: 'Take the pressure of parliament off a minister, and before he knows was is happening, he becomes part of the establishment that he was elected to control.'

The Special Branch

A middle-aged bespectacled man in civilian clothes was seated behind a desk. He showed me a police identification card. He asked if I was interested in helping the police with secret and confidential information and I asked what he meant. He asked me about my political allegiance and I refused to answer. I asked him about the purpose of his visit. He said he wants to know about political activity in the college. He offered me financial incentives tax-free and told me I would not be seen publicly with him and that any information I gave would be treated in strict confidence. I was asked to sign a copy of the Official Secrets Act, but I refused.[34] [Robert McNeil (20), statement to Paisley College of Technology governors.]

The Special Branch (this artless word 'special' recurs continually in discussions of secret organizations) was founded in 1883 at Scotland Yard to deal with the Fenians, and together with the Indian Intelligence Bureau, formed the colonial nucleus of what has grown in less than a century into a rather elaborate political police, more or less nationally organized, 1,600 strong, probably possessed of files on more than one million people, and working in an obscure but symbiotic relationship with MI5, the security service. Until recently, the size of the Special Branch was regarded as yet another State secret and the extraction of some simple numbers has taken a good deal of persistence.

Robin Cook, a Labour MP, brought the subject up every year, in 1977, 1978 and 1979, in an adjournment debate — this is a procedure whereby an MP can hold forth briefly on a pet topic, often a constituency matter, and a government spokesman of some sort will reply. The Labour Home Secretary, Merlyn Rees, having been forced to ask himself the question 'Why keep the numbers secret?' could not think of a convincing answer, and was eventually honest enough to do something about it. He gave the figures, for London (about 450 men) and for the rest of England. His colleagues gave the figures for Northern Ireland and Scotland. Clearly he also circulated local Chief Constables with the passages from Hansard setting out his views, for over the next year about half of England's Chief Constables suddenly included a report of sorts on their local Special Branch complement, some giving the numbers.

It is the more important among politicians and officials to stress the autonomy of local Chief Constables, because the Special Branch in fact spends much of its time feeding information to and taking instructions from Scotland Yard and MI5, and is thus much more centralized than most police activities. Obscurantism is still present; the chairman of the police committee for West Yorkshire, a municipal committee which approves the budget and exercises nominal control over its local Chief Constable, refused in June 1978 to give numbers, on the grounds it would 'impair the efficiency of the police and aid criminal elements'. The South Yorkshire force next door openly gave the number as 27, although no migration of subversives across its borders was observed afterwards.

Nor has the new openness led to the commander of the Special Branch at Scotland Yard being prepared to enter into harmless conversation. When Deputy Assistant Commissioner Bryan was appointed in 1977, I put this to the test by suggesting a newspaper interview. The negotiations, such as they were, were handled through Scotland Yard's News Group Controller, David Bryant. He first asked for a written list of topics and questions. It was duly submitted. Back came a stalling reply: 'DAC Bryan is not willing to give an interview at the moment. However he will be happy to consider the idea again, say in three months, when he has had time to settle into his new post.' I requested this in writing, and almost a year later resubmitted a request for a conversation. 'Certainly not', came the answer. 'It is not practice and never has been.'

The growth in size of the Special Branch has been recent; in the early 1960s, there were only some 200 officers at Scotland Yard. Rees says the 'numbers game' is highly misleading, because it takes three men to guard one prominent person's life. Politicians tend to dissolve into rumination here about the IRA, the PFLP, the Iraqis, the Baader-Meinhof Gang, the Angry Brigade, the Red Brigade, the Bulgarian hit-squads, and all the other perfectly genuine threats to the tranquillity of a world capital such as London. A sizeable headquarters staff spend their time on 'threat assessment' — working out who might want to assassinate each visiting foreign leader; at least 100 men must be working full-time on guarding members of the Cabinet, the Royal Family, Opposition leaders and exposed diplomats.

This still leaves a large number of policemen, however. They work at ports and airports, interrogating passengers (routine comings and goings are reported direct to MI5 by immigration officers). In Dyfed-Powis, for example, which includes in its area the Irish port of Fishguard, the Port Unit made only five arrests in 1978 under the Prevention of Terrorism Act, but it 'submitted 3,964 reports on persons of criminal and security interest: more than 10 a day ...'[35]

The Special Branch acts as the arresting arm of MI5, and in its turn supplies it with intelligence. Its own sources of information on local political activity are in part routine; ordinary police pass on details of all political meetings that come to them, together with what details about the personalities involved they can glean. The rationale is to monitor likely 'public disorder'. Special Branch officers often figure in allegations at universities and factories that they try to recruit informers, with copious invocations of the Official Secrets Act and offers of cash, in efforts to provide data on perfectly legal political activities. When a vetted juror was excluded in 1979 from a trial of anarchists, on Special Branch information which the Crown claimed showed he would be biased against the anarchists (they were ostentatiously trying to be fair), he turned out to be Mr David Myddleton, an Old Etonian professor of finance, who was once treasurer of the harmless right-wing Society for Individual Freedom and participated in a demonstration outside the Bank of England in 1970 for the right of individuals to buy gold — he was one of only six people there.

The problem about policemen, not all of whom may be as sophisticated as the charming and well-read officers deputed to act as ministerial bodyguards, is that they seek promotion by demonstrations of zeal. When the task is, as the Chief Constable of Manchester puts it, to act as an 'intelligence gathering agency' for 'terrorist activities' and 'public order situations' then their zeal will emerge by successfully compiling lists of names. Coupled with the natural wish of informers to be seen to give value for money, the likely outcome is that bucket-loads of material, irrelevant, mistaken, or just ordinarily nosey, will be submitted as 'reports'. The reports are placed in increasingly sophisticated computer systems. This makes it rather important that members of the public (a) know what type of information is being compiled about them; (b) how it is being stored; (c) to whom it is distributed; and (d) whether it is right or wrong.

This topic will be discussed in the chapter on privacy, but as far as the Special Branch is concerned it is worth noting here that it is precisely this information which is carefully kept secret. In November 1979 the Tory junior minister at the Home Office, Leon Brittan, said loftily: 'Mr Cook speculated about the number of files and other matters. Little credence can be given to those figures.'[36] He did not say to what figures credence might be given. The Metropolitan Police 'C' Department computer, ordered in 1979, is reported to have places for 1.4 million Special Branch files, although full computerization is said to be going very slowly. The *New Scientist* (18 January 1979), reported that only 600,000 Special Branch files would be computerized by 1985, and that to date, only 350,000 files had been inserted including intelligence material from drugs, immigration, serious crimes and fraud squads.

The Special Branch is not the KGB, which is a comprehensive, extremely centralized and powerful body operating in a totalitarian system and probably inhibited from doing exactly what it likes only by bureaucratic rivalries. But it is a political police, and one of its main tasks is officially defined, over and again, as dealing with 'subversion'. Any activity is subversive in the eyes of the government if it 'threatens the wellbeing of the State and is intended to undermine parliamentary democracy by political or industrial means'.[37] This, in the usual sweeping fashion of British officialdom, goes well beyond violent or illegal behaviour, and could certainly be construed to cover such harmless activities as writing this book.

Having gathered dossiers, by secret means, the Special Branch may again, officially or unofficially, secretly distribute the information. It certainly works in cooperation with MI5 and with bodies like the Jewish Defence League (when dealing with Fascists) and industrial employers (when dealing with trade-union militants). It is very difficult to stop policemen passing on information contained in their files, despite the Official Secrets Act, to former colleagues working as private detectives or industrial 'security officers'; to other government departments, or to interested businessmen. In 1979 alone there were three exposed examples of police material being passed: to a casino firm to help drum up trade; to a dishonest financier about the extent of information on a business partner; and to an armed robber about the dossier on which he was to be prosecuted. The recipients were an employee of Ladbrokes; the late Sir Eric Miller; and a convict called Roger Denhardt. Those concerned, a policeman, a detective superintendent and an employee of the Official Receiver, were prosecuted.

Academics and administrators may wish to know if would-be lecturers are reds; works managers if would-be labourers are agitators. Government prosecutors may wish to know if any members of a jury are likely to be left-wing. One's anxiety in this area is not lessened by the existence of privately funded bodies such as the Economic League which keep industrial blacklists. The League's activities have apparently been discussed in the press once too often, for in 1979 they openly conceded the blacklist's existence: 'The League puts considerable effort into monitoring the activities of subversive groups and individuals striving to undermine free enterprise and State-controlled industry ... it has amassed a substantial store of information about the activities of subversive groups and individuals prominent in them.'[38] Where does it all come from? Do they trade material with the Special Branch? There were documents published before the war suggesting informed contacts with the police and more recent reports that the League had access to criminal records.

Ministers make soothing noises about the Special Branch; Leon Brittan said in the 1979 debate:

> We should face the fact that much of the work of the Special Branch precludes it from being conducted in the full glare of public scrutiny. It would be idle to pretend the contrary ... Those who seek to undermine our democratic institutions or put the public to fear often operate covertly and by stealth. Police action to counter that cannot be effective if it is conducted in public. It would not be in the public interest for detailed accounts of Special Branch operations to be given, as these are often bound to be concerned with matters affecting security.

This is another of those extendable arguments; it could be applied in precisely the same form to justify a policy of secrecy about the activities of the ordinary police. Burglars, after all invariably 'operate covertly and by stealth'.

The case for moving in the opposite direction towards less secrecy, is buttressed by the evidence that policemen, who by the nature of their occupation, think exclusively in terms of social control, are envisaging the future application of a great deal of it to the rest of us. James Anderton, Chief Constable of Greater Manchester, delivered himself of the following oration on 16 October 1979, on a BBC television programme:

Question: What in the panel's opinion is now the greatest threat to the preservation of law and order in this country?
Anderton: This is a far-reaching and wide question and cannot be answered really in simple terms. My own personal view, quite frankly is this, that we are fast approaching a situation in this country where people are beginning to lose confidence in the ability of those in authority, those who have the job like me of preserving order, to do it effectively in the wider public interest. There are at work in the community today — and I say this quite openly — factions, political factions, whose designed end is to overthrow democracy as we know it. They are at work in the field of public order, in the industrial relations field, in politics in the truest sense. And I think from a police point of view that my task in the future, in the 10 to 15 years from now, the period during which I shall continue to serve, that basic crime as such, theft, burglary, even violent crime will not be the predominant police feature. What will be the matter of greatest concern to me will be the covert and ultimately overt attempt to overthrow democracy, to subvert the authority of the State, and in fact to involve themselves in acts of sedition designed to destroy our parliamentary system and the democratic government in this country.[39]

If this kind of situation is going to come about, we had better find out enough to deal with it in an informed way. And if by some hypothetical mischance, Chief Constable Anderton should be mistaken, or even raving mad, we had better find out enough about his anti-subversive operations to be able to keep a supervisory eye on them. Either way, such remarks are a clarion-call for less secrecy.

Telephone Tapping

I apologize for not leaving my name and address but I was forced to sign the OSA as a term of employment. I work in the main exchange for the telephone area and I used to wonder why (when I was young and naïve) a clerk from a distant office would phone in a couple of wiring coordinates (usually you are inundated with forms and paperwork) for you to connect up. It seemed very strange to me and one day I asked a wise old mentor why this was so, 'It's the Home Office lad', he said, 'They're tapping some poor bugger's phone.'[40]

As everyone knows their phones are liable to be tapped, this is a form of surveillance only useful against the careless and stupid — which all of us are liable to be at times. The British security services therefore make a considerable fetish of the need for absolute secrecy about phone tapping in the hope that this will encourage people to be foolish. They hope, one imagines, that either everyone will assume their phone is tapped continuously and thus be put to the inconvenience of leaving subversive messages in hollow trees; or else that wicked persons will suspect phone tapping is all a bluff and not bother to be discreet. From the point of view of a policeman, these considerations perhaps make a certain amount of sense.

But from any other point of view, it is hard to see how a supposedly democratic political process with all that implies by way of balance, countervailing opinion and consultation with the citizenry, could seriously produce in Britain for enactment by Parliament, such a grotesque law as this:

> If any person discloses any information relating to the obtaining of information by interception of telecommunications conversations ... he shall be guilty of an offence. It shall [not] be a defence ... to prove that before the time of the alleged offence, the information had been made available to the public ... (Maximum penalty two years imprisonment).

This was the proposition of the Protection of Information Bill, introduced in 1979, and mercifully dropped by an embarrassed government after the small print was pointed out to them. It would have meant total control by officials of every scrap of knowledge about telephone tapping. Considering that the knowledge we already possess shows an alarming discrepancy between the facts and what the government claims in public, this would be dangerous.

Telephone tapping is probably illegal if ordinary people do it.

The Post Office Act 1969 (S.77 Schedule 5) provides a defence for engineers doing what the government tells them. If the government does order a tapping on a ministerial warrant, the courts will not intervene, taking the view that government phone tapping is on a legal par with eating one's lunch; there is no law against doing it as often as you like, and that is that.

In 1957, after a privacy outcry because police intercepts about a barrister were passed to the Bar Council, a committee of Privy Councillors was set up to inquire into British tapping. Privy Councillors who take an oath of secrecy, are favourite candidates for such 'sensitive' work (although one might have hesitated to have entrusted too much of the nation's welfare to a committee of certain Privy Councillors of the past). The report of the Birkett committee[41] was, rather surprisingly, published by Harold Macmillan although the evidence it took was not. For 23 years, ministers, flourishing mildewed copies of the Report, refused to make themselves accountable, claiming its provisions were strictly adhered to. What holes have been cut in the veil of secrecy, suggest this is quite untrue. It is highly significant that Merlyn Rees, a Labour Home Secretary who prided himself on a sympathetic understanding of the needs of the security services and police, then moved to the view that all may not be well. In November 1979, during a tortuous speech on the Blunt affair, he told MPs:

> If I were Home Secretary ... I should also be considering separately, whether the time had come to examine the question of interception as Birkett did 20 years ago. I believe that that should be done as well. The best way is for this to be undertaken by a team from the Security Commission.[42]

From a man who had just spent several years nominally in charge of the Home Office and theoretically signing every warrant for a tap, this was headier stuff than it perhaps appears at first sight.

The Birkett Report made a number of confident statements. Telephones were tapped by three bodies, it said: the police; Customs and Excise; and the Security Services. This is perfectly true if one includes the army among the security services. It said that every application for a warrant was given 'personal consideration' and signed by the Home Secretary.

This was unlikely to have remained true even before the Home Office admitted in Spring 1980 how out of date Birkett had become. First, the quantity of surveillance increased greatly since 1957 both on serious crime, where police have focused on the idea of 'criminal intelligence' and on political subversion. The New Left, various forms of international terrorism and the dramatic revival of the IRA, pushed up the manning of the Special Branch six-fold over twenty years. A Home Secretary might be physically able to make inquiries on 242 warrants a year, the 1957 maximum figure Birkett gave. If he were to give say, ten minutes consideration to each, he could, by setting aside an hour a week, go through a batch of half a dozen. But it is hard to imagine him setting aside a whole afternoon a week, or even a full day. Estimates of 1,200-1,500 taps a year have been made, but there is no way to substantiate this figure. Ministers will not be drawn in public although there has been, at the time of writing, no denial that the five-storey centralized GPO tapping centre in Ebury Bridge Road, Chelsea, has a minimum simultaneous capacity of 1,000 lines, and sophisticated voice-recognition and computer print-out facilities, developed by GCHQ since the late 1960s.[43]

Secondly, when a rare provable case of tapping came to the High Court in 1979, of an antique dealer who said he was being unlawfully harassed, the police and the Home Office, refused to produce a signed warrant on the grounds of 'Crown privilege'. Nor would they produce directives issued to the police on the procedure for obtaining consent.

Finally, Chapman Pincher in his journalistic memoirs shared this scepticism:

> Statements in parliament have given the firm impression that no person's phone can be tapped without the written authority of the Home Secretary in the form of a warrant. This is misleading in the extreme. I have established, by questioning security officials who have obtained warrants, that the Home Secretary himself is rarely involved. He delegates the responsibility to one or more senior officials. Only when another minister, an MP or an important public figure is suspect does the Home Secretary himself have to sign the warrant.

The Birkett Report went on to say that only the Home Secretary or his stand-in did the signing. This cannot be true today. Any minister can legally authorize a warrant. MI6 will act through the Foreign Office if it wants to intercept domestic communications. The electronic activities of GCHQ Cheltenham, through the 'Composite Signals Organization' in Britain, will involve continuous domestic interception via either the Foreign Office or the Ministry of Defence. Successive Northern Ireland Secretaries authorize widespread phone tapping in Northern Ireland, under the name of an 'emergency' which has now lasted ten years. Army intelligence is unlikely to be self-denying either in this regard. So there is not one minister nominally in charge of tapping; there are at least four.

Birkett assured the public that the telephones of innocent citizens were never tapped, only those of suspected major criminals and suspected major Russian spies: 'Under the safeguards we have set out, the telephone of the ordinary law-abiding citizen would be quite immune, as it always has been.' Private conversations were sifted by 'carefully chosen' officials, the Report said; matters not strictly relevant to criminal investigation were destroyed, and the rest kept strictly secret. Only about six policemen had access to sifted material in a criminal investigation. Only two officers of MI5 were allowed to see a transcript, although material 'of security interest' was put on file for circulation.

None of this is true today. I will give one case from personal knowledge. In 1977, in Northern Ireland, a government information officer, Tommy Roberts, who recently died, got very drunk one day, and described to a respected British journalist the details of an embarrassing personal quarrel the journalist had had over the phone with a lover. The government is always tapping journalists' phones in Ireland, in the hope of catching them talking to members of the IRA, or in the hope of getting some hold over them. In 1972, it was alleged although not proved that police threatened a *Railway Gazette* employee with tapes of a sexually embarrassing phone conversation; the police were in pursuit of leaks of confidential documents, not about national security, but about railway closures. The authors of the Birkett Report would, one imagine, be shocked by such breaches.

Birkett quite failed to mention ways open to the security service and police of eavesdropping without either obtaining a warrant or queuing for a police vacancy. The 'printermeter' or 'tiger machine' will be attached to a phone informally by the Post Office, and it records all numbers dialled, though not the content of conversations. The other form of eavesdropping is to attach a 'bug' or to use the domestic phone as a 'combined tap and bug'. To set this up a man has to come round and pretend to mend the telephone, which is awkward; it will then function as a microphone and pick up all conversation in the room.

We can detect something of an argument behind one section of

Birkett. The Report published all telephone-tap statistics up to 1957, in a global fashion, showing that no more than 242 had ever been authorized in a year. But then it bowed to the displeased security men, and recommended quite irrationally that no one should ever repeat the exercise: 'It would greatly aid the operation of agencies hostile to the State if they were able to estimate even approximately the extent of interceptions of communications for security pruposes.' This illogicality is a reliable sign of the secrecy obsession. Birkett gave no reasons why criminal statistics, as distinct from security ones, should not be given every year, but they also continue to be kept secret. 'Agencies hostile to the State', which presumably meant the Russians, must have been able to guess approximately what was going on from Birkett's figures, unless they were deliberately misleading, in which case they could scarcely be reassuring to the public in any event. The 'useful to an enemy' argument is capable of infinite expansion. Just as one could argue that it is useful to an enemy to know the location of London, so one could argue it is useful to an enemy to know the number of MI5 men, or the number of Special Branch men, or the number of ordinary policemen in Britain. The Birkett Report was, in its way, a rare exercise in open government, but it was still capable of being infected by nonsense. The argument would look slightly more wholesome if it were stood on its head as a principle of open government: 'It would greatly aid the operations of citizens who are members, and indeed nominally controllers of the State, if they were able to estimate, even approximately, the extent of interceptions of communications for security purposes.' (In spring 1980, the Government released the statistics. 'Never again, however', they parrotted.)

The Report did make one definite recommendation towards openness. It was unable, it said, to see why the Home Office make a fetish of never introducing phone-tap evidence into Court, thus keeping the practice a total secret. The Home Office ignored this recommendation.

Thus, it was twenty years before anyone found the evidence to make a legal challenge to tapping; the police and the security services merely used tapping as an intelligence device, with some notion of not embarrassing the government. James Malone,[44] an antique dealer accused of handling offences, realised that a testifying detective had, contrary to his orders, put details of Malone's phone conversations in his notebook. Malone then claimed in the High Court that the practice was unlawful, and that he had been persecuted thus for years. The Vice-Chancellor Sir Robert Megarry saying the situation 'cries out for legislation', pronounced 'England is not a country where everything is forbidden except what is expressly permitted; it is a country where everything is permitted except what is expressly forbidden', which brought hollow laughter from all journalists who had ever clashed with the 'uncertain crime' of contempt of court. Because the warrant was not produced, no avenue was opened for any future citizen to try to discover if his phone was tapped.

This *laissez-faire* approach is, once again, probably in breach of the European Convention on Human Rights. The European Court does not allow governments to conduct secret inspections of their citizens as the mood takes them. In 1978, the Court professed itself satisfied with German supervisory arrangements for tapping.[45] The German parliament nominated five MPs to a control board. The board appointed a regulatory commission of three members to report to it. The system, said the Court 'may in the circumstances of the case be regarded as enjoying sufficient independence to give an objective ruling'.

The signatory countries did not 'enjoy an unlimited discretion to subject persons within their jurisdiction to secret surveillance', the Court said. In the name of the struggle against espionage and terrorism, they could not adopt what measures they pleased, because the Court was 'aware of the danger such a law poses of undermining or even destroying democracy on the ground of defending it'. Whatever system was adopted, had to provide 'adequate and effective guarantees against abuse'. The Court said: 'In a field where abuse is potentially so easy in individual cases and could have such harmful consequences for democratic society as a whole, it is in principle desirable to entrust supervisory control to a judge.'

Harold Wilson, much to the suspicion of some security men, 'peremptorily stopped' MI5's habit of tapping MPs phones when he came to power in 1964, and they were never tapped between then and 1970. This certainly removed the one possible source of public pressure about tapping during that period, but it did little for the rest of us.

The British citizen has no way of finding out if his phone has been tapped. If he should find out, he has no guarantees against abuse whatever, either through the courts or through Parliament. Non-elected officials have merely to persuade one of a group of ministers, who will never have to answer publicly for what they do, to accede to their wishes. Perhaps they can even act autonomously. A secret warrant arrives at the Post Office, and the Post Office employees, bound by the Official Secrets Act, do what they are told. It is a very pure form of bureaucratic Utopia; the official is kept invisible, and the citizen stripped naked.

Secret Propaganda

Looking at the spies and secret policemen, it is easy enough to see that a cloth of secrecy may disguise mistakes, incompetence, threats to civil rights, unaccountable power centres and unbalanced political attitudes. The history of the secret propaganda enterprises of the Foreign Office shows one or two further consequences of secrecy — bureaucratic immortality, and a poisoning of the wells of journalism.

As the Cold War began, Christopher Mayhew, a junior minister in the Labour Government persuaded Attlee and Bevin, the Foreign Secretary, to set up a propaganda department[46] which would convince foreigners and key domestic figures such as trade unionists, that the Russians were a menace and were telling a great many lies. These assertions were, in 1947, entirely correct, and counter-propaganda was an intelligent idea. The covering of its workings in secrecy was less intelligent.

Mayhew recognized the difficulty. On 6 December 1947, he sent an outline to Bevin, classified 'Top Secret' of the way he proposed to create a 'Communist Information Department in order to concoct the special material required for our publicity'. It was to concentrate on Europe, the Middle East and Asia, and attack Communism by promoting social democracy as a 'third force'. The worker's paradise of the USSR was to be presented as a 'gigantic hoax'.

Mayhew wrote,

> You will appreciate that one of the main dangers involved in the scheme proposed arises from the fact that as soon as the campaign is launched, we become officially responsible for a number of controversial anti-Communist and anti-capitalist statements put out by our publicity machine. From time to time, mistakes may be made and a statement may be put out which can be effectively refuted [and] seriously discredit the campaign in the early stages.

Mayhew's instinct was to be honest: 'proceed quietly at first, being careful to stick to the truth, and to balance anti-Communist with anti-capitalist arguments, so as to reassure the Parliamentary Labour Party'.

But the road of secrecy was taken instead. By the following July, Mayhew was reporting that 'the new Information Research Department is now turning out a fairly steady stream of anti-Communist propaganda material'. IRD material was not only being sent out to overseas embassies, but was in a 'discreet and personal' way being peddled to trade unionists via Transport House, the Labour Party headquarters. Plans were afoot for covert subsidy of an anti-Communist trade union newsletter. A memo to Bevin marked 'Secret' of 6 January 1949 said of the newsletter:

> It would have been strictly non-official, but at the same time a good deal of material would have come from us and we would have assisted in its translation and distribution through our information services. We would not give it direct financial assistance, but had worked out an arrangement for purchases of the newsletters on a scale and at a price sufficient to guarantee its financial soundness.

Mayhew still wanted to go public. On 14 April 1949 he was explaining an ambitious plan to Bevin (memo marked 'Secret' of 14 April 1949) for the worldwide sale of millions of copies of an anti-Communist booklet:

> To achieve this circulation it will be necessary to acknowledge the Foreign Office origin of this booklet, and thus acknowledge the fact that the Foreign Office is conducting a regular campaign of anti-Communist propaganda — a fact which, miraculously enough, is still not publicly known. The step would be an unusual one, but we are living in most unusual times and I would recommend we face up to a certain amount of political and diplomatic fuss and go ahead.

But it was too late, IRD was set on a secret course which it was to follow for 30 years. It was too late in another respect. Mayhew had wished on him by a ministerial colleague Hector MacNeil, the services of a young diplomat whom he sacked after two months for being 'dirty, drunk and idle'. It is hardly likely that Guy Burgess, the diplomat in question, was too idle to tell the Russians, by whom he was employed, exactly what IRD was engaged in. Over the years, as IRD grew bigger and bigger — with the CIA joining in the propaganda war and IRD men scattered across embassies of the globe subsidizing, bribing and broadcasting — they were merely deceiving people who read books and newspapers (and sometimes those who actually wrote for them) about what was going on in the world.

The CIA, which had a great deal of money, was uninhibited in its work. It is now clear that it was barely possible to move in the 1960s and early 1970s without stumbling across a CIA-sponsored research foundation, publishing house, news agency, radio station or individual journalist. Marchetti notes that, as the CIA moved from 'grey propaganda' (which is merely slanted) into 'black' untruths, native American researchers and scholars were solemnly compiling accounts of foreign affairs based on false stories 'planted' in complaisant overseas newspapers.[47] There was no way of stopping the process, and it was rationalized as part of the general contribution to blackening the image of Communism, *ipso facto* a good thing.

Had IRD gone public, the risk to national security would have been nil. The risk to national interests, in so far at least as the Russians would have been alerted, would have been inconsiderable. From 'two or three devillers', IRD swelled into a body whose Soviet section alone had more than 60 members. Even in its declining days it occupied a 12-storey tower-block on Millbank, Riverwalk House, and spent around £1 million a year. It took a full 30 years for IRD, shielded from public scrutiny and bending carefully to the bureaucratic winds, to be closed down as secretively as it had been launched.

IRD also became an instrument of news management among British journalists. From its own point of view, there was no such thing as objective journalism — only propaganda. A typical IRD operation would be to comb the Eastern bloc press for stories about drunkenness, and work them into a feature implying that Communists were so miserable that they all became alcoholics. It was then up to overseas IRD men to get the story into a local paper, no matter how. At the same time, IRD became by the very nature of its operations, a large reservoir of interesting factual material about, first the Russians, and eventually the Irish and any country the British or Americans wanted to influence. They approached British journalists discreetly, suggesting they had special intelligence material and were prepared to make it available to such fine persons as the journalists in question. They were rather a hush-hush research department, so the material could not be seen to be traced back to them ...

The effect of this offer of a special relationship was pernicious. Of the 60 or so newspaper, television and BBC and radio journalists on the IRD mailing-list in 1977, some were knowing conduits for intelligence material and committed cold warriors. Some were bright enough to see very well the dangers of Foreign Office unattributable material, but supped with a cautiously long spoon. After all, they were scarcely equipped to read the Albanian press or obscure Soviet military journals for themselves. And some were deceived. When I proposed to print an analysis of the rise and fall of IRD in the *Guardian,* one distinguished journalist flatly refused to believe that her valuable data-bank was a deliberate propaganda operation. Only when I showed her Foreign Office documents that put it beyond doubt, did she fall silent.

Like all Foreign Office dealings with journalists, the relationships established by IRD were essentially manipulative. If journalists wrote or behaved in a way that displeased them or did not accord with what were taken to be the aims of HMG, all 'help' was withdrawn. Conversely, detailed information was showered on 'anti-Communist' writers, and it was the presence of so many of these on IRD's mailing-list that was eventually to prove their undoing *post détente,* post-Watergate, with the 1974-9 Labour Government.

The apparatus of secrecy was, in the absence of any real question of national security, merely a structure of petty mendacity. The name, 'Information Research Department', was a thin cover, because the Foreign Office lists also described a genuine research department, and genuine information departments. Employees were briefed on the 'need to know' principle, and ordered not to disclose even to other Foreign Office staff the identity of their department. Memos to the staff were stamped 'Secret' — the second highest security classification signifying a danger of serious injury to the nation. Regular propaganda material was sent in plain envelopes to the private homes of journalists, and correspondence from the Foreign Office came marked 'Personal' with no title or departmental heading but merely a telephone number. One circular, from Ray Whitney, then head of IRD and later to become a Conservative MP, said of 'the understanding on which we send you these papers':

They are prepared in the Foreign and Commonwealth Office primarily for members of the Diplomatic Service, but we are allowed to give them on a personal basis to a few people outside the services who might find them of interest. While the material they contain may be freely used, they are not statements of official policy and should not be attributed to HMG, nor should the titles themselves be quoted in discussion or in print. The papers should not be shown to anyone else and they should be destroyed when no longer needed.

The material that was mailed carried no identifying marks of origin. It included elaborate lists of 'Communist Front organizations', a thick manual prepared in 1972 and up-dated thereafter on the aims, policy and tactics of the IRA with potted biographies of IRA personalities, and regular background briefs on such topics as *détente:* 'Communist leaders evidently do not see the pursuit of international *détente* as imposing any constraint on their aim of imposing world revolution, though they remain determined to insulate their own people against non-Communist political ideas' or China: 'The African continent is the main focus of China's interest in the developing world and the recipient of most of her foreign aid'; or the Indian Ocean: 'Since early 1972, regular Soviet use has been made of Berbera's alongside berths for maintenance, replenishment and harbour training'.

In 1971, the then Permanent Secretary, Sir Denis Greenhill, pruned IRD ruthlessly. Its money from the Secret Vote and the CIA, and its freelance attitudes made it a target for bureaucratic hostility — although this was plainly a much less dangerous enemy than scrutiny by Parliament. It became less exclusively anti-Communist, but instead a more wide-ranging covert propaganda arm of British government — a faintly questionable idea. In 1976, another reforming official, Sir Michael Palliser, brought the former Canadian High Commissioner, Sir Colin Crowe, out of retirement to conduct a secret inquiry. This was shortly before the 'Think Tank' toured the Foreign Office, looking for economies. As outsiders, they were the victims of some battening down of hatches by IRD. Only two 'safe' members of the team were allowed into the department, and IRD staff were warned that other members of the 'Think Tank' were not to be given 'sensitive' information.

Sir Colin proposed a study of 'a more coordinated and focused information/propaganda effort'. IRD overseas offices should be scrapped, 'individual operations, publications and distribution lists should be kept under regular scrutiny', and the department's venerable anti-Communist terms of reference should be rewritten. This meant that IRD was to be inspected a second time under Labour ministers who had already insisted on the removal of the more notoriously right-wing of IRD's journalistic clients.

At the end of 1977, under David Owen, the whole operation was closed down as a clandestine agency. Many of its staff were pensioned off and a new integrated department, called just as enigmatically, the Overseas Information Department, was inaugurated. It was supposed to be much smaller, not so secret and not engaged in domestic propaganda. Owen announced that as his contribution to open government, the series of background analyses produced by OID, and other Foreign Office research papers would be made available to all journalists and members of the public. Typically, the Foreign Office resisted the idea, proposed by Owen's political adviser, that journalists who had disclosed IRD's history should be invited to the press conference to announce these developments. It preferred to deal with the house-trained diplomatic correspondents.

It was difficult, naturally, to announce the closure of IRD as such in Parliament. (Perhaps not impossible, but it would have raised a semantic difficulty or two.) After the history of IRD was disclosed in the *Guardian,* the Foreign Office gave Evan Luard, the junior minister, the following brief to answer a parliamentary question demanding when and why IRD had closed: 'The operation of the Information Research Department was terminated on 30 April 1977, as a result of a reorganization of the FCO information departments undertaken for both policy and economy reasons.' That may have been uninformative; but it is even more interesting to compare the public answer given by the Foreign Office about IRD's duties, with the internal document proposing to water them down. The first document is the 'written answer' distributed to journalists at the House of Commons. The second is a Foreign Office internal memorandum, dated 6 August 1976, and itself written in a guarded and emollient Whitehall jargon. The first document means nothing whatever, the second has a relationship of sorts to the truth. The first document is for public information. The second constitutes a State secret.

1 February 1978
Mr Neil Kinnock (Bedwellty): To ask the Secretary of State for Foreign and Commonwealth Affairs, what were the precise

terms of reference of the Information Research Department of his department in 1975 and 1976 in relation to journalists and broadcasters writing and broadcasting in the United Kingdom.

NO. W27

Mr Evan Luard

The terms of reference of Information Research Department in 1975/76 were:

'Responsibility for the compilation of information reports for Her Majesty's Missions abroad'

Background papers were produced by the Department for the use of our missions overseas, but copies were also sent to a number of interested people in the United Kingdom including some journalists and broadcasters.

SECRET

ANNEX

REVISED TERMS OF REFERENCE FOR IRD
PROPOSED BY SIR C CROWE

IRD provides the unattributable element of HMG's information effort in support of British foreign policy. It has a positive role, in common and in coordination with the information programme as a whole, to influence decisions being taken abroad in matters affecting our economic, defence and political interests and to persuade international opinion of our case where specifically British interests are at stake, e.g. Northern Ireland, Southern Africa, or in bilateral disputes to which the UK is one of the parties. Its major role however is defensive, exposing and countering of threats both to the home base, the UK, coming from abroad, and to the interests of our allies and alliances, notably the EEC and NATO. This defensive role carries with it the capacity to counter-attack, to counter activities which damage British interests abroad or hamper the acceptance of HMG's foreign policy.

SECRET

The Government Underground

In 1978, two Conservative MPs, Robin Hodgson and Robert Banks, complained in a booklet that governments had been gambling since 1968 that civil defence could be reorganized in a crisis. Quoting military estimates that 36 million people would survive a 200-megaton strike if adequately warned, but only 20 million otherwise, they said civil defence planning 'is an ill-coordinated shambles surrounded by a fog of secrecy, largely ministerially imposed'.[48]

Among its more expensive secret activities, the British Civil Service under successive ministers has in fact, over the last 40 years, seen to the construction of a series of 'hardened' tunnels, command posts and bunkers, to be used in conjunction with an increasingly sophisticated emergency system of regional civil-military government.

The rationale both for the activity and the secrecy surrounding it, has been that the Russians are coming. The Russians have not yet come, and the whole of this area of military preparedness is a thorny one which ought to be openly discussed. Instead we have seen in the last generation some sporadic whistleblowing and some appreciable public unease. On a purely practical level, it would affect one's personal attitude towards the Third World War considerably to know whether there was a good chance of surviving it, or whether as the radioactive dust settled, troops of Permanent Secretaries, Chief Constables, minor members of the Royal Family and lady traffic wardens were going to emerge from holes in the ground, as lonely monarchs of all they surveyed.

Moreover, there is no opportunity to discuss whether all this digging in is leading us in the direction of a police state. The lines appear to be blurred between the emergency brought about by a Soviet military attack, and the more probable future civil emergency caused by a prolonged strike or social upheaval. Say the army grew tired of sitting in Northern Ireland watching the antics of irresponsible left-wing governments. A very different group, the 1944 German military conspirators, planned to use the existing emergency systems to take over Germany, after assassinating Hitler. A variant of this anxiety is found in the suspicion among radical left-wing groups that a popular revolution is now technically impossible. The apparatus of the State has become physically invulnerable. But the question is really one for all of us who value democracy; if the machine of government is truly impregnable, then we only vote and change administrations by courtesy of the administrators. They might simply stop cooperating one day, retire into the bunkers and start governing by decree. Where is the Bastille we would be forced to storm? Three hundred feet underground on Salisbury plain? The basement of the Department of the Environment in Marsham Street?

The atmosphere of secrecy starts with the newspapers. D-notice No. 8, still extant, is headed 'National Defence — War Precautions and Civil Defence'. It reads:

> The purpose of this notice is to safeguard a number of key buildings, structures and installations which are essential to national defence. Most of them are below ground, and have a peacetime use from which it may be possible to deduce their wartime function; nevertheless it would be damaging to our national interest to disclose their defence purpose, to publish details of their precise location, structural details, approaches or identifiable surface work.
>
> The buildings, structures and installations fall broadly into the following categories:
>
> a) underground installations for the storage and movement of emergency reserves of oil;
>
> b) sites of headquarters or communications centres of government above local authority level in time of war;
>
> c) underground cables or other communications equipment intended for emergency use;
>
> d) underground flood-gates that are not in public view on the London underground railways.
>
> You are also requested not to identify or publish the purpose of the Mobile Emergency Control of Railways or of the buildings or sites earmarked for the Emergency National Grid Control Centre or the NATO Wartime Civil Agencies for Oil and Shipping; or the capacity of any non-commercial oil storages or pipelines.
>
> This notice will have particular application when the subjects of war precautions and civil defence are under consideration. Much has already been written about these subjects, so it would be easy to assume that little or no security interest was at stake; in all cases of doubt, or when no official release of information has been made, you are requested to seek advice through the Secretary of the Committee.[49]

It is not the purpose of this book to try to tease out the network of government citadels under London and around the countryside, or the exact tracery of official emergency planning. For those who want to try their hand at the guesswork, three useful whistleblowing books are available: *Beneath the City Streets,* by a technical journalist, Peter Laurie; *The Political Police in Britain* by Tony Bunyan and *Review of Security and the State,* by State Research.[50] What becomes clear in all of them is the sheer intricacy of the planning, physical and institutional, which has built up since the events of the General Strike and the Second World War, and the difficulty of making sense of it in the face of a denial of information by the government. The first chief periods of building seem to have been in the early 1950s, at the height of the Cold War, when telephone exchanges, communications tunnels and bunkers were constructed under London to withstand atom bombs, which had been recently acquired by the Russians. Laurie estimates the cost at between £9 and £18 million at 1953 prices — out of about £100 million spent in those four years on civil defence overall. Of the Kingsway telephone exchange built under Chancery Lane tube station in 1950, which he was many years later allowed to inspect, Laurie remarks, awestruck:

> Kingsway has its own artesian well and reserves of fuel and food to allow it to function in complete isolation for more than six weeks. It is entered through an inconspicuous door in High Holborn. Its size — to walk round it all takes at least an hour and a half — its cleanliness, order and quietness, are an impressive testimony to the government's determination to protect itself. It is also extraordinary to think that this bright busy world of technicians lay almost unsuspected beneath one of London's busiest streets for more than a quarter of a century. If the government can hide this from us, it is plain it can hide almost anything.[51]

In the early 1960s with the advent of the H-bomb, somewhere between 50 to 100 rural bunkers were excavated — one estimate of the cost is £1,400 million — to provide a system of parallel military-civilian regional commands, and subregional controls (known then as Regional Seats of Government). They are probably linked by the GPO's conspicuous microwave towers among other means of telecommunications. Military, civil defence and ordinary civilian communications systems are all part of the same national system, the one buried in the fibres of the other. Because telecommunications are so important, the Post Office is a key arm of government, and the Official Secrets Acts are rigorously applied to GPO engineers. In 1963 the Campaign for Nuclear Disarmament ran into a government determined to keep its secrets. Although demonstrations at nuclear air bases were smartly dealt with by taking the Official Secrets Act spying clauses and announcing that they also applied to 'sabotage', the Regional Seats of Government were exposed. A group called Spies for Peace named 13 sites, and newspapers breached the D-notices to report a demonstration at one, Warren Row (which has since been vacated).

The genuinely awkward clash between civilian interests and those of the State was obvious enough; people are likely to be mutinous if they know that an imminent nuclear war will leave them unprotected — but on the other hand, unless the government is in a position to show the Russians it can survive a strike and launch a retaliatory one, it is not doing its best to minimize the danger of the war actually happening.

The government has abandoned any systematic expenditure on shelters and civil defence since the late 1960s when nuclear stalemate was accepted. The Heath administration of 1970-4 changed tack, beset as it was by strikes and preoccupied with internal security. It launched training for local councillors at the Home Office Home Defence College in York, and local authorities (who constitute the civilian unit below subregional controls) have composed their own contingency plans. These moves demonstrate a certain deliberate confusion between wartime problems (withdrawing emergency services from target areas and waiting for the fall-out to die down) and peacetime issues (strikes, insurrections, revolution, floods or plagues of frogs).

Home Office Circular ES/1/72 issued on 22 March 1972 from the Emergency Services division of the Home Office remarked: 'It is considered there is much common ground between war planning and the preparations required for, and the organization appropriate to, a major peacetime emergency or natural disaster. Accordingly there are many advantages in creating a closer relationship than hitherto in local planning for different emergencies of peace and war.' What this meant in plain English was that 'civil defence' was no longer to emphasize the protection and rescue of the citizenry (the idea being a waste of time); it was to concentrate on the continued successful government and control of those still available to be governed. This was not a policy of civil defence, but of internal security. To emphasize it, the same circular asked each council to nominate an emergency HQ 'irrespective of the degree of protection' against nuclear attack. One can argue as devil's advocate that this assertion is simply logical — either a city is not bombed, in which case the HQ will be useful, or it is bombed, in which case even a protected HQ would not survive, or would only survive surrounded by contaminated devastation and might as well simply be bypassed from the beginning in favour of the subregional control excavated out in the countryside. The whole issue would be interesting to have debated in public, rather than have secretly decided by the Home Office, because one can also argue that these decisions represented an unacknowledged scheme to nullify strikes, disguised as a 'civil defence'.

For our purposes, what is relevant are four levels of perceivable secrecy about 'emergencies'. First there is the pompous or furtive attitude of municipal officials towards what they suspect are stimulating documents. As David Chambers, a Nottinghamshire County Councillor wrote in complaint to *The Times* in November 1979: 'I have attended the Home Defence College course for councillors. In chairing the final session of the course with members from all over the UK, I was astounded at the different classifications given to their authorities' contingency plans. While I had our *published* booklet from Notts., some councillors had experienced great difficulty in seeing theirs and many were overprinted "Top Secret".'

Secondly, there is a relaxed attitude by central government to the material it puts in front of local authorities. The councillors are urged to restrict the circulation of their course documents at York, but this is the merest reflex action by the Home Office, equivalent in normal society to yelling at the top of one's voice. Clearly the Home Office does not mind the non-mandarin world knowing, for example, that one of its schemes provides 'during a peacetime emergency' for the elegant 'Post Office Telephone Preference System'. Under this, only people 'necessary to maintain the life of the community in a peacetime emergency' will be able to make telephone calls in and out. Everyone else ('Category 3') will only be able to receive incoming calls — presumably from the important persons in Categories 1 and 2. That the government can thus silence its citizens at a stroke gives it an awesome air of invulnerability to subversives, which is no doubt gratifying to civil servants. In an open society, one might be able to enquire precisely what peacetime emergencies the Home Office have in mind that require the commandeering of most phone lines in the country. A war, when trunk cabling would be switched to military use, is a different matter. Who would take the decision to pull out the plugs in peacetime — the Prime Minister? The Cabinet Secretary? The Civil Contingencies Committee of the Cabinet? The House of Commons? How do you get your name on the Category 2 list? Could you still get the Speaking Clock? The questions are so fascinating that one half wishes we were not tormented by these unexplained gifts of information. (The Speaking Clock lines are actually taken over only in case of imminent nuclear attack, when they carry signals to activate the wartime sirens in police stations — a system installed for £4 million in the early 1960s and maintained at an annual cost of £1 million.)[52]

The available material does gesture at a third category of information — that which the Home Office finds genuinely rather sensitive. The York notes say, for example:

> The main problems of law and order as foreseen at present are (a) to provide a force numerically adequate to deal with the additional tasks arising in war. (b) to be able effectively to keep the law in the best possible democratic way consistent with post-attack conditions. Some modification of the penal code might well be called for. (c) to be able to exercise justice in a practical and equitable way. Plans do exist to provide for these problems, but for obvious reasons are classified.

One is struck by the phrase 'obvious reasons'. What does it mean? It may be a reference to the plans which existed for the post-holocaust police in 1967, where heavy emphasis was laid on the need to round up 'potentially subversive people'. It may merely be a sensitivity to the public discussion of firing-squads for looters.

The fourth tier of secrecy is the genuinely important one — the location of all the Regional Seats of Government; the estimates of postwar damage under different scenarios; the precise peacetime contingencies under which particular aspects of the plans come into play; the lists of who is to be arrested and who is to be sheltered; the strategic policy considerations which motivate the whole exercise; the alternative policy options which were considered but discarded. And, if one is to end this list rhetorically, disclosure of which is considered the greater danger — Russian saboteurs or some of us.

The ABC Affair

Whistleblowing on the American pattern was something which the British secret world tried to stop in the late 1970s. In the process it demonstrated admirably what a discreditable impression it was capable of giving of itself. Confronted with rule-breakers — chaps who simply wouldn't play the game — the extravagant legal resources of the British authorities proved to be limited by political reality. In 1978, at the end of what came to be known as the ABC affair, the groups concerned with secret activity in the MOD-FO-Home Office-Cabinet Office complex, had the following achievements behind them.

Three people had been kept out of or removed from Britain, with the impression given that they were more or less traitors in the pay of international Communism. The first was Winslow Peck, a former analyst with the National Security Agency, who had supplied information about the radio surveillance empire of the NSA to a London radical magazine, *Time Out*. He was held at Heathrow airport on arrival in June 1976, and refused entry under the 1971 Immigration Act on the grounds that his presence was not 'in the national interest'.

The second was a young American journalist, Mark Hosenball, the son of a middle-class family, who wrote for *Time Out* throughout 1974 and 1975 when the magazine occupied itself naming members of the large CIA station in London, describing in detail the operations of the British SIGINT organization, and exposing the CIA connections of Forum World Features, a London news agency supplying material to Third World newspapers. He was deported at the request of MI5 by the Labour Home Secretary, Merlyn Rees, under the 1971 Immigration Act for 'obtaining for publication information harmful to the UK, including information prejudicial to the safety of servants of the Crown'.[53] This unexplained reference may have meant that his work with ex-CIA whistleblowers was enabling him to name British agents — an activity as likely to sterilize them on the payroll as to lead to their deaths. Hosenball returned to New York, his career as a professional journalist improved if anything by his brief notoriety.

Third was Phillip Agee, a former CIA agent whose Latin American experiences appeared not only to have disillusioned him but infected him with socialism. He spent four years writing an exposé of the CIA, completing it in London in 1974 and vowing to continue his efforts to disrupt Britain's senior partner: 'If it is successful, I shall be able to support other current and former CIA employees who want to describe their experiences and to open more windows on this activity.'[54] He used London as a base for his crusade, and in September 1976 went to Jamaica where he announced that a classic 'destabilization' campaign was being waged against the Social Democrat Prime Minister Michael Manley. He named seven CIA agents at the US Embassy. There is no doubt that, as a former British colony, Jamaica remains in the sphere of influence of M16. Were such operations with secret agents taking place, MI6 was certainly involved, and could therefore present Agee to ministers as a threat to specifically British interests. (Britain could scarcely be seen to harass people merely at the behest of the CIA. It would be shaming.)

Rees deported Agee and Hosenball together, quoting from his brief that Agee, 'maintained regular contacts harmful to the security of the UK' and 'continues to be involved in disseminating information harmful to the UK' and, 'has aided and counselled others in obtaining information for publication which could be harmful to the security of the UK'. Agee eventually went to Germany and settled down to continue working with radical groups in Hamburg; the deportation probably hampered his activities a good deal. In 1980, the United States withdrew his passport as well.

In Britain itself, one junior whistleblowing soldier and two more left-wing journalists were prosecuted. Two more radical magazines, *The Leveller* and *Peace News* were prosecuted along with the magazine of the National Union of Journalists, for naming military personnel.

Duncan Campbell, an Oxford physics graduate, was the son of a Presbyterian economics professor and a mathematician mother (who monitored German transmissions during the war from Special Communications Unit No. 3 near Bletchley — one of SIGINT's precursors). He brought to journalism an unusually dangerous scientific background; it was not necessary for him to seek out dependent relationships with Whitehall news managers, because he already knew something of what he was talking about. He contributed to *New Scientist* and the *Sunday Times*.

Campbell wrote a great deal of the article on SIGINT which appeared in *Time Out*. He had a flat in Brighton stacked high with photographs and files on the telephone, radar, radio and signals systems which intrigued him — much of it culled from technical journals and manufacturers' literature. His association with *Time Out* led theatrically to the dock of No. 1 Court at the Old Bailey when Agee's supporters overreached themselves. They had set up a defence committee to protest at the Agee-Hosenball deportations, which MI5 immediately put under surveillance (as later events demonstrated).

Campbell was arrested by the Special Branch after he inescapably breached the Official Secrets Act by talking to an ex-soldier during the defence campaign. His flat was ransacked and the Attorney-General was persuaded to sanction charges of: (a) spying by collecting secret information in his research as a journalist; (b) spying by interviewing the ex-soldier about his work in SIGINT, and (c) breaking the catch-all Section 2 provision of the Official Secrets Act, by listening to a disclosure of official information. The first charge, fascinating in its implication that journalism was the same as espionage, was dropped halfway through the trial after it became clear that much of the supposedly 'Top Secret' material was publicly available, or selectively passed to other journalists in an unattributable way. The second charge was thrown out by the judge on the grounds that Campbell was not a spy and it was 'oppressive'. On the catch-all charge that remained, Campbell was duly convicted, and discharged without punishment by the judge. Had he accepted hints to plead guilty to the final technical charge, he could probably have also avoided an order to make a contribution to legal costs of almost £5,000. The uproar brought him the offer of a staff job on the *New Statesman* and a reputation as a minor hero.

A second young journalist, Crispin Aubrey, also worked for *Time Out;* arranged for Campbell's assistance in interviewing the soldier who wished to talk about SIGINT; naïvely furnished the Special Branch with evidence of the conversation by using a tape-recorder he had been given as a Christmas present; and was arrested alongside Campbell. He too was charged with journalism in so far as (a) he committed an act preparatory to spying by making an appointment; (b) he abetted Duncan Campbell's spying (or interviewing), and (c) he broke the catch-all regulations by preparing and abetting a disclosure of official information. He too, saw the spying charges dropped, was duly convicted on the technical charge and sent home without punishment on a conditional discharge. He was ordered to find costs amounting to £12,000; he came from a fairly affluent middle-class background. Aubrey peacefully resumed his career as a reporter.

A third journalist, Peter Laurie, again with a mathematical background, was caught up in the attempts to silence whistleblowers. Laurie, now Editor of *Practical Computing,* was revising a reprint of his 1969 book, *Beneath the City Streets,* which broke original ground by trying to trace buried government citadels and communications systems. Much of his research was similar to

Campbell's; indeed they were cooperating. The book derives from the application of intelligence to public sources — putting together all the bits and pieces available from officials, technical journals, from the telephone directory, from foreign parallels and from walking around fields and installations.

The arrest of Aubrey and Campbell alarmed Laurie's publishers, Hutchinson. The manuscript was submitted to the secretary of the D-notice Committee, Rear-Admiral Kenneth Farnhill. Farnhill, taking counsel from his Whitehall mentors, who were in a high state of excitement about the Campbell affair, implied they were unhappy. He could not say it contravened D-notices to republish the book (the D-notice system accepts that once something has been printed, at least in Britain, it is in the public domain). But 'he had to point out that some parts might be useful to terrorists, and he would ask that we consider whether publication were advisable in the national interest'.

Hutchinson dropped the book. Laurie says: 'It would be easy to be bitter, but one must remember that publishers exist to make a profit, and a book like this although of great interest to the author and *aficionados* of the subject, is a marginal affair in publishing terms, not worth the odium of an Official Secrets Act prosecution.'

This is an exact demonstration of the epidemic nature of secrecy in Britain. All the laws bearing on information are so wide — libel, contempt, official secrets — that they are unpredictable. One has to try to elicit an attitude from the authorities, about what is thought 'acceptable' and what undesirable at a particular moment. A word, a gesture, a frown at the right juncture and it simply ceases to be worthwhile to risk publication. Books do not appear, newspaper articles are spiked, distributors do not care to handle a magazine. No single book or article is that important after all ... There are more ways of killing a cat than dragging it through the courts in an expensive and possibly embarrassing prosecution. This is why protestations from Whitehall that there are very few actual trials under the Official Secrets Act deserve to be treated with contempt. The number of court cases is of no significance.

Laurie was someone who failed to subside. He decided to publish the book himself, and resubmitted the new parts to Farnhill. By now Campbell had been committed for trial on the novel charge of collecting available information about defence communications, for a purpose 'prejudicial to the safety or interests of the State' and which could be helpful to an enemy. Farnhill, obviously in some difficulty, said the book did in fact contravene D-notices; that it raised questions about the whole scope of the Official Secrets Act; that Laurie should look to the outcome of the ABC trial; and that 28 pages contained offensive material which he could not further specify.

Laurie attempted to get a ruling as to whether his publishing plans constituted an illegal act or not. The police would not help, the Metropolitan Commissioner replying: 'It is not part of the duties of the Commissioner of Police to judge in advance whether the publication of any material would be a criminal offence.' The Home Secretary did not reply. The Ministry of Defence inspected the manuscript. They took two months. Then they replied that they could not suggest specific amendments:

> The fact is that the new material which you have researched is in a category, Defence Communications, where for security reasons neither the Defence Secretary nor any other ministers can confirm or deny its accuracy or give any measure of clearance for its publication. But there is no doubt that information of this sort would be of great assistance to any enemy.

The Attorney-General's office endorsed this form of words, with its veiled hint at possible prosecution.

Knowing the mental habits of civil servants, it is perfectly possible that they feared Laurie was engaged in a plot of some kind to tease public statements about SIGINT from them. Once the D-notice system has broken down, there is simply no basis of trust available on which to whisper, 'This is OK old boy, but that isn't.' Laurie asserted he merely wished to get his book published, without helping terrorists do his country harm: 'By threatening prosecution for unauthorized disclosure of what journalists know already, while refusing to say what may or may not be said, the government makes it in effect dangerous to write anything that is not a handout from a Ministry', he complained.

Eventually, the 'collection' charges against Campbell collapsed, and Laurie informed the Ministry he intended to go ahead and publish, removing only those sections about specific SIGINT and defence microwave link sites which he thought might 'damage national security'. The new edition of the book was published (by Granada), without government comment. It received slightly more attention than it would have done in the absence of the ABC affair.

The seventh person caught up in this drive against

whistleblowing was an ex-corporal of signals, John Berry who seven years previously had been one of 1,000 men on Cyprus for SIGINT. He had sat behind a receiver, eavesdropping on Iraqi transmissions. Since leaving the Army, he had become a rather left-wing social worker and he took a dim view of his former employers:

> Both the extent of intelligence activities of this nature and the resources which the British government deploys in this area are largely unknown to the public. The fact that they remain unknown is due in no small measure to the considerable pressure placed on people who have or have had access to the facts. It appears to me that secrecy is one of the most important keys to power and the existence of an organization spending vast sums of money in the total absence of public control should do much to dispel any illusions about the democratic nature of our government.

This idealistic letter was written to the Agee-Hosenball defence committee, who were, of course being watched by MI5. Berry was arrested, held in prison, and had some difficulty in obtaining bail. The fruits of his three-hour conversation with Aubrey and Campbell, describing all he could remember about his SIGINT duties, was later described by the trial judge as stale, relatively low-level, but still of potential value to an enemy. It was described by the security authorities (who had already obtained from the Home Secretary the deportations of Agee and Hosenball) in a different fashion (they were seeking to persuade the Labour Attorney-General Sam Silkin of the need to bring spying charges against all three):

> Mr Berry was a former soldier from a unit with very high security characteristics, who had solemnly undertaken never to reveal the work he had been doing, either while in the service or after leaving it. The advice which I was given was that any breach of those undertakings could do damage, ranging from serious to exceptionally grave to the national security.[55]

Berry was charged with spying by passing on information to the two journalists and, under the catch-all Section 2, of making an unauthorized disclosure of official information. The spying charge, like the others, was thrown out by the judge, who instructed the jury to convict on the catch-all charge, of which Berry was plainly guilty. Mr Justice Mars-Jones sent him home with a suspended six-month sentence. Berry kept his social worker's job and asserted later: 'We have won a battle and the war will go on. The ABC trial has marginally exposed the secret State within the State. There were powerful agencies behind this prosecution and they are not responsible to anyone.' He had spent a week or two in prison, and an uneasy 18 months facing the prospect of receiving a sentence of up to 14 years. He also achieved a platform of sorts to declare from the witness-box a view which may have been at the root of Whitehall's difficulties in the whole affair: 'No one can classify my mind.'

The security services for their part achieved the satisfaction of hearing the judge announce, by way of an official moral: 'We will not tolerate defectors or whistleblowers from our intelligence services, who seek the assistance of the press or other media to publicize secrets, whatever the motive.' The sentences however, had been pointedly derisory.

This then is a list of official achievements in the two-year affair: a London nucleus of disaffected intelligence men and sympathetic journalists was temporarily scattered and, to an extremely limited extent, made to suffer. The price paid by Whitehall was high. For deporting Agee and Hosenball while refusing to produce the evidence against them — it may have been from informers, or bugs, or even falsehoods — the Labour Home Secretary Merlyn Rees faced a hail of parliamentary criticism, to which he could only reply, 'You must trust me.' The experience was an unpleasant one for him, and badly dented his political credit.

The Attorney-General, Sam Silkin, faced even harsher criticism for sanctioning the ABC prosecutions at the urging of the security-intelligence complex. His reputation was assailed and he was held responsible for an expensive fiasco; held guilty of political hypocrisy over the Official Secrets Acts themselves; held himself to be the secret inventor of the sinister practice of jury-vetting. (Jury-vetting came to light in a sensational way during the (trial.)

The security services themselves were somewhat discredited in the eyes of the public. Silkin's decision to drop the 'collection' charge and Mr Justice Mars-Jones's decision to throw out all the remaining spy charges made it appear that the defence complaint of a 'bogus veil of secrecy' was entirely justified. Although the conversation at issue was dramatically played over *in camera,* the ploy of putting up a SIGINT colonel, Hugh Johnstone, to testify anonymously about the vital necessity of total secrecy, was to misfire in a ludicrous fashion. Colonel Johnstone was not apparently still active in place; the Crown refused to present their first choice of signals commander, 'Col A', as a witness, if his name was to be given to the defence. They produced Colonel Johnstone instead, but insisted he publicly testify at committal proceedings, as 'Colonel B'. *Peace News, The Leveller* and *The Journalist* coolly named him, and were charged with contempt of court. A group of undeferential MPs then again named him under parliamentary privilege, provoking a minor constitutional crisis. The DPP appeared to think the other newspapers should not report what the MPs said. But this was to stretch the elastic attitudes of Fleet Street to breaking point. His name was printed everywhere. There was a brief fashion for label badges saying 'H.A. Johnstone'. The three original journalistic culprits were fined by the Lord Chief Justice, Lord Widgery, but acquitted on appeal to the House of Lords, thus knocking a small hole in the archaic law of contempt. Col. Johnstone was then allowed by his superiors to testify under his own name, like everyone else, at the opening of the main trial. Lord Hutchinson cross-examined him hard, setting against his assertion that SIGINT was a total secret to the public, article after article, photograph after photograph. As Sam Silkin said morosely afterwards:

> Anyone with any knowledge of the courts knows that, however thoroughly a prosecution may prepare its case, witnesses don't always measure up to expectations — particularly when skilfully, some have said brilliantly, cross-examined.[56]

It emerged fairly rapidly that the Russians, Fleet Street defence correspondents, and every peasant on the island, knew that the sovereign base area of Cyprus housed a British radio interception station. The trial came to an abrupt halt as the subterranean muttering about jury-vetting culminated in a television disclosure that the jury foreman was a former member of the SAS and not well-disposed towards the defendants. The television company was cited for contempt, but Sam Silkin — feeling, one imagines, that he had enough on his plate — declined to prosecute.

The second trial, with a new jury, also had a new judge, Mr Justice Willis having fallen ill. 'He took a view which the first judge had not evinced', said Mr Silkin afterwards. He threw out the spying charges. Mr Silkin meanwhile felt obliged to disclose the so-called guidelines for jury-vetting he had drawn up in secret three years before. They resulted in a fresh bout of criticism directed at Silkin and the whole nature of the justice system.

The political damage done by the affair to the ambitions of Whitehall to steer secrets law reform in the right direction, was very great. The history of the legislation is dealt with elsewhere in detail, but at the point when these arrests were made, it was at a delicate stage.

The last celebrated prosecution of journalists had been in the 1971 *Sunday Telegraph* case. That too had been a fiasco. The judge had attacked the wide and vague Acts, saying Section 2 ought to be 'pensioned off'. Newspapers were enraged at the threat of prosecution for mere 'receipt' of some document which had already been leaked. The Franks Committee conducted an inquiry and duly recommended that 'receipt' should not be an offence, and information would have to be adjudged specifically damaging before its future distribution became a crime. Whitehall was not enthusiastic about the Franks Report, and even less so about 'Freedom of Information'. Merlyn Rees had just announced that 'mere receipt' would be done away with in order to implement Franks (tardily enough). To charge journalists, once again, with 'mere receipt' under Section 2, looked to the public like an act of incomprehensible perversity.

What became clear as a result of the case, was that the promise to abolish 'mere receipt' had been a completely cosmetic scheme in the first place. The phrase annoyed newspapers; but small print yet more catholic and threatening in its effects was intended to replace it. Campbell had been 'inciting' and 'interrogating' and 'pumping Berry dry', said Silkin indignantly. Given some allowance for colourful description he was speaking of a journalistic interview. 'The upper half of Section 2 will remain law if Franks is enacted', said Silkin afterwards, correctly. But it may have been as a result of this political outcry against the use of the old Section 2 that Silkin at that point allowed himself to be persuaded into the unprecedented step of laying Section 1 espionage charges against journalists. It was a means of demonstrating to the world that Campbell and company were highly dangerous and even traitorous people.

Silkin presented it afterwards as a step forced on him by the shocking nature of the facts which called for serious punishment. 'I cannot be held responsible for the accuracy of the estimate of damage', he said.

> I am not a military security expert, or an international relations expert or a communications expert … I personally and critically questioned those who made that assessment … I asked [leading counsel] to satisfy himself independently about the damage assessment … for several months I declined to give my consent to the prosecution until I felt as sure as anybody can be on a study of only one side of a case that the damage assessment was sufficiently accurate to rely on. I may say that I was criticized for that very delay. It hardly needs to be stated that if I publish vital defence secrets in the press I may do just as much harm to our national security as if I sell them to the Russians. How could any responsible Attorney-General ignore the unanimous views presented to me that disclosure of both the [Campbell 'collection'] material and the Berry material could do damage ranging from serious to exceptionally grave to the national security?[57]

This oratory was all very well, but it did not explain one piece of secret pre-trial manoeuvring. Campbell, Berry and Aubrey suggested through counsel that they might plead guilty to the minor Section 2 charges if the prosecution agreed to drop the Section 1 charges. And Sam Silkin agreed. It might have affected the jury's mind a little, as they listened to Crown speeches about the wickedness of the trio, to know that the Crown would have traded the espionage charges for the sake of a quiet conviction on the small-scale indictment. Perhaps Silkin had grown uneasy once again at the point when he considered this offer of a plea-bargain.

One can see why it was important to him to believe the ABC trio were a menace; but why was it so important for the security men to have Aubrey, Berry and Campbell charged with Section 1 offences? To suggest that it was an outraged vendetta by Sir Leonard Hooper, former head of GCHQ and at the time coordinator of intelligence and security in the Cabinet Office, seems misguided. But some explanation is needed after all; it would have been easy to get convictions and two-year jail sentences on the minor Section 2 charges alone, and that would have been quite enough to stop journalists talking to soldiers.

One can perhaps reconstruct from subsequent political events. The catch-all provisions of Section 2 were slowly, but inevitably, proceeding towards reform. It will be remembered that Sir Martin Furnival-Jones, then head of MI5, was emphatic to the Franks Committee that blanket protection should remain. He was sufficiently perturbed about the kind of material journalists pick up and pass on to coin the memorable phrase 'espionage by inadvertence'. As far as security and intelligence work went, the replacement Section 2 proposed by Franks was not planned to give blanket protection. It would only protect documents classified 'Secret' and above, and confirmed in their classification by a minister. Journalists who had conversations with sources would be awkward to prosecute; one would have to prove they knew that what they were being told was material of a high security classification. (The original sources would be easy enough to get — they would presumably know the status of the information they were conveying.)

But, with the disappearance of a satisfactorily comprehensive Section 2, perhaps Section 1 could be made to work a little harder for its living? It had already been extended to take in CND subversives demonstrating at airbases. They had been adjudged by the Lords to be 'saboteurs' and within the section. It would be much easier to charge whistleblowing journalists with communicating information that might be 'useful to an enemy', than with some laborious post-Franks Section 2 formulation. It would be much easier than having to demonstrate the classification of each bit of information conveyed in a conversation or even contained in a book. (It will be remembered that the only information the Ministry of Defence was prepared to volunteer to Peter Laurie was a categorical statement: 'There is no doubt that information of this sort would be of great assistance to any enemy.')

The equation in this theory is that, following the failure of the ABC Section 1 prosecutions, Merlyn Rees announced an important change to Franks. Henceforth, all items of security information were 'deserving of the highest protection'. An accumulation of small facts, harmless in themselves, could be dangerous he said. And so, when the draft Bill emerged into the arms of the successor Tory Government, it contained the Draconian proposal that all security information should be *ipso facto* 'protected information', and never to be disclosed. Section 1 had turned out to be useless

against journalists. A dramatic re-vamp of the new Section 2 was
therefore required. And precisely because the ABC prosecution had
so discredited the military and security services approach to official
secrecy, the new Bill was regarded with great suspicion, and the
new small print about the security services was read with some
hostility. Attempts to legislate that even information already
publicly available should remain 'protected' from further
disclosure were greeted with incredulity. In some ways the Blunt
affair provided a useful excuse for the government to ditch a Bill
against which a heavy campaign of opposition was beginning to
roll. And the security services were back to square one.
Whistleblowing was still a workable idea in Britain, and 'national
security', like 'patriotism', continued to be a phrase rightly regarded
with a fish eye.

6
Freedom of Information: Reform and Its Enemies

The freedom of the press is a term which really means the citizen's right to knowledge. Instead of giving freedom of expression an honoured place in British constitutional conventions, the history of our institutions has thrown up a dangerous idea that the press has no rights, no privileges, and no special restraints. The press and its representatives are merely considered to be an interest group, like other subjects, with no claims other than its general rights under the law. The theory is false: the press is, or ought to be, a democratic transmission mechanism, specially protected. The myth is not carried out in practice; there are a few special privileges for the press, such as early access to some government papers and arrangements to mingle with politicians and other power-holders (protected from ordinary members of the public by policemen). There are a greater number of special vetos: newspapers cannot report many things the ordinary citizen can drift into a courtroom and listen to; because of the laws of libel, they cannot report the myriad critical or offensive remarks that members of the public and officials make to each other quite freely; they cannot publish to the world, in theory at least, the 'State secrets' that are the gossip of ministers' clubs and house parties.

But it suits power-holders to peddle this myth. The provision of the European Convention on Human Rights naming the right to give and receive information has not been incorporated into English law by a Bill of Rights, as it ought to be. If freedom of expression was given the weight it should have in British political conventions, the secrecy landscape would look very different today. As it is, the last ten years have seen a great growth in the realization that we need (a) less secrecy and (b) a law that gives the public a right to information. As the campaign has flowed, it has mysteriously run into the sands time and again. While other Western countries draft public access, data and privacy laws (and refine existing ones), Britain faces the 1980s with the prospect of nothing. This is the way politics work in Britain; every time the traditional mechanisms start up — official inquiries, open lobbying by pressure-groups, even the writing of party manifestos — a ghostly hand reaches out for the brake.

As good a starting point as any is the Fulton Report on the Civil Service; it began work in 1966 — fifteen years ago — and set the tone of meaningless verbiage, punctuated by pilgrimages to Sweden and the US, which has continued ever since: Fulton said:

> It is particularly important for a professional civil service to keep in mind that, in carrying out the tasks of modern government, it should remain the servant of democracy and be responsive to the control of Ministers ...
>
> We think the administrative process is surrounded by too much secrecy. The public interest would be better served if there were a greater amount of openness. The increasingly wide range of problems handled by government, and their far-reaching effects upon the community as a whole, demand the widest possible consultation with its different parts and interests. We believe such consultation is not only necessary in itself, but will also improve the quality of ultimate decisions and increase the general understanding of their purpose.
>
> We welcome the trend in recent years towards wider and more open consultation before decisions are taken; and we welcome too, the increasing provision of the detailed information on which decisions are made. Both should be carried much further; it is healthy for a democracy increasingly to press to be consulted and informed. There are still too many occasions where information is unnecessarily withheld and consultation merely perfunctory ... it is an abuse of consultation when it is turned into a belated attempt to prepare the ground for decisions that in reality have been taken already.[1]

Fulton conceded that there had to be some secrecy when ministers and officials were debating possible courses of action. But, apart from this temporary veil, and a ban on national security matters, trade secrets and knowledge which would enable outsiders to make money out of government decisions, Fulton wanted factual material made available to the citizenry as well as to the administrators. This was presented, half-heartedly, as a simple aid to communication; the community would be able to see how well it was being governed without any tiresome misunderstandings. But there was no vagueness about what Fulton was proposing; a system of downright 'open government' on the Swedish pattern, with the way paved by a government inquiry covering, among other things, the Official Secrets Act and designed: 'to make recommendations for getting rid of unnecessary secrecy in this country'.

The Fulton Report said what all its spiritual successors were to say: 'Civil servants, and perhaps also ministers, are apt to give great and sometimes excessive weight to the difficulties and problems which would undoubtedly arise from more open processes of administration and policy-making. In this connection therefore, we wish to draw attention to practice in Sweden...'

Over the next twelve years, Fulton's call for open government was side-tracked and suppressed. Both political parties paid lip-service to it when out of power, and colluded with Whitehall when in. Senior politicians and civil servants did not believe in open government then, and do not now. There is little in it for them.

Sweden, the US, Canada and the Rest of the World

In an increasing number of other countries these matters are ordered differently. In Sweden, anyone, even a foreigner, can walk into the Ministry of Defence HQ and see two lists — one of all the correspondence and reports which reached the Ministry that day, open for inspection, and the other, rather shorter, listing all the titles of secret military documents which are not on public view.[2] In most ministries and public bodies, government documents are available on demand. The Swedish press agency, TT, plods around each morning, calling at the Prime Minister's office to read the incoming mail and visits the other government departments. As a consequence, the simplest way for a journalist to get information about government activity in Sweden is to ring up a civil servant, who will most likely tell him. Why argue when the journalist has an enforceable legal right at the end of the day?

The history of public access goes back to 1766, when Sweden's Freedom of the Press Act was passed in the name of public enlightenment.[3] It does not mean everything is promiscuously on display in Sweden, where there is a much more sophisticated structure of privacy law and press professional discipline. What it does mean is that the guiding principle is the opposite of Britain's: government information belongs to the public with certain detailed exceptions. The costs are negligible, because governing has traditionally been carried out this way and is manageable in a small country. The process of policy formation is much more open, and citizens have a right to inspect many of the dossiers held on them (with restrictions on awkward files such as medical records), and an independent data inspectorate to scrutinize security service files on their behalf.

Elsewhere in Scandinavia, the Swedish example began to be followed in the 1960s and 1970s, sometimes in more limited ways. Denmark, for example, set up public access laws to great cries of fear and alarm from civil servants. The laws are mild; departments did not originally have to register the existence of documents, which destroyed much of the point. But the perceived drawbacks so far have been apparently nil, after a thorough government review and in 1979 the law was being steadily developed.

In the US, a larger country than Britain, a strong constitutional principle of freedom of speech is once again the base-line. There has none the less been a long struggle against the US's many bureaucracies, punctuated by whistleblowing exercises over the Pentagon papers, which charted misconduct in Vietnam; over Watergate, which toppled an unscrupulous President Nixon; and over the CIA, whose disaffected employees painted over time a detailed picture of a secret organization almost manically out of control. All this added to public mistrust of government. Congressional hearings in the 1950s catalogued many ways in which the executive manipulated information, and a Freedom of Information Act was finally passed in 1966, giving public access to government documents.

The Act did not work very well, because officials could still 'classify' whatever they liked as secret without court review; refuse to produce any document not specifically identified; and stall or overcharge for research as much as they pleased. It was 1974 before amendments giving the Act teeth were passed along with privacy legislation giving the citizen the right to inspect investigatory files about him. By January 1978, 48 States had passed similar local access laws. President Carter's administration also announced instructions to limit profligate over-classification in the first place, and provide for six-year declassifying reviews.[4] Although there have been great efforts to lobby by organizations such as the FBI, which claims its work is being hampered and that the expense is enormous, there is no indication that US public opinion wants to go back on the laws.

Estimates of the true cost have ranged between 150 million

dollars and 30 million dollars a year, with the most recent estimate of a mere 12 million dollars a year based on a June 1978 report from the US Comptroller General. In trying to assess the figures, it is important to remember that US departments have resisted the legislation and have every incentive to exaggerate by, for example, treating all public inquiries for information as formal FOI requests, or trying to smuggle their public relations' budget into the figures. Canada, trying to plan its own legislation by studying the US, guessed its own annual costs would be 10.5 million dollars annually, although the Canadian Bar Association did their own research and produced an absolute maximum figure for Canada of 3 million dollars.[5]

Scaling up these figures for Britain's greater population would suggest a guesswork figure between £4 and £13 million annually, which might, in fact, be far lower in practice. The Scandinavian approach is so cheap that there are no identifiable costs at all; departments are organized to answer most requests informally. In the US there have been many retrospective requests for material on such historical *cause célèbres* as the Alger Hiss case; attempts by rival firms to get hold of commercially valuable material or stop other firms getting hold of it; and the extensive use of the courts to arbitrate with the executive — all these complicate the American scene, and make it disingenuous to point to aspects of it and shudder, as British officials have a habit of doing. And after all, the British government budget for its own authorized information publicity and propaganda services was £23.3 million within the UK in 1978, and £71.9 million abroad.[6] It is a well-known newspaper tag that news is what somebody doesn't want you to print — all the rest is public relations. Britain spends a great deal on public relations.

Like Australia, New Zealand, the Netherlands and even France in a limited way, Canada was planning freedom of information laws at the end of the 1970s, embodying the key principle that everything is public unless specifically exempted. At the end of 1979, a Bill was introduced by one Conservative Government, and was expected to be reintroduced by the next liberal administration, which suddenly won power. A series of lobby groups had to campaign for it, and the US example probably helped. But many Western democratic bureaucracies were taking the same road — it was obviously a common response to the way complicated, high-technology societies were developing in the 1960s and 1970s.

What is important from the British perspective is that legislation on the Canadian pattern cannot be excused away by British power-holders in the way that it can with the US or Sweden. The US has a formal constitution with separation of powers between judges, officials and law-makers in which 'FOI' is just one more check on an otherwise invulnerable executive machine. Sweden does not have the same link as there is in Britain between government departments and MPs. The minister in a department is merely the head of a tiny policy-making unit while the main business of administration is carried on by semi-independent agencies — the Prisons Board, for example, or the Immigration Board — controlled only through their budget and the appointment of their heads.

In Britain, as White Papers never tire of telling us, we have 'ministerial responsibility' to Parliament for the work of the entire executive machine. This is a myth, as I hope has been fairly shown by now, and one of the myth's functions has been to be trundled out like the giant statue of a god, every time someone proposes upsetting Whitehall habits. But Canada has exactly the same constitutional framework as Britain, with ministerial responsibility and so forth, even down to a borrowed version of the Official Secrets Act. Canadian government is modelled, apart from its federalism, on British government.

Canada proposes a right of public access to government files; enforcement by an Information Commissioner or Ombudsman with a last resort right to go to Court; a right of access to one's own personal files; and exemptions from universal disclosure for military, foreign affairs, law enforcement, commercial, personal and 'policy advice' documents.[7] This is the skeleton of a full-scale Freedom of Information Act which could be borrowed by Britain tomorrow.

Wasting Time, 1968-74

The Fulton Report was published in 1968 under Harold Wilson's Labour Government of 1964-70. As far as open government was concerned, Whitehall's first response was simple enough. It affected to misunderstand the whole proposal. An interdepartmental Whitehall study was set up in deference to the Fulton recommendations and it published a self-congratulatory White Paper[8] explaining what was perfectly obvious — that the government already pumped out a great deal of information (in 1967 the idea of Green Papers was introduced — consultative documents about issues on which the government had yet to make up its collective mind). Although the White Paper confirmed a trend which has developed more or less slowly and unsatisfactorily ever since — to increase the amount of material the government decides to release of its own accord — it was otherwise pure stonewalling. The paper explained how important it was that civil servants and ministers should be able to talk frankly among themselves. In a piece of wilful misunderstanding, the White Paper explained for the benefit of such misguided persons as the members of the Fulton Committee that the Official Secrets Acts were 'not in any way a barrier to open government'. They merely related to *unauthorized* disclosures.

Such immobilism left it open to the Conservative opposition to promise less secrecy in government as part of their General Election campaign. But once the Heath Government came to power in 1970, it was clear it did not understand what was meant by open government. It merely set up, alongside the Younger Inquiry (the study of privacy launched by the dying Labour Government), a trio of reform exercises on existing information law — Faulks on libel, Phillimore on contempt and Franks on the Official Secrets Act. Although Franks produced four thick volumes of fascinating evidence about the official and ministerial mind,[9] its terms of reference have already ruled out the question of open government.

The committee members took themselves off, in what was becoming the usual way, to Sweden, the US and two countries then without access laws, France and Canada.

A small number of witnesses ... suggested introduction of legislation to give a general right of access to certain kinds of official information ... it was put to us that such legislation would 'positively assist the public to obtain information about government'. This was an interesting suggestion, but we decided on reflection it was not one we should adopt ... this suggestion raised important constitutional questions going beyond our terms of reference. Accordingly we have not gone fully into the possibility of such legislation in the UK, in the sense of treating it as if it fell within our terms of reference. Such laws simply cannot be transplanted into the very different British context without consideration of the constitutional repercussions. Moreover, as we have said, the law is not one of the most important influences on openness in government.[10]

Thus the basic Franks proposal — to work out for once what was really supposed to be secret in government in order to protect it — was fatally divorced from a public right of access to the rest of Whitehall's files; from privacy law which was also being considered in isolation; from questions of a drastic cut in the 30-year quarantine period for records, already reduced from 50 years in 1970; and from any idea of legislating free expression and a free press into a more central role in the British machinery of politics.

Politicians and civil servants did not indeed find the idea altogether unattractive of using Franks to construct a new secrecy law which could, as had been the case in the 1908-11 period, be made efficient enough to put a genuine bite on the press. In the later, notorious, phrase of the Labour Home Secretary Merlyn Rees, they could design, in place of the old blunderbuss, an Armalite rifle.

The ruminations of the Franks Committee thus took on an unexpectedly prophetic air:

> A democratic government ... has a task which is complicated by its obligations to the people. It needs the trust of the governed. It cannot use the plea of secrecy to hide from the people its basic aims. On the contrary, it must explain those aims: it must provide the justification for them and give the facts both for and against a selected course of action. Nor must such information be provided only at one level and through one means of communication. A government which pursues secret aims or which operates in greater secrecy than the effective conduct of its proper functions requires, or which turns information services into propaganda agencies, will lose the trust of the people. It will be countered by ill-informed and destructive criticism. Its critics will try and break down all barriers to preserve secrecy, and they will disclose all that they can, by whatever means, discover...[11]

Franks divided all government information in effect into two classes — that which was merely secret in so far as an official could be dismissed for revealing it without authority, and that which was very secret, in so far as the indiscreet official in question should be sent to prison for disclosures. The proposals would have left Section 1 of the Official Secrets Act as an unmodernized espionage act, and replaced the catch-all Section 2 by a list of types of legally protected information.

The list was a beginning, although it was too vague. It included, for example, all Cabinet documents, whether they were really secret or not, as a deferential nod in the direction of 'collective responsibility'. It left the category of 'Confidential' information about firms and private individuals as a blithely catholic loophole. It reflected a temporary obsession with sterling rates by proposing to make all material about currency and the reserves protected by law. And it granted cover to all material about defence, spying, civil defence, surveillance and foreign affairs, so long as it was classified at least 'Secret', without allowing any way to challenge the classification made in the first place (provided the responsible minister fell in with what his civil servants had done).

In any event, the Heath Government collapsed in 1974 without doing anything whatever about Franks — or for that matter, Younger and Phillimore.[12] (Faulks reported and was shelved the following year.)[13] Meanwhile the Labour Party had in Opposition taken up the torch of liberty. The manifesto on which Harold Wilson returned to power contained a fine promise to introduce real freedom of information by a measure, 'to put the burden on the public authorities to justify witholding information'. Some of the US lobbying for public access, and the work of campaigners like the notorious consumer advocate Ralph Nader, had wafted across the Atlantic and this was the fruit. Prime ministers and permanent secretaries were faced with a bigger threat to their entrenched habits than at the outset of the previous administration. The time had come, not for inertia, but for a campaign of outflanking and sabotage.

The Labour Government, 1974-9

An intriguing preview of the tactics likely to be used in Whitehall had come not only in the wash of self-justification presented to the Franks Committee, but in an odd little defeat in 1962. Until then, civil servants conducted planning inquiries by submitting reports to the minister in secret, who then announced his decision without giving reasons. In 1957, Ministry of Housing and Local Government officials argued strenuously to a committee (also chaired by Lord Franks) that to publish the reports would cause embarrassment, be a hindrance to sound policy-making and would cause administrative difficulties amounting almost to chaos.[14] The committee disagreed, the civil servants dropped their resistance, and the atmosphere surrounding these appeals became much healthier.[15]

The Home Office, a deeply obscurantist ministry, was to be the 'lead department' in 1974 because it was in charge of the laws prohibiting information; the gamekeepers were to turn poacher. The pilgrimages abroad began again; Roy Jenkins, the new Home Secretary, travelled to the US with his Permanent Secretary, Sir Arthur Petersen. They returned, letting it be known that the Freedom of Information on the US pattern looked highly expensive and disruptive, and only appeared to benefit big corporations. Although Jenkins gave a public lecture backing the idea in principle, very little serious attention was paid to it by the Cabinet.

The political problem was that, as soon as the Franks proposals for trimming the Official Secrets Act emerged from the Whitehall digestive system, it would become obvious that nothing was being done about the more important issue — public access. Franks sat unattended on the shelf for two more years. It was now four years since it had reported, and six since a government committed to reform the Acts took office. Harold Wilson retired as Labour Prime Minister in 1976. James Callaghan succeeded him. There was continuing backbench pressure for open government, as promised; in April 1976, a Cabinet committee was set up on the secrecy problem — neither its existence not its membership were, of course, disclosed.

Naturally, Jenkins was a member. So, reportedly, were David Owen the Foreign Secretary, who made some practical efforts to open up the Foreign Office,[16] and Tony Benn, the Energy Secretary and constant campaigner for grass-roots democracy.[17] It was chaired by Callaghan himself, the arch non-discloser, whose views had not become more libertarian since his 1971 testimony to Franks: 'I sometimes think we make it almost impossible to govern at all in this country.'

Roy Jenkins moved on to an EEC post in Brussels, taking a perhaps exaggerated reputation for liberalism with him. Merlyn Rees, a Callaghan protégé and former Northern Ireland Secretary (where security and intelligence men rode high), replaced him. As far as can be traced from subsequent events, it had by now already been decided to scuttle any notion of public access and concentrate on Official Secrets Act reform. The only problem was 'presentational', as Whitehall phrases these things, or, in harsher language — how to get away with it.

Instead of issuing a White Paper explaining the government's settled intentions, Rees issued a temporizing statement in November 1976,[18] outlining merely the plans for Official Secrets

Act reform. This move did not go down very well. Backbenchers, Labour and Liberal Party workers, academics and pressure-groups woke up very sharply to the likelihood they were simply not going to see the Labour Government fulfil its commitment. The water had been publicly tested by ministers, and it was uncomfortably hot. As the Cabinet committee resumed its secret meetings, a flanking manoeuvre was attempted. If civil servants could be persuaded somehow to separate factual material from the policy options and proposals they put up to ministers, the material could be published at Whitehall's discretion. Hey presto: 'open government' would have arrived, as a free gift from the Civil Service to the public — on the governors' terms.

On 6 July 1977, the head of the Home Civil Service, Sir Douglas Allen, circulated an announcement to all departments designed to enforce Callaghan's professions of 'openness'. (It was, naturally, not published, although it was later leaked):

Dear Head of Department,   6 July 1977
DISCLOSURE OF OFFICIAL INFORMATION

1. ...I am writing in terms which the Prime Minister has specifically approved ... to ask you to ensure that your Department gives effect to it. You may wish to let your Minister see this guidance, drawing particular attention to Paragraph 10.

2. The change may seem simply to be one of degree and of timing. But it is intended to mark a real change of policy even if the initial step is modest ... there is, of course, no intention to publish material which correctly bears a current security classification or privacy marking ...

3. In effect, what is proposed is an increase in the already considerable amount of material put out by departments. The additional material will mainly consist of deliberate presentations in the later stages of discussion and will probably take the form of Green Papers ... consideration should also be given to the issue of bibliographies or digests so that interested parties are advised what material is available.

4. ...When Ministers decide what announcement they wish to make, therefore, they will also wish to consider whether and in what form the factual and analytical material may be published since there may be, as the Prime Minister made clear ... circumstances in which Ministers will not wish to disclose such material.

5. It is not the intention to depart from the present practice of not disclosing PARS nor identifying them publicly. ['Programme Analysis and Review'— audits of departmental performances, introduced as a reform and subsequently downplayed, in any event, to the point of invisibility.]

6. ...Re-writing material specially for publication is wasteful and expensive in staff time. Therefore, when policy studies are being undertaken in future, the background material should be written in a form which will permit it to be published separately.

7. ...There should be a charge for all material ... to include all aspects of reproduction and handling ...

8. The government's decision on this question is in a form which should not involve substantial additional work but which could all too easily be lost to view. There are many who would have wanted the government to go much further (on the lines of the formidably burdensome Freedom of Information Act in the USA). Our prospects of being able to avoid such an expensive development here could well depend on whether we can show that the Prime Minister's statement had reality and results. So I ask all of you to keep this question of publicizing material well on your checklist of action in any significant area of policy formation, even at Divisional level; and to encourage your Ministers to take an interest in this question.

9. Since the Prime Minister may well be asked what effect this announcement has had ... I should be grateful if you could arrange to have some kind of record kept ...

10. The greater publicizing of material can hardly fail to add to one cost — that of responding to the additional direct correspondence to which it may well give rise ... Departments must do their best in these matters, and should inform a correspondent if the timescale for a reply is likely to be longer than normal.

This was Hamlet without the Prince: an access system without any legal right of access. But the letter was well intentioned enough. Sir Douglas, when he retired, gave a radio talk urging that greater consistency and stability in policy would result from more openness.[19] Well intentioned enough too, is the civil servant's ESTACODE which tells them how to behave. Until recently a 'Restricted' document, it says:

The need for greater openness in the work of government is now widely accepted. Openness in this context means two things:

a) The fullest possible exposition to Parliament and to the Public of the reasons for government policies and decisions *when those policies and decisions are formulated and announced.* [My emphasis.]

b) Creating a better public understanding about the way in which the processes of government work and about the factual or technical background to government policies or decisions.

The Times undertook a laborious monitoring exercise and found the post-Allen flow of documents entirely unconvincing[20] — the Cabinet office even refused to release the 'background papers' to its eventual anodyne White Paper, on the grounds they consisted of 'confidential exchanges with foreign governments'. This did not prevent the government boasting rather unsteadily a year later:

> Since that time ... much has been done to explain energy policy; the facts relevant to the Windscale debate on nuclear expansion, have been placed fully before the public; there is a growing dialogue on education; the Home Office has made public an internal review of Criminal Justice policy ... to meet the increasing demand for more and better information about road plans; the presumption now is that the evidence available to the department will be accessible ... except where its release might be damaging to individuals. The instructions ... will need time to achieve their full effect [they] do not mean that all announcements of government decisions will or should be accompanied by an appendix of supporting government papers.[21]

Disclosure of energy policy, the apparent jewel in this crown, was rather vitiated by the Energy Secretary's later assertion that his civil servants tended to keep relevant information, not only from the public, but even from him.[22]

Finally, on 19 July, in its dying days, the Labour Government put out its White Paper.[23] Last minute pressure and nothing else led to a few remarks about open government being tacked on to the draft. They stupefied the campaigners. The token paragraphs said, as though it were an idea that had suddenly occurred to them, that open government laws were a scheme that had been mentioned. Willing, of course, to listen to novel proposals, the government would, at some point in the future, for investigation purposes, despatch observers to Sweden...

There is a Yiddish word, *chutzpah;* the best definition of it is that it is the quality shown by a young man who, having murdered both his parents, throws himself on the mercy of the court on the grounds that he is an orphan. The Callaghan White Paper demonstrated a good deal of *chutzpah*:

> A present day government works in a climate different from that, of for example, 20 years ago. Government departments already make public or make available on request a great deal of information ... an ever-increasing flow of Green papers and other consultative documents ... in our system of Government, the executive is under continuous scrutiny by Parliament...
>
> It is settled Government policy to continue to expand the flow of information to Parliament and the public, in particular setting out the background to major decisions...
>
> So the Government accepts an obligation to publish more information and will continue to develop its practice accordingly. The question is whether to go further, perhaps by creating a statutory right to information on the lines of the legislation in force in some other countries, notably in the United States and Sweden...
>
> Legislation on these lines would completely change the nature of the Government's obligations: instead of accepting a declared obligation to make more information available, operating on a voluntary and discretionary basis, the Government would be under a statutory duty to disclose...
>
> Legislation to put the Government under a statutory duty to disclose information on demand would have wide implications. First resource costs. While there have been differing estimates of the cost of US legislation, it is clear that it has been unexpectedly high.
>
> Perhaps more fundamentally, it is at least for consideration how far the analogy from foreign experience should be pressed. In order to achieve the reasonable objectives of open government in the British context, where the policies and decision of the executive are under constant and vigilant scrutiny by Parliament, and Ministers are directly answerable in Parliament, it may be neither necessary nor desirable to proceed to legislation of a kind which may be justifiable in other and often very different contexts — for instance that of the United States.

This is a matter on which the Government has come to no conclusion and has an open mind. The Government recognizes that its proposals do not go as far as the Labour Party Manifesto of October 1974, which proposed that the Official Secrets Act should be replaced 'by a measure to put the burden on public authorities to justify withholding information'. We regard however, the reform of Section 2 of the Official Secrets Act 1911, on the lines set out in this White Paper as a necessary precursor of further change ...

Before deciding whether to go further we shall initiate a more detailed study than has so far been possible of overseas experience ... and we shall announce our conclusions from this study in due course.[24]

No factual analyses behind this decision were, of course, published. The secret was that there were almost none in existence.

Such a process of silence followed by betrayal might not have seemed, on the face of it, very much of an advertisement for the system of government about which the White Paper purported to boast. But Rees, Callaghan, the Cabinet Office and the Home Office must have calculated that the general public were ignorant of the issues at stake. As Merlyn Rees coolly put it to one outraged MP: 'When my Honourable Friend talks about people outside being worried, I can only express the wish that, at the Election, he finds more than two or three people in his constituency who are concerned about it.'[25]

A committee of officials was set to pack their suitcases for the cosmetic new 'open government' study. This was the fifth such trip in ten years — members of the Fulton Committee had gone in 1968; members of the Franks Committee in 1972; Roy Jenkins and his Permanent Secretary in 1975; and Sir Douglas Allen himself in 1977.

Meanwhile, the Labour Government pressed ahead with the drafting of a new secrets law, both attractive in itself (the 'Armalite' theory) and another preemptive means of undermining the continued public access campaign. That autumn, after the Queen's speech outlining the programme of a minority government likely to be forced to the polls very soon, the usual 'non-attributable background notes' were distributed to the Westminster lobby.

The Civil Service Department press office, reminding the lay journalists of recent history, wrote defensively: 'The Government said ... reform of the Official Secrets Act would not be a barrier to greater openness.' It was a curiously atavistic phrase — perhaps even a Freudian slip — because that wording harked back to the notorious 1969 White Paper, *Information and the Public Interest,* which had busily defended the even more indefensible. The White Paper had said the Official Secrets Act themselves were: 'not in any way a barrier to greater openness'. The non-attributable note of 1978 added winningly: 'The Government is very much committed to greater openness.'

There were signs, in the specific proposals to draft a new Official Secrets law, that the Whitehall lobbyists had also been at work there. As the time had passed, it became obvious that Franks' obsession with the sterling balances was no longer relevant. The Frank Field affair[26] had shown that attempts to prosecute people for leaking Cabinet documents, as such, would be so politically embarrassing as not to be a practical proposition. In what was presented as a liberalizing step, these two categories were dropped from Franks proposed list of information crimes. But all personal files were still to be barred, in the name of 'privacy', even from the people about whom they were compiled. So too was all industrial information to be protected by law if it was 'Confidential'. These two classes are in fact good candidates for including, with proper safeguards, in public access laws; dangerous or dirty industrial habits and unscrupulous dossier-building are two of the most important areas a public access law would open up.

In some rather tortuous passages, obviously the outcome of a mandarinate argument by the Ministry of Defence and the Foreign Office, the White Paper appeared to suggest that, although nothing in these areas would be illegal unless classified at least 'Secret', there were plans afoot to lock up many more papers than that. Some information was not, it said, classified 'Secret' to save effort; but it really ought to be.[27]

Strangest and most ominous of all, it seemed that behind the curtains, MI5, MI6 and GCHQ were writing themselves a legal charter against journalism — having failed to achieve much in the contemporaneous ABC secrets trial except to make themselves look ridiculous. Franks had naturally included the activities of these bodies in his category of defence secrets, provided exposure of the information in question actually threatened 'serious injury to the nation'. Not so, said the White Paper:

The Government has concluded that information relating to security and intelligence is deserving of the highest protection, whether or not it is classified. This is preeminently an area where the gradual accumulation of small items of information, apparently trivial in themselves, could eventually create a risk for the safety of an individual or constitute a serious threat to the safety of the nation as a whole. Information about security and intelligence matters will therefore be a separate category in the Bill.[28]

The Labour Government limped to a close. The Civil Service Department men compiled, after all their travels, a 150-page book, explaining how public access was done in Sweden, the US, Denmark, Norway, Canada, France, Holland and Australia.[29] The drafting of a new Section 2 of the Official Secrets Act ground on, unfinished and uncontrolled, in the Home Office. Callaghan put a characteristic obituary stamp on the strange chronicle of events between 1974 and 1979. At the Party Conference in October 1979 he was asked from the floor about his government's refusal to grant public access. With a straight face Callaghan told his questioner in the Brighton Conference hall that the government had been unable to introduce a Freedom of Information Act because it lacked a parliamentary majority. As one MP, Chris Price, wrote acidly at the time: 'Come off it, Jim ... to play the ingenu to the party faithful on this one is a bit much.'[30]

The Conservatives, 1979

The Labour Government was defeated in the May 1979 General Election, and the Conservatives under Margaret Thatcher came to power on a primitive right-wing platform. Their essentially manipulative approach to political information was signalled by the appointment of a long-serving political 'hawk', Angus Maude, as a minister with a specific brief to coordinate the output of propaganda by ministers and the timing of announcements by Whitehall press officers. All ideas of open government were scrapped. So was the half-way stage of a voluntary 'code of practice' which was being floated by some timid lawyers and civil servants.[31]

In the autumn of 1979, the custodians of the Official Secrets Acts themselves returned to play out a brief, comic coda. The Home Office's Protection of Official Information Bill emerged from the machinery and landed in Mrs Thatcher's lap. It was a few days before journalists mastered the small print. Naturally enough, the

'Lobby Guidance Note' of publication day, 19 October 1979, had been deeply misleading:

> The Government undertook ... to introduce ... provisions appropriate to the present time. This Bill ... fulfils that undertaking ... This Bill differs from the Franks Report in a number of respects. For example, Cabinet documents and information about the currency and reserves will not as Franks envisaged be protected.

The note listed the categories of 'protected information', failing to point out that some material *not* envisaged by Franks was being thrown in; there were defence and international affairs matters likely to cause serious injury or endanger the safety of a citizen; 'confidential' industrial and personal material; and a law enforcement clause. But there were also the novelties, some hinted at in the White Paper, some not. There was 'security and intelligence'; confidential matters received from foreign governments; and another whole new category called 'the authorized interception of telecommunication or postal communications'.

The lobby note breezed unattributably on:

> The private citizen's offence is more limited than the other two offences, e.g. in respect of knowledge that the information was protected information ... Clause 7 provides, in the case of certain categories of information only, a defence in respect of the offences under the Bill that the information in question was already publicly available.

This 'guidance' was in fact describing a series of clauses under which it became: (a) possible for the first time since the 1908 Whitehall débâcle to jail journalists for printing so-called protected information, regardless of its origins; and (b) *no defence at all* to prove that material about security matters, phone-tapping and classified defence and international issues *had in fact already been made public*.

Altogether the Bill as drafted said the following things: Apart from government announcements, it would henceforth be a crime to print any information whatsoever about the activities of the Special Branch, MI5, MI6 or GCHQ, no matter how it had been obtained or whether it had been published before. It would similarly be a crime to print any information whatsoever about government telephone-tapping, signals interception, bugging or letter-opening, no matter why it was being done, no matter how the information was come by, and no matter whether it had been made public before. It would henceforth be a crime, merely on the assertion of the minister concerned, to print any information about military or 'international relations' matters that was thought 'likely to cause serious injury to the interests of the nation', no matter how acquired, or even if had been already published.[32]

As was eventually pointed out by shocked journalists and MPs, this appeared to make it a crime to complain that one's telephone was being tapped, and a crime to print the complaint. The Foreign Office, the Ministry of Defence, the Home Office, the spies and the political police appeared to have written themselves an apparatus of censorship unparalleled in the Western world. If this was supposed to be a reform, it was difficult to imagine what Whitehall would consider an act of repression.

It was amusing to watch the usual processes of news management at work. The Bill was published on a Friday as often happens — MPs are leaving for the weekend, and tend not to study complex legal drafting which is often made deliberately obscure. The newspapers' senior lobby men do not always attend on Fridays, because nothing normally happens and the Palace of Westminster closes down at teatime. The morning papers have little space on a Friday night, because lack of advertising and lower sales of Saturday papers always mean a cut in the number of pages. And there to hand is the 'lobby guidance note'.

No newspaper the following morning appeared to grasp what was being proposed. Among the less frivolous newspapers, the conservative *Daily Telegraph* handed the task of explanation to its legal correspondent. In a routine story, 'Prosecution risk narrowed in secrets Bill', the cadences of the 'lobby guidance note', could be seen, sometimes word for word; 'For certain categories of information only, there is a defence under the Bill that the information in question was already publicly available.' The *Financial Times* too, did not perceive the novel clauses, novel offences and prohibitions on free speech. Its political staff even remarked: 'Under its provisions — which go slightly further than proposed either by the Franks Committee in 1972 or the last Labour Government's White Paper — only a narrow range of specified information will be protected against disclosure.' Nor was the *Guardian* exempt from this bamboozling; its political staff and a leader-writer made an effort to analyse the Bill, but only managed to consider two points about its clauses: (1) that it was not a Freedom of Information Act; (2) that ministers were to be their own judge and jury of the 'serious injury test'.[33] Reading the papers the following morning, ministers and officials must have been pleased. The Bill's reception was muted and it had obviously not been understood.

Eventually, other journalists obtained texts of the Bill, read it carefully and explained what it meant. There was, late in the day, great outrage. Editors, journalists' unions and lobbyists for press freedom began to plan a campaign of considerable weight. *The Times,* off the streets through a dispute when the Bill was published, returned in November with an angry leading article hinting that it might flout such a law if the public interest demanded it.[34] As discussed in the previous chapter, there was a sudden *furor* over MI5 and the long-concealed Soviet 'mole' Anthony Blunt, which had two consequences; it added fuel to the public campaign against the Bill, and it provided embarrassed Conservative ministers with an opportunity to rid themselves of this unconsidered legislative albatross. Mrs Thatcher announced dramatically, at the height of the Blunt uproar, that the Bill would be withdrawn.[35]

It was dead. Freedom of Information was dead. Contempt law had not been reformed and was likely to be little better or worse, when it was. Libel law reform was apparently dead too. Privacy law was not even gestating. A considered report on the need for data protection laws was already beginning to moulder. The European Human Rights Convention clauses on free expression had not been written into English law. In fourteen years, the British political process had gone round in circles and generated exactly nothing.

What Freedom of Information Might Mean

Despite the blocking manoeuvres of ministers and senior officials, there had by 1980 been at least eight systematic attempts to draft a workable Freedom of Information Act, or to outline proposals for one. Most of them were based either on a draft worked out by the Labour Party's machinery of government subcommittee of the National Executive Committee; or on the work of the Outer Circle Policy Unit, which is headed by a historian, James Cornford. This Unit is funded by the Rowntree Trust and has prominent Liberal connections. A number of MPs had tried to bring in private member's Bills, including Robin Cook and Michael Meacher from the Labour Party, and Clement Freud from the Liberal Party. An all-party Freedom of Information Group was in operation at Westminster, headed briefly by a Conservative Sir Bernard Braine and involved at one point (in an unhappy testimony to MPs' lack of research resources) with the Scientologists. The list of declared supporters of public access was a long one; it included, for example, the Law Society; Justice, the British section of the International Commission of Jurists; the indefatigable National Council for Civil Liberties; Sir Robert Mark, former Commissioner of the Metropolitan Police; the Child Poverty Action Group; the National Consumer Council, the Fabian Society, the Liberal Party; and the Editors of the *Guardian* and *The Times*.

From this growing demand, the outlines of a potentially coherent information law have become clear, although the emphasis and the boldness of the proposals has varied. Some people find it hard to shake off their paternalism. I remember one liberal leader-writer saying anguishedly: 'But can we trust the popular press with freedom of information?' A public access law is not complicated in essence. It would say: (a) Every document possessed by every public body is public property; (b) There are some exceptions to this; and (c) There is a machinery for enforcement. We can perhaps add: (d) Some of the exceptions are so important their disclosure must actually be made illegal.

What are the exceptions to be? The guiding principle most useful here is probably, 'Don't trust the Government an inch.' It will be a key task when public access does arrive to draft exemptions as narrowly as possible. The lesson of all information laws in Britain is that, sooner or later, those in authority will try to exploit them to the hilt.

Franks's labours provide a basis. There ought to be an exemption for important military matters, preferably drawn in narrow detail and working on the premiss that *tactical* information about codes and operations tends to be more genuinely secret than matters of policy. The information that a lorry-load of soldiers will drive to Crossmaglen at 4.30 p.m. on Friday is, temporarily, a genuine secret. That Britain intends to sell H-bombs to South Africa, were it the case, should be made public.

Similarly, in foreign affairs, negotiations to release a British businessman held by an unfriendly country would probably be worthless unless conducted in conditions of great, if temporary secrecy. On the other hand, if Britain conducts itself in subservience to say the US, as occurred during the Vietnam war, it is important for the public to know why and how this is occurring.

The same tests apply to law enforcement material. No one would claim the right to know who the police plan to arrest tomorrow, or how the guard rosters work at Long Lartin high-security prison. But we do have the right to know how jury-vetting is carried on; what instructions prison governors receive; and the type of information held on file by police and security men.

Civil servants would like to claim wide exemptions for 'policy advice'. This must be resisted. If officials are trying to persuade a minister, for example, to increase maximum lorry weights or to build nuclear power stations, then the public should know that that is the attitude of the department. There may be a case for protecting minutes of internal meetings in a department, and minutes of Cabinet and Cabinet committee meetings. There is not a good case, but only a mythological one, for protecting deliberate and considered options put before ministers, or before Cabinets and their committees — or comments and pressures on a department from outside lobbyists and from other departments.

There should not be an exemption for legal opinions given by the Law Officers to other government departments, except where questions of individual privacy arise — 'privilege' is a misused word in legal circles. Nor should reports of police complaints investigations that are not proceeded with by the DPP be automatically exempt.

Although there are an appreciable number of statutes already limiting disclosure of information obtained from companies, a 'confidence' exemption must be extremely tightly drawn; 'commercial confidence' is a fetish which will probably not always stand up to close examination. Individual privacy, unless properly analysed, is a concept which could also be used to blow a huge hole in any public access law. First of all, there must be a right of access for individuals to files held about themselves — this includes medical records, social security files, tax records, school and university dossiers and police records of a factual nature (convictions, complaints, contacts with the police). For particularly sensitive records where a right of inspection would be self-defeating — psychiatric files, criminal intelligence files, security files, telephone intercept files — there will have to be an independent body on the lines of the Swedish Data Inspection Board, with the right to see all files in order to check that improper types of information are not being kept, such as gossip, records of legitimate political activity, or improperly obtained material.

As well as an individual-access clause, there will need to be a public-rights clause — that information can be disclosed to the general public if the public interest in its disclosure outweighs the damage to individual or commercial privacy. Without such a provision, any document with the name of an individual or a firm on it is in danger of being kept secret. There may also be a case for disclosing short-lists for patronage jobs — judges, chairmen, heads of boards. This is a more awkward area; it is possible the solution lies in a parliamentary examination of ministerial appointees before confirming them in office, which takes us out of the direct information field.

So far we have talked about exemptions for types of information. There may be a case for exempting types of organizations too, at least at first. It would be prudent to phase-in public access, starting with central government departments, and moving out to State agencies, nationalized industries and local authorities. Similarly, it would make more sense not to throw open the last 30 years of records at once, but to have phased retrospection. Otherwise, there would be a danger that Whitehall would write itself an exemption for the whole of the last generation's files, on the grounds that not only would it be unfair to do otherwise — it would also be expensive, hard work.

If that covers the past, there will also have to be regulations about the future. Granted a category of 'closed information', there will have to be regular reviews so that material can be released as soon as it is no longer sensitive. Cabinet minutes as such might last five years under protection; some operational military material might be secret for no longer than a week; commercial secrets might need protection for no more than a year or two. As soon as security material is considered irrelevant, it should be released to the individual concerned — or it may need full protection for 30 years, or longer. Exemptions will survive raggedly into the future in this way; there may be a case for fixed reviews at say, one, five, ten and twenty-year intervals.

Machinery for enforcement will also need some thought. There will need to be regulations to compel departments to make indexes, both of open and allegedly exempted material; to respond to requests within time-limits; and make copying facilities available. Beyond this, someone will have to police the boundaries. Is a document properly exempted? It will be through refusals and challenges that an exact frontier line will be drawn in the broad swathes laid down by law. The consensus so far appears to be that an ombudsman figure should be used as the first resort for appeals. He would be quick, cheap and flexible. Beyond that stand, either the courts, or for those who suspect judges and prefer Parliament, a Parliamentary Commission answerable to the House of Commons, and equipped with powers to order disclosure if need be. The burden would be on public authorities to justify refusals. They would have to show first that the documents refused originally belonged in an exempted category; second that it was also at the time against the public interest to disclose them; and third that, after proper review procedures, they still merited protection.

And this legislation itself will only be a beginning, if a crucial one. We shall also need a reformed Espionage Act, a Bill of Rights enshrining free expression; a contempt law so narrowly drawn that it does no more than penalize those who vilify the defendants in a criminal trial; a law of libel that allows the press to speak more openly; and a code of privacy that gives the weak some redress and the mighty no protection. Then we will have really moved the frontiers of secrecy.

Postscript

Since this book was finished, the frontier-lines of British secrecy have been far from peaceful. In a few of the more sensitive areas the secrecy-mongers have given a little ground, notably on phone tapping, prison administration, historical records and jury vetting. But there have been counter-attacks in other parts of the forest which bear out in an interestingly exact fashion some of the warnings given in the course of this book. Supposedly discredited legal notions — contempt of court, the Official Secrets Act, and the law of confidence — have been wielded against the media in altercations that, at the time of writing, were still some way short of final resolution.

The most spectacular retreat, on the face of it, came over telephone tapping, on 1 April 1980. Ever since the Malone case in Britain, and the Klass judgment of 1978 at Strasbourg, the Home Office had been labouring behind the scenes to head off a clash with the European Court of Human Rights, and also to deflect the Royal Commission on Criminal Procedure who were anxious to examine tapping. William Whitelaw, the Conservative Home Secretary, published a White Paper which purported to describe the tapping system and to give the very statistics on 23 years of interception which ministers had always refused to reveal. He also announced that, although there would be no legislation giving a proper basis of safeguards, and although there would be no right to discover whether the citizen's phone had ever been tapped, a senior judge would be appointed, to publish only one report giving his opinion of the general system, and thereafter to report to the Home Office who would publish what, if anything, they thought fit.

The skimpy White Paper (Cmnd. 7873) confirmed many of the allegations in this book. It turned out that it was not the Home Secretary but his officials who decided whether taps should be instituted, modified or renewed. It gave figures showing the number of warrants had more than quadrupled over the years to a peak of 467. The figures were meaningless in fact; not only did they omit all mention of Foreign Office surveillance through GCHQ and informal taps through meters and bugs, they also excluded Northern Ireland and its ten years of blanket interception, on 'security' grounds. Most subtle of all, while admitting that 'public order' was a criterion along with genuinely serious crime, and that organizations with more than one phone could be tapped on a single warrant, the White Paper omitted to show how many multi-phone 'organization' warrants were thus being issued. Behind a show of retreat, furtive unaccountability was plainly alive and well.

On prisons, Whitelaw fell in with some of the May recommendations, for the appointment of outside inspectors and lay members of the Prisons Board. These may prove to be useful institutional steps towards openness. The Cabinet Office also appeared to have dropped some of its more fatuous historical restrictions by the spring of 1980: a few immediate post-war documents began to appear in the Public Records Office at Kew under the 30-year rule, although they mentioned the existence of MI6 in passing. Nothing of any serious content about MI6 was apparently released, but to admit its existence was a tiny step towards the real world.

The question of jury vetting continued to reveal a deep split in the judiciary, once it had ceased to be secret. By May 1980 this had led not only to criminal appeals being lodged against vetted convictions, but also to an embarassing public denunciation by the Master of the Rolls, Lord Denning, of the whole practice. He said it was an invasion of privacy and unconstitutional (Times Law Reports, 8 May 1980).

These relatively wholesome events were probably of less long-term importance than some direct attacks on the press and television companies. The law of contempt of court was invoked by the Home Office in May 1980 in novel fashion. In an attempt to prevent further publication of the Prison Department papers discussed in Chapter 3 of this book, they announced, after winning the first stage of a test-case brought by the NCCL, that they would prosecute the NCCL solicitor, Harriet Harman for contempt of court. The Home Office claimed that she must have been my personal source from which, as a journalist, I received copies of the papers in question. Although the papers and photographs had all been exhibits and evidence in a public court case, their claim was that no lawyer was entitled to show them to a third party — thus hoping by the back door to regain the secrecy they had lost when the court originally ordered the Home Office to disclose the material. It was a gratuitous attempt to make it hard for journalists to collect material supposedly for the public record.

Two other legal tank-traps were dug around this time for 'World in Action', the Granada TV programme. They became involved in a development of the one-man war waged against the world of British spies by Duncan Campbell, veteran of the ABC secrets trial. After the *New Statesman* and the *Daily Mirror* printed long disclosures of security leakages, possible Chinese penetration and widespread frauds on the taxpayer, allegedly taking place at the GCHQ Hong Kong radio monitoring station, Granada set out to emulate the press. The IBA, who had years before excised references to GCHQ from TV documentaries, coolly announced that, in their view, the programme was a breach of the Official Secrets Act, which could prejudice 'national security'. They ordered it not to be shown, as planned, on 19 May 1980.

Even more serious was the attempt, backed by appeal court judges, of a state industry, the British Steel Corporation, to force Granada to disclose one of their sources — a senior member of BSC who had anonymously handed over, in what he took to be the public interest, documents showing poor management and secret government intervention around the time of an unprecedented national steel strike. The papers were used in a 'World in Action' programme.

The influence of Sam Silkin's earlier attempts to extend the irrelevant ideas of the law of confidence to censor memoirs, became clear. The judges accepted that it was a 'breach of confidence' by Granada's source to take the documents. Granada having churlishly not given the BSC an opportunity to exercise what the US press calls 'prior restraint' — an injunction to ban the programme — BSC had to be allowed another remedy. The appeal court ordered Granada to name their source, on pain of contempt of court. This, of course, flew in the face of basic journalistic ethics and Granada announced they would appeal against the decision to the Lords.

What was most disturbing was the lack of any regard by the judges for the public good of free expression. They painted a picture of an information landscape devoid of democratic values and populated by old fictions of the common law. Lord Justice Templeman asserted: 'Granada deliberately broke the common law by publishing information confidential to BSC ... no principle of public policy or of freedom of the press or freedom of information or journalistic ethics justifies resistance in these circumstances to BSC's claim.'

Lord Denning himself set himself up as a freelance licenser of the press: 'In order to be deserving of freedom, the press must show itself worthy of it. A free press must be a responsible press ... If a newspaper should act irresponsibly, then it forfeits its claim to protect its sources of information.' Lord Denning announced that he did not care for the way Granada had conducted their interview with the BSC chairman, or the way they had made it hard for BSC to get an advance injunction to ban the programme: 'I cannot think it right that their want of responsibility should enable them to make this damaging attack on the Steel Corporation and on the Government.'

It was Judge Jeffreys who once ruled in the seventeenth century, 'That no person could expose to the public knowledge anything that concerned the affairs of the public, without licence from the king, or from such persons as he may think fit to entrust with that power.' Confronted with British attitudes towards secrecy, one must go back a long way to find their political roots.

Notes

Chapter 1

1. Itzhak Galnoor (ed.), *Government Secrecy in Democracies,* Harper & Row, New York, 1977, pp.281-4.
2. Harold Wilson, *Final Term: The Labour Government 1974-76,* Weidenfeld & Nicolson/Michael Joseph, 1979, p.237.
3. *Guardian,* 8 May 1978.
4. Cecil King, *Diary, 1970-74,* Jonathan Cape, 1975, p.31.
5. Hansard, 21 November 1979.
6. Ibid.
7. *The Times,* 4 April 1978.
8. *The Times,* 4 May 1978.
9. *Times Educational Supplement,* 24 September 1976.
10. Wilson, *Final Term,* p.223.
11. *Guardian,* 25 January 1980.
12. *Fourth Report of the Committee of Public Accounts, Session 1974-75,* HMSO, pp.244-8.
13. Ibid., pp.xv-xvii.
14. Leslie Chapman, *Your Disobedient Servant: The Continuing Story of Whitehall Overspending,* Penguin, 1979.
15. *Second Special Report of the Inquiry into Evidence Given to the Committee of Public Accounts, Session 1974-75,* HMSO.
16. This restriction was still operating on 7 November 1979. See letter to *The Times* of that date.
17. *Observer,* 8 December 1979.
18. Home Office, *Reform of Section 2 of the Official Secrets Act 1911,* Commons Paper 7285, HMSO, July 1978, pp.19-21; Lord Fulton (Chairman), *The Civil Service: Report of the Committee,* Cmnd. 3638, vol. I, HMSO, June 1968, p.93 (hereafter referred to as Fulton Report, 1968).
19. Richard Crossman, *Diaries of a Cabinet Minister,* vol. 3, Hamish Hamilton, 1975.
20. Barbara Castle, entry for 25 February 1969, *The Castle Diaries,* Weidenfeld & Nicolson, 1980.
21. Chapman, *Your Disobedient Servant,* p.70.

22. Lord Franks (Chairman), *Report and Evidence of the Departmental Committee on Section 2 of the Official Secrets Act 1911,* Cmnd. 5104, vol. II, HMSO, September 1972, pp.9-12 (hereafter referred to as Franks Report, 1972).
23. Ibid.
24. Wilson, *Final Term,* p.198. 'Even the Cabinet table was the wrong way round', he said.
25. Hansard, 16 June 1977.
26. Franks Report, vol. III, p.319.
27. Ibid., vol. IV, p.190.
28. Tony Benn, *Arguments for Socialism,* Jonathan Cape, 1979.
29. Franks Report, vol. III, pp.316-39.
30. Ibid.
31. First printed in the *New Statesman,* 10 November 1978.
32. *The Times,* 22 August 1978.
33. Stafford H. Northcote and C.E. Trevelyan, *Report on the Organisation of the Permanent Civil Service,* 23 November 1853.
34. Fulton Report, p.14.
35. R.W.L. Wilding, 'The Professional Ethic of the Administrator', *Management Services in Government,* vol. 34, no. 4, Civil Service Department, November 1979.
36. Reprinted *Guardian,* 4 February 1980.
37. Franks Report, vol. I, Appendix iii.
38. Ibid., vol. I, p.24.
39. Ibid., vol. III, p.261.
40. Ibid., vol. III, p.13.
41. Ibid., vol. II, p.15.
42. Ibid., vol. III, p.134.
43. Lord Radcliffe, *Report of the Committee on Ministerial Memoirs,* Cmnd. 6386, HMSO, 1976.
44. Ibid.
45. Harold Wilson, Hansard, 22 January 1976.
46. Gain *v.* Gain, All ER 63; Chatterton *v.* Secretary of State for India 1895 2QB 189; Duncan *v.* Cammell Laird 1942 All ER 149; Asiatic Petroleum *v.* Anglo-Persian Oil 1916 1KB 822; Ellis 1953 2 All ER 149; Rogers 1972 All ER 1057.
47. Williams *v.* Home Office, High Court 25 February to 25 March 1980.
48. Margaret Gowing, *Independence and Deterrence,* vol. 1, Macmillan, 1964, ch. 2.
49. Hansard, 24 January 1980.
50. See Outer Circle Policy Unit, *An Official Information Act,* OCPU, 1977.
51. *Sunday Times,* 12 November 1967; *The Times,* 12 December 1967.
52. *Sunday Times,* 8 October 1972.
53. *Guardian,* 20 March 1979. One Departmental minute was quoted; William Rodgers, Transport Minister, refused to publish the others.
54. *New Society,* 17 June 1976.
55. See James Michael, *The Politics of Secrecy: The Case for a Freedom of Information Law,* NCCL, 1979; Outer Circle Policy Unit, *An Official Information Act; Sunday Times,* 2 December 1979; *Guardian,* 20 August 1979.
56. Michael, *Politics of Secrecy.*

57. *Guardian,* 2 August 1979.
58. *Daily Telegraph,* 5 May 1978.
59. Sir Norman Lindop (Chairman), *Report of Data Protection Committee,* Cmnd. 7341, HMSO, December 1978.
60. Tony Benn, 'Mr Benn's Secret Service' in 'World in Action', 4 January 1980; *Guardian,* 7 December 1979, report of Cabinet leak on Whitehall's deliberate low profile over nuclear power station sitings. See also Hansard, 6 December 1979.

Chapter 2

1. Official Secrets Act, 1920.
2. Official Secrets Act, 1911.
3. Franks Report, vol. I, HMSO, 1972, p.118.
4. Chapman Pincher, *Inside Story: A Documentary of the Pursuit of Power,* Sidgwick & Jackson, 1978.
5. Attorney-General *v.* Times Newspapers, 22 July 1975.
6. Franks Report, ibid.
7. Jonathan Aitken, *Officially Secret,* Weidenfeld & Nicolson, 1971.
8. *New Statesman,* 1 February 1979.
9. *Sunday Times,* 8 October 1972.
10. *New Society,* 17 June 1976.
11. Shelter housing conference, London, 28 July 1978.
12. *Sunday Telegraph,* 23 May 1976.
13. Lord Radcliffe, E. Shinwell and S. Lloyd, *Report of the Committee of Privy Councillors Appointed to Inquire into 'D' Notice Matters,* Cmnd. 3309, HMSO, June 1967, p.270 (hereafter referred to as Radcliffe Report).
14. Ibid., p.273.
15. Ibid., p.288.
16. Ibid., p.26.
17. *Daily Telegraph,* 31 June 1973.
18. Lord Denning, *Report in the Light of the Circumstances Surrounding the Resignation of the Former Secretary of State for War, Mr J.D. Profumo,* Cmnd. 2152, HMSO, September 1963, p.86.
19. Radcliffe Report.
20. Ibid., p.41.
21. Dated 16 November 1974.
22. 5 April 1976.
23. 27 July 1978.
24. 11 December 1975.
25. Cabinet documents released to the Public Records Office 1978.
26. Hugo Young, *The Crossman Affair,* Hamish Hamilton, 1976, p.65.
27. 1969 AC 910.
28. Attorney-General *v.* Times Newspapers, 22 July 1975.
29. Young, *The Crossman Affair,* p.209.
30. Geoffrey Robertson, 'Law for the Press' in J. Curran (ed.), *The British Press: A Manifesto,* Macmillan, 1978.
31. *UK Press Gazette,* 28 January 1980.
32. P. Chippindale and D. Leigh, *The Thorpe Committal,* Arrow Books, 1979.

33. 8 May 1979.
34. Lord Justice Phillimore (Chairman), *Report of the Committee on Contempt of Court,* Cmnd. 5794, HMSO, December 1974 (hereafter referred to as Phillimore Report).
35. 1973 3WLR 298.
36. 24 April 1978.
37. 30 March 1979.
38. *Contempt of Court — A Discussion Paper,* Cmnd. 7145, HMSO, 22 March 1978.
39. 1974 AC 273.
40. Hayward *v. Sunday Telegraph,* 9 November 1979.
41. *New York Times v.* Sullivan, 376 US 254.
42. Mr Justice Faulks (Chairman), *Report of the Committee on Defamation,* Cmnd. 5909, HMSO, 1975.
43. See Richard Ingrams, *Goldenballs,* Private Eye/Deutsch, 1979.
44. *Guardian,* 25 February 1980.
45. Harold Wilson, *Final Term,* Weidenfeld & Nicolson/Michael Joseph, 1979, pp.225-6.
46. Ibid., p.143.
47. Attorney-General *v.* Times Newspapers, 22 July 1975.
48. Franks Report, vol. IV, p.187.
49. Ibid., vol. II, p.71.

Chapter 3

1. Tony Parker, *The Frying Pan: A Prison and Its Prisoners,* Panther, 1971, pp.86-7.
2. Pat Arrowsmith, *Breakout: Poems and Drawings from Prison,* Edinburgh University Student Publication Board, 1975.
3. Sidney and Beatrice Webb, *Prisons Under Local Government,* 1922.
4. Mr Justice May (Chairman), *Report of the Committee of Inquiry into the United Kingdom Prison Service,* Cmnd. 7673, HMSO, 1979, para. 6.64 (hereafter referred to as May Report).
5. Stan Cohen and Laurie Taylor, *Prison Secrets,* NCCL/Radical Alternatives to Prison, 1978.
6. Graham Zellick, 'Prisoners and the Law' in S. McConville (ed.), *The Use of Imprisonment,* Routledge & Kegan Paul, 1975, p.2.
7. May Report, para. 6.69.
8. Quoted in Taylor and Cohen, *Prison Secrets,* p.56.
9. Ibid., p.68.
10. May Report, para. 5.96; *R. v.* The Board of Visitors of Hull Prison (*ex parte* Cotterill and others) and *R. v.* The Board of Visitors of Wandsworth Prison (*ex parte* Rosa).
11. Cohen and Taylor, *Prison Secrets,* p.44.
12. *Guardian,* 21 June 1979.
13. Franks Report, Cmnd. 5104, HMSO, 1972, vol. IV, pp.299-300.
14. May Report, para. 8.2-3.
15. Ibid., paras. 10.56-7.
16. Ibid., paras. 5.20-80.
17. Cohen and Taylor, *Prison Secrets,* p.86.

18. Franks Report, vol. II, pp.354-7.
19. 13 August 1975.
20. *Daily Telegraph,* 22 November 1979.
21. *Guardian,* 16 November 1978.
22. *Guardian,* 7 December 1979.
23. Home Office, *Prisons and the Prisoner,* HMSO, 1977.
24. *Guardian,* 10 January 1980.
25. May Report, paras. 5.91-104.
26. Cohen and Taylor, *Prison Secrets,* p.27.
27. Ibid., p.81.
28. Ibid., pp.84-5.
29. *Guardian,* 15 February 1977.
30. May Report, para. 5.62.
31. Ibid., para. 5.9.

Chapter 4

1. *R. v.* Armstrong 1922.
2. Ellis *v.* Deheer 1922, 2 KB 113.
3. Lord Morris of Borth-y-Guest, *Report of the Committee on Jury Service,* Cmnd. 2623, HMSO, April 1965.
4. *Observer,* 21 June 1959.
5. Morris Report.
6. Criminal Law Revision Committee, 10th Report, *Secrecy of the Jury Room,* Cmnd. 3750, HMSO, 1967.
7. *Sun,* 9 January 1973.
8. *Times Law Reports,* 27 February 1967.
9. *Daily Telegraph,* 9 January 1978.
10. *Guardian,* 14 January 1974.
11. *Guardian,* 12 April 1976.
12. See Sir Robert Mark, *In the Office of Constable,* Constable, 1978. The 1978 statistics showed even fewer — below 10 per cent of Crown Court defendants — being acquitted by juries. See Zander, *Guardian,* 10 January 1980.
13. *Sunday Times,* 1 October 1978.
14. *Members of the Jury,* NCCL, 1978.
15. 25 July 1979.
16. *New Statesman,* 27 July 1979.
17. *Report of the Royal Commission on Legal Services,* Cmnd. 7648, HMSO, October 1979.
18. 'World at One', BBC Radio, 27 September 1979.
19. Society of Labour Lawyers Meeting, Labour Party Conference, Brighton, October 1979.
20. Phillimore Report, Cmnd. 5794, HMSO, December 1974.
21. Lord Scarman, Attorney-General *v. The Leveller, Peace News* and the National Union of Journalists, 1 February 1979, House of Lords (19 May 1978, Divisional Court).
22. *Times Law Reports,* 16 January 1980.
23. Morris Report.
24. *R. v.* Armstrong, 1922.

25. Lord Justice James, *The Distribution of Criminal Business Between the Crown Courts and the Magistrates' Courts,* Cmnd. 6323, HMSO, November 1978.
26. Blackstone Lectures, 1978.
27. All ER 240, 1973.
28. *Daily Telegraph,* 5 October 1973.
29. Four such people were challenged on 16 January 1973 at the Old Bailey 'Nasty Tales' pornography trial.
30. *Listener,* 11 August 1966.
31. *R. v.* Dawton, Bennet, Mills, Ladd, Carr and Stevenson, 1 September 1979, the 'anarchists' trial.
32. Jeremy Bentham, *Elements in the Art of Packing,* 1821.
33. Association of Chief Police Officers, November 1978.
34. Gordon Honeycombe, *Adam's Tale,* Hutchinson, 1974, p.253. See also Barry Cox, Martin Shirley and John Short, *The Fall of Scotland Yard,* Penguin, 1977.
35. Geoffrey Robertson, *Reluctant Judas,* Temple Smith, 1976 (a study of the Lennon case concerning a Special Branch informer, by a barrister).
36. Hansard, 3 March 1974.
37. Hansard, 19 May 1975, 'It is not the practice of the Crown to object to jurors on the grounds of their political beliefs as such. Political views are only relevant to the extent that, depending on the nature of the charges, political views held to an extreme may impair the impartiality of jurors, or give rise to the possibility of improper pressure.'
38. Personal communication.
39. Society of Labour Lawyers Meeting, Labour Party Conference, Brighton, October, 1979.
40. 'Man Alive', BBC TV, October 1979.
41. Statement by the Attorney-General, 10 October 1978. For the text see Harriet Harman and John Griffith, *Justice Deserted: The Subversion of the Jury,* 2nd edn, NCCL, 1980.
42. Hansard, 13 November 1978.
43. See Harman and Griffith, *Justice Deserted.*
44. See Anna Coote, *New Statesman,* 22 September 1978.
45. *Daily Telegraph,* 19 September 1978.
46. Harman and Griffith, *Justice Deserted,* Appendix 2.
47. E.P. Thompson, 'The State and its Enemies', *New Society,* 19 October 1978.
48. Letter to D.E. Thomas, Plaid Cymru MP for Merioneth, 17 May 1979.
49. Liberal Assembly, Margate, 27 September 1979.
50. *Guardian,* 21 December 1979.

Chapter 5

1. Incognito evidence, 5 November 1971, to Franks Report, vol. III, Cmnd. 5104, HMSO, 1972.
2. Press conference, Washington, 24 May 1978.
3. D-notice No. 10 issued August 1971. See Chapter 2.
4. Harold Wilson, *The Governance of Britain,* Weidenfeld & Nicolson, 1976.

5. Chapman Pincher, *Inside Story: A Documentary of the Pursuit of Power,* Sidgwick & Jackson, 1978, p.23.
6. Franks Report, Cmnd. 5104, vol. III, HMSO, 1972.
7. *Observer,* 12 August 1979.
8. Debate on Sir Anthony Blunt. See Hansard, 21 November 1979.
9. Bruce Page, David Leitch and Phillip Knightly, *Philby, the Spy who Betrayed a Nation,* Sphere, 1977.
10. Pincher, *Inside Story,* pp.185-7.
11. Ibid., p.28.
12. Victor Marchetti and John D. Marks, *The CIA and the Cult of Intelligence,* Coronet 1976, p.264.
13. Philip Agee, *Inside the Company: CIA Diary,* Penguin, 1975, p.582.
14. *Observer,* 9 December 1979.
15. D-notice No. 11, August, 1971. See Chapter 2.
16. *Observer,* 13 August 1978.
17. Hansard, 25 May 1978.
18. Richard Lee and Colin Pratt. *Operation Julie: How the Undercover Police Team Smashed the World's Greatest Drug Ring,* W.H. Allen, 1978.
19. See note 8.
20. Denning Report, HMSO, 1963, p.79.
21. Ibid., p.79.
22. Franks Report, vol. III, pp.243-66.
23. Denning Report, vol. III, pp.79-80.
24. Andrew Boyle, *The Climate of Treason: Five Who Spied for Russia,* Hutchinson, 1979; see also note 8.
25. Blunt debate, see note 8.
26. Andrew Boyle, *Observer,* 20 January 1980.
27. So too was Jack Jones, General Secretary of the TGWU and mainstay of the Labour Government. Tony Benn was thus informed in 1975, as Industry Secretary, when he considered offering Jones the Chairmanship of the National Enterprise Board. Personal communication.
28. Franks Report, vol. III, p.243-66.
29. Denning Report, p.77.
30. *Sunday Times,* 11 January 1980 and Barbara Castle, *The Castle Diaries,* Weidenfeld & Nicolson, 1980.
31. Blunt debate, see note 8.
32. Personal communication.
33. Blunt debate, see note 8.
34. Robin Cook MP for Edinburgh Central, Hansard, 7 November 1979.
35. State Research, *Review of Security and the State,* Julian Friedmann, 1979.
36. Leon Brittan, Hansard, 7 November 1979.
37. Ibid.
38. State Research, *Bulletin,* no. 15, December 1979.
39. Ibid.
40. Letter to *The Leveller,* 16 June 1978.
41. Sir Norman Birkett (Chairman), *Report of the Inquiry into the Interception of Communications,* Cmnd. 283, HMSO 1957.
42. Blunt debate, see note 8.

43. Merlyn Rees, in a February 1979 'lobby terms' briefing, told some journalists that there were at least 2,000 taps a year.
44. James Malone *v.* Commissioner of Metropolitan Police.
45. Klass and other *v.* Federal Republic of Germany.
46. Documents made available by Christopher Mayhew.
47. Marchetti and Marks, *The CIA,* pp.193-209.
48. *Britain's Home Defence Gamble,* Conservative Political Centre, Smith Square, London SW1.
49. D-notice No. 8. See Chapter 2.
50. Peter Laurie, *Beneath the City Streets,* Panther, 1979; Tony Bunyan, *The Political Police in Britain,* ch. 5, Julian Friedmann, 1976; State Research, *Review of State Security.*
51. Laurie, *Beneath the City Streets,* pp.202-4.
52. Ibid., p.149.
53. Debate on Agee-Hosenball deportations, Hansard, 3 May 1977.
54. Agee, *CIA Diary.*
55. Notes for a speech first delivered by Silkin to his Dulwich constituency Labour Party.
56. Ibid.
57. Ibid.

Chapter 6

1. Fulton Report, HMSO, 1968, pp.91-2.
2. The register or 'day-list' for 29 August 1978, listed 17 defence documents which had either arrived in, or were being despatched from, the Defence Ministry. The secret list was about the same length and gave serial numbers, dates, destinations and brief titles of the secret papers. They included for example, a seismic profile of areas of Sweden containing installations. Only three were marked 'Top Secret'; they were about planned troop dispositions.
3. See Itzhak Galnoor, *Adminstrative Secrecy in Developed Countries,* ISAS, Macmillan, 1979; Donald C. Rowat, *Government Secrecy in Democracies,* Harper & Row, 1977 and; Home Office, *Disclosure of Official Information: A Report on Overseas Practice,* HMSO, 1979, for detailed accounts of foreign practice.
4. Executive Order 12065, drafted 1977.
5. Compare James Michael, *The Politics of Secrecy,* NCCL, 1979, Trevor Barnes, *Open Up! Britain and Freedom of Information in the 1980s,* Fabian Society, 1980 and Home Office, *Reform of Section 2 of the Official Secrets Act 1911,* Commons Paper 7285, HMSO, 1978.
6. See Michael, *Politics of Secrecy.*
7. See Rowat, *Administrative Secrecy* and OCPU, *An Official Information Act,* OCPU, 1977.
8. Cabinet Office, *Information and the Public Interest,* Cmnd. 4089, HMSO, 1969.
9. Franks Report, HMSO, 1972.
10. Ibid., vol. I, pp.35-6.
11. Ibid., p.12.

12. Younger Report, HMSO, 1972; Phillimore Report, HMSO, 1974.
13. Faulks Report, HMSO, 1975.
14. Lord Franks (chairman), *Report of the Committee on Administrative Tribunals and Inquiries,* Cmnd. 218, HMSO, July 1957.
15. Ronald Wraith, *Open Government: The British Interpretation,* Royal Institute of Public Administration, 1977, p.18.
16. Owen completed the close-down of IRD (see previous chapter) and announced that the hitherto confidential and unattributable 'background briefs' would be made available, starting with one on the Italian Red Brigades. He also declassified and put on public display a number of miscellaneous internal studies.
17. See Barnes, *Open Up.*
18. Hansard, 22 November 1976.
19. BBC Radio, 13 August 1978.
20. *The Times,* 14 November 1979.
21. Home Office, *Reform of Section 2 of OSA.*
22. See Chapter 1.
23. Home Office, *Reform of Section 2 of OSA.*
24. Ibid., pp.19-21.
25. Hansard, 19 June 1978.
26. See Chapter 2.
27. Home Office, *Reform of Section 2 of OSA,* p.12.
28. Ibid., p.16.
29. Civil Service Department, *Disclosure of Official Information.*
30. See *New Statesman,* 8 October 1979.
31. Anthony Lincoln (chairman), *Freedom of Information: A Report by Justice,* Justice, 1978.
32. The Bill listed six categories of protected information:

(a) information relating to defence or international relations the unauthorized disclosure of which would be likely to cause serious injury to the interests of the nation or endanger the safety of a citizen of the UK and Colonies; (b) information relating to security or intelligence; (c) information obtained by reason of the interception of postal packets or telecommunications conversations, messages or signals in pursuit of a requirement imposed or authorization given on behalf of the Crown, and information relating to the obtaining of information by reason of any such interception; (d) information which is likely to be useful in the commission of offences or in facilitating an escape from legal custody or the doing of other acts prejudicial to the safe keeping of persons in legal custody, or the unauthorized disclosure of which would be likely to impede the prevention or detection of offences or the apprehension or prosecution of suspected offenders; (e) subject to subsection 3 below, information which is obtained from a government of another State, from an organization of which States, the governments of States, or the organs of any such government or organization and which is held ... on terms requiring it to be held in confidence or in circumstances in which it would be reasonable to expect it to be held in confidence; and (f) information which relates to or is obtained from any of the persons mentioned in subsection 4 below and which is held ... on terms or in circumstances requiring it to be held in confidence or in circumstances in which it would be reasonable to expect it to be held in confidence.

The information covered is that which 'is or has been held' by a Crown servant. Subsection 3 releases 'in confidence' information, but not the other sorts, if the requirement has become out of date. Subsection 4 grants the protection of the 'in confidence' clauses to partnerships, companies, State agencies, foreign corporate organizations and private individuals — in fact, to everybody and everything outside government.

33. *Daily Telegraph, Financial Times* and *Guardian,* 20 October 1979.
34. *The Times,* 14 November 1979.
35. Hansard, 21 November 1979.

Bibliography

Agee, Philip, *Inside the Company: CIA Diary,* Penguin, 1975.

Aitken, Jonathan, *Officially Secret,* Weidenfeld & Nicholson, 1971.

Arrowsmith, Pat, *Breakout: Poems and Drawings from Prison,* Edinburgh University Student Publications Board, 1975.

Association of Chief Police Officers of England, Wales and Northern Ireland, *Evidence to the Royal Commission on Criminal Procedure,* Part II, *The Criminal Trial,* HMSO, November 1978.

Barnes, Trevor, *Open Up! Britain and Freedom of Information in the 1980s,* Fabian Society, 11 Dartmouth St, London SW1, 1980.

Benn, Tony, *Arguments for Socialism,* Jonathan Cape, 1979.

Boyle, Andrew, *The Climate of Treason: Five who Spied for Russia,* Hutchinson, 1979.

Boyle, Jimmy, *A Sense of Freedom,* Pan, 1977.

Bunyan, Tony, *The Political Police in Britain,* Julian Friedmann, 1976.

Cabinet Office, *Information and the Public Interest,* Cmnd. 4089, HMSO, 1969.

Castle, Barbara, *The Castle Diaries,* Weidenfeld & Nicolson, 1980.

Chapman, Leslie, *Your Disobedient Servant: The Continuing Story of Whitehall Overspending,* Penguin, 1979.

Chippindale, Peter and Leigh, David, *The Thorpe Committal,* Hutchinson, Arrow Books, 1979.

Civil Service Department, *Disclosure of Official Information: A Report on Overseas Practice,* HMSO, 1979.

Cohen, Stan and Taylor, Laurie, *Prison Secrets,* National Council for Civil Liberties/Radical Alternatives to Prison, 186 Kings Cross Rd, London EC1, 1978.

Cox, Barry, Shirley, Martin and Short, John, *The Fall of Scotland Yard,* Penguin, 1977.

Denning, Lord, *Report in the Light of the Circumstances Surrounding the Resignation of the Former Secretary of State for War, Mr J.D. Profumo,* Cmnd. 2152, HMSO, September, 1963.

Faulks, Mr Justice (chairman), *Report of the Committee on Defamation,* Cmnd. 5909, HMSO, March 1975.

Franks, Lord (chairman), *Report and Evidence of the Committee on Section 2 of the Official Secrets Act 1911,* 4 vols., Cmnd. 5104, HMSO, September 1972.

——, *Report of the Committee on Administrative Tribunals and Inquiries,* Cmnd. 218, HMSO, July 1975.

Frazier, Howard (ed.), *Uncloaking the CIA,* Collier Macmillan, 1978.

Fulton, Lord (chairman), *The Civil Service: Report of the Committee,* 4 vols., Cmnd. 3638, HMSO, June 1968.

Galnoor, Itzhak (ed.), *Government Secrecy in Democracies,* Harper & Row, New York, 1977.

Gowing, Margaret, *Independence and Deterrence,* vol. 1, *Policy Making,* Macmillan, 1964.

Crossman, Richard, *Diaries of a Cabinet Minister,* 3 vols., Hamish Hamilton, 1975/6/7.

Hain, Peter (ed.), *Policing the Police,* vols. 1 & 2, John Calder, 1979, 1980.

Harman, Harriet and Griffith, John, *Justice Deserted: The Subversion of the Jury,* 2nd edn, National Council for Civil Liberties, 186 Kings Cross Rd, London EC1, 1980.

Hewitt, Patricia (ed.), *Computers, Records and the Right to Privacy,* National Council for Civil Liberties, Input Two-Nine, 1979.

Hogg, John (translator), *The Vulnerability of the Computerized Society,* Sarbarhetskommitten, Ministry of Defence, Stockholm, 1978.

Holm, Niels Elschou, 'The Danish System of Open Files in Public Administration' in *Scandinavian Studies in Law,* 1975.

Home Office, *Reform of Section 2 of the Official Secrets Act 1911,* Commons Paper 7285, HMSO, July 1978.

——, *Prisons and the Prisoner,* HMSO, 1977.

Honeycombe, George, *Adam's Tale,* Hutchinson, 1974.

James, Lord Justice (chairman), *The Distribution of Criminal Business Between the Crown Courts and the Magistrates' Courts,* Cmnd. 6323, HMSO, November 1978.

King, Cecil, *Diary, 1970-74,* Jonathan Cape, 1975.

Laurie, Peter, *Beneath the City Streets,* revised edn, Panther, 1979.

Lee, Richard and Pratt, Colin, *Operation Julie: How the Under-*

cover Police Team Smashed the World's Greatest Drugs Ring, W.H. Allen, 1978.

Lewin, Ronald, *Ultra Goes to War: The Secret Story,* Hutchinson, 1978.

Liberal Party, *Public Access to Official Information,* 1978.

Lincoln, Anthony QC, (chairman), *Freedom of Information: A Report by Justice,* Justice, British Section of the International Commission of Jurists, 1978.

Lindop, Sir Norman (chairman), *Report of Data Protection Committee,* Cmnd. 7341, HMSO, December 1978.

McDermott, Geoffrey, *The New Diplomacy and Its Apparatus,* Plume Press/Ward Lock, 1973.

Marchetti, Victor and Marks, John D., *The CIA and the Cult of Intelligence,* Coronet, 1976.

Mark, Sir Robert, *In the Office of Constable,* Collins, 1978.

Marwick, Christine M. (ed.), *Litigation Under the Amended Federal Freedom of Information Act,* Fourth edn, Center for National Security Studies, 122 Maryland Ave NE, Washington DC 20002, 1978.

May, Mr Justice (chairman), *Report of the Committee of Inquiry into the United Kingdom Prison Services,* Cmnd. 7673, HMSO, 1979.

Michael, James, *The Politics of Secrecy: The Case for a Freedom of Information Law,* National Council for Civil Liberties, 1979.

Morris, Lord of Borth-y-Guest, *Report of the Committee on Jury Service,* Cmnd. 2623, HMSO, April 1965.

National Council for Civil Liberties, *Members of the Jury,* NCCL, 186 Kings Cross Rd, London EC1, 1978.

Nixon, Richard M., *The White House Transcripts,* introduced by R.W. Apple Jr. of the *New York Times,* Bantam, 1974.

Nordenson, Ulf K. (translator), *The Freedom of the Press Act* and *Amendements to the Freedom of the Press Act,* Constitutional documents of Sweden, published by the Swedish Riksdag, Stockholm, 1975 and 1978.

Northcote, Stafford H. and Trevelyan, C.E., *Report on the Organization of the Permanent Civil Service,* 22 November, 1853.

Outer Circle Policy Unit, *An Official Information Act,* OCPU, 4 Cambridge Terr, London NW1, 1977.

——, *Official Information Bill,* OCPU, July 1978.

Page, Bruce, Leitch, David and Knightley, Phillip, *Philby, the Spy who Betrayed a Generation,* Sphere, 1977.

Parker, Tony, *The Frying Pan: A Prison and Its Prisoners,* Panther, 1971.

Phillimore, Lord Justice (chairman), *Report of the Committee on Contempt of Court,* Cmnd. 5794, HMSO, December 1974.

Pincher, Chapman, *Inside Story: a Documentary of the Pursuit of Power,* Sidgwick & Jackson, 1978.

Radcliffe, Lord, *Report of the Committee on Ministerial Memoirs,* Cmnd. 6386, HMSO, 22 January 1976.

——, Shinwell, E. and Lloyd, S., *Report of the Committee of Privy Councillors Appointed to Inquire into 'D' Notice Matters,* Cmnd. 3309, HMSO, June 1967.

Robertson, Geoffrey, 'Law for the Press' in J. Curran (ed.) *The British Press: A Manifesto,* Macmillan, 1978.

Rowat, Donald C. (ed.), *Administrative Secrecy in Developed Countries,* International Institute of Administrative Sciences, Macmillan, 1979.

Sedgemore, Brian, *Mr Secretary of State,* Quartet, 1978.

State Research, *Review of Security and the State,* Julian Friedmann, 1979.

Thompson, E.P., *The Making of the English Working Class,* Pelican, 1977.

US Department of Justice, *Attorney-General's Memorandum on the 1974 Amendments to the Freedom of Information Act,* US Government Printing Office, February 1975.

——, *Freedom of Information Case List, A Short Guide to the Freedom of Information Act,* February 1978 edn., Office of Legal Counsel, Department of Justice, Washington DC.

Vinge, P.G., *Experiences of the Swedish Data Act,* Federation of Swedish Industries, Stockholm, 1975.

Webb, Sidney and Beatrice, *Prisons Under Local Government,* 1922.

Williams, David, *Not in the Public Interest,* Hutchinson, 1965.

Wilding, R.W.L., 'The Professional Ethic of the Administrator', *Management Services in Government,* vol. 34, no. 4, Civil Service Department, Whitehall, London SW1, November 1979.

Williams, Marcia, *Inside Number 10,* Weidenfeld & Nicolson, 1972.

Wilson, Harold, *The Labour Government 1964-70: A Personal Record,* Weidenfeld & Nicolson and Michael Joseph, 1971.

——, *The Governance of Britain,* Weidenfeld & Nicolson, 1976.

——, *Final Term: The Labour Government 1974-76,* Weidenfeld & Nicolson and Michael Joseph, 1979.

Wraith, Ronald, *Open Government: The British Interpretation,* Royal Institute of Public Administration, 1977.

Wynn, H.P., 'Freedom of Statistical Information', *Journal of the Royal Statistical Society,* vol. 141, part 1, 1978.

Young, Hugo, *The Crossman Affair,* Hamish Hamilton and Jonathan Cape, 1976.

Younger, Kenneth (chairman), *Report of the Committee on Privacy,* Cmnd. 5012, HMSO, July 1972.

Zellick, Graham, 'Prisoners and the Law' in S. McConville (ed.), *The Use of Imprisonment: Essays in the Changing State of English Penal Policy,* Routledge & Kegan Paul, 1975.

Index